HOW LOVE
WINS

Also by Doug Carnine

Saint Badass
Personal Transcendence in Tucker Max Hell

Saint Badass: Personal Transcendence in Tucker Max Hell tells the inspiring story of Doug Carnine—a meditation teacher and lay Buddhist minister—and his unlikely friendship with four prisoners—three murderers and one alleged rapist—at Tucker Max, in their own words, and follows their journey as they rediscover their humanity in one of the most inhuman places on Earth.

An illuminating and hopeful account of inmate rehabilitation through Buddhist teachings.

— Kirkus Reviews

Make no mistake, Saint Badass is an incredibly gritty read which is often uncomfortable, but that is also its great strength. No punches are pulled, the prisoners are allowed to speak their minds without censorship, and that makes the resulting transformations even more compelling — and inspiring — than they would have been otherwise.

Whilst readers won't always like what they read in Saint Badass, they cannot fail to be transformed by it.

— BuddhistBookReviews.com

Coming in 2021

Lasting Happiness
A Guide for Teens and Young Adults

Lasting Happiness: A Guide for Teens and Young Adults, is a practical template for the development of kindful habits that nurture happiness in individuals and their communities. Using personal narratives from youth in diverse circumstances, who have found kindfulness to be an asset and including incarcerated, homeless and LGBTQ voices, all readers will recognize the emotional and social dynamics that are affecting their lives. This book gives youth the opportunity to change their self-defeating habits through mindful kindness. The book's research documents the critical role of mindfulness and kindness in nurturing relationships, which are the gate way to lasting happiness.

HOW LOVE
WINS

DR. DOUG CARNINE

How Love Wins
Doug Carnine

© 2020 Choose Kindness Foundation

Published by Choose Kindness Foundation
Eugene, Oregon

Second Edition
ISBN: 978-0-9980509-8-0
ISBN: 978-0-9980509-9-7 (ebook)

Library of Congress Control Number: 2020902436

Contents

Contents

Contents

A Note From the Author

It is the end of June, 2020. The Pandemic has crippled the world and for the last several days racial uprisings are taking place around the world, but especially in the US. This seems like the least likely time to be writing about *How Love Wins*. We will choose, intentionally or not, to lean into love and kindness or fall into fear, anxiety, helplessness and anger. This book is all about the 'whys' and 'hows' to lean into love and kindness—simple to understand, but challenging to do:

- Live a happy, healthy, and meaningful life through close, caring relationships.

- Use mindfulness/meditation to break unkind habits and build kind habits.

- Develop kind habits for the benefit of self and others through being friendly, offering help, showing appreciation, and reaching out to those in need.

- Share this key message with others.

Preface

> Both mindfulness and compassion are vital to the process of growth and transformation; but, while mindfulness is the servant of the awaking heart of compassion, it is the force of compassionate motivations that reorganizes the mind and sets in motion lasting change.
>
> — PAUL GILBERT AND CHODEN, *MINDFUL COMPASSION*

> There isn't time, so brief is life, for bickerings, apologies, heartburnings, callings to account. There is only time for loving, and but an instant, so to speak, for that.
>
> — MARK TWAIN

> It is one of the most beautiful compensations of this life that no man can sincerely try to help another without helping himself.
>
> — RALPH WALDO EMERSON

When I was nineteen, the love of my life dumped me. For a few months I was a miserable sophomore at the University of Illinois, consumed and upset by feelings of dejection, jealousy, anger, and resentment. I recycled the same hopeless thoughts over and over in my mind: *How can I get her back? I can't survive without her! Should I make the four-hour drive to beg her in person?* These thoughts and feelings were constantly on my mind, whether I was washing my hands, brushing my teeth, eating breakfast, walking to class, or waiting to cross the street. I was miserable, desperate for relief.

Fortunately, a good friend happened to be reading *The Essentials of Zen Buddhism*, by D. T. Suzuki. I was intrigued by what he told me about the book, and I began to hope that Buddhism could help me feel better. I didn't yet know anything about Buddhism or meditation, but I understood enough to realize that most of my unhappiness was coming from my own negative thoughts and feelings. And while I knew I couldn't make my girlfriend take me back, I thought maybe this Buddhism thing could help me take control of my own feelings.

Two years later, I was engaged in a regular meditation and mindfulness practice. Only gradually did I begin to see just how much of my own unhappiness, and some of the unhappiness I caused others, came from my own unkind habits, like anger. But at that time, I did not believe I could change those habits. My self-centered ways of thinking, feeling, and acting kept me from realizing the harm they were causing. Over the next few years, I gradually began to soften some of my unkind habits; for example, greatly reducing the heat of my anger.

It was only much later in life that I realized how deeply I wanted to change. I was ordained as a lay minister at the Eugene Buddhist Priory, volunteered at a hospice center, and became a meditation and spiritual mentor to men in prison for violent crimes. Through these experiences, I became aware of the tremendous power of kindness. As I kept studying, practicing, and reading medical, anthropological, and social science research on meditation, mindfulness, and kindness, I became convinced that all of us are capable of changing our unkind habits and building kind ones. This book is about how you can make those changes.

I hope that my more-than 40 years of experience as both a professor of education and as a student and practitioner of Buddhism[1] have helped me to write a book that will be helpful to readers of all levels. Although I myself am a practicing Buddhist, I wrote this book for readers who are interested in meditation and kindness, but who are not looking for religious instruction. In fact, this book is about a universal idea that applies to Buddhists, Christians, followers of other major religions, and atheists alike: the revolutionary impact that mindful kindness can have on all of our lives.

Acknowledgments

Over a 13-year period, many individuals have made invaluable contributions to the development of this book. I am grateful to my wife, Linda, who has supported me in too many ways to list. Jerry Silbert has been a colleague on many projects for over 40 years and made general and specific suggestions on the six earlier versions of this book. Another friend, Alex Granzin, guided me toward making the book more readable. Two friends, who are Buddhist monks, deepened my thinking about the content: Rev. Oriana LaChance and Rev. Helen Cummings, both members of the Order of Buddhist Contemplatives. Editor Ilima Loomis not only improved the readability of the book but also pointed out my conceptual gaps. Geri Larkin was the "big idea" source for the book's title, provided input on what would stay and what would go, and helped recruit collaborators Ilima and illustrator Alex Alviar. Barbara Gates gave me the encouragement and direction that moved me forward and kept me going. Limelight Department designed the book cover. Susan Jerde created the art on pages 21, 87, 88, 222, and 223. Alex Alviar created all the other art in the book. Tina Wells organized the production and did the final proofing. The book's design comes from Lynda Gansel. Ashly Cupit handled the book's production. Mauricio Valadrian created the video about the book, and Julie Hutchings helped develop the feedkindness.com website. Many friends have given me feedback along the way, including Bernadette Solano, Ed Kame'enui, Larry Weinerman, John Noell, Marty Sheehan, David Newman, Elena Rudy, Mary Opalenik, Claire Migdal, Sakre Edson, Alex Holding, Lindsey Leo, Dave Howe, Karen Fierman, Geoff Colvin, Ben Cook, Malka Simcha, Kathleen Rice-Reed, Duana Welch, Cage Campbell, Tom Maloney, Kathleen Heinz, Lynne Anderson, and Deb Jones. Thanks to Anita Archer for inspiration.

And finally, I am deeply indebted to the meditation and mindfulness classes and ceremonies of the Order of Buddhist Contemplatives at Eugene Buddhist Priory and Shasta Abbey in Mt. Shasta, California, as well as the religious guidance of the Buddhist teachers there; without these experiences, this book would not exist. In addition to the research on both mindfulness and kindness, this book is based on my experiences and those of my wife and partner, Linda; my correspondence with the men I mentor in prison, especially Roy Tester; and my relationship with the hospice patient Jeremy, whose last name I am withholding to protect his privacy

While it takes a village to raise a child, it takes a community to keep raising an adult. My gratitude extends to all those who are part of my community, in small and large ways.

The Case for Mindful Kindness

D o you find yourself wondering if there is more to life than what you've found? Despite your searching, do you continue to find that at times life lacks the meaning you crave, and happiness[i] is hard to grasp? Perhaps you spend too much time complaining, feeling resentful and irritable. Or maybe you are tired of the regrets racing around in your mind, or the anxiety you feel about a new phase of your life on the horizon, such as finding a partner, switching jobs, retirement, health problems, or living without a loved one. While many of these worries and fears are driven by genuinely important concerns, allowing them to overtake you and dominate your thoughts only serves to make you more agitated and miserable—while doing nothing to actually help the situation.

Achieving what society often teaches us to want in life—a slimmer waistline, the newest model car, a larger income—may help us to solve short-term problems and distract us for a while, but they don't help us come to a deeper understanding of our purpose in life. We are left with a feeling of emptiness, even if we have accomplished everything that society has told us we need to be happy.

Reading this book can change your purpose in life and what is meaningful to you. To see if such changes actually take place, you have to first answer these two questions now before you go through the book. Here are the two questions to answer: What are your purposes in life? What is meaningful to you in your life? To see if your answers to these questions change as you go through the book, you need to write down your answers. I recommend you pick a notebook that you dedicate as your practice journal to write answers to the exercises that appear throughout the book. For now, write your answers to these two questions on the last

---

i. Historically, in other cultures, "happiness" has meant fortunate external events. In the US, the term refers to an internal feeling based on, for example, the five elements identified by Penn State psychologist Martin Seligman: positive emotions, engagement, relationships, meaning, and achievement.

page of your practice journal. You will revisit your answers as you go through this book.

In this book, I will show you how to make your life more purposeful, healthier and happier, by fostering closer relationships, and practicing kindness. Many scientific studies have validated the importance of close relationships in human health and happiness. One longitudinal study conducted by researchers at Harvard University began with sophomores in 1938 (later, men from inner-city Baltimore were added to the study), to find out what makes for a happy, long life. Many health experts were surprised at the results reported by the study's director, Robert Waldinger, a psychiatrist at Massachusetts General Hospital and a professor of psychiatry at Harvard Medical School. "Close relationships, more than money or fame, are what keep people happy throughout their lives," he said in an interview with the *Harvard Gazette*. "Those ties protect people from life's discontents, help to delay mental and physical decline, and are better predictors of long and happy lives than social class, IQ, or even genes."[2] And what happens without close relationships? "Loneliness kills," he said. "It's as powerful as smoking or alcoholism."

The Benefits of Kindness in Building Close, Caring Relationships

How do you develop close, caring relationships? The answer, "being kind," may seem too simple.

KINDNESS
The quality of being friendly, giving, and considerate.

The scientific research about the power of kindness in developing close, caring relationships is compelling. For example, in a famous 1998 study, John Gottman, a psychology professor and researcher at the University of Washington, interviewed and observed 130 newlywed couples as they carried out everyday tasks, such as cooking, cleaning, listening to music, and talking to each other. Eighty percent of the time, Gottman was able to accurately predict whether the couple would still be together in six years into the future. How was he able to make the prediction? By observing the degree to which the couples were kind to each other. Gottman's findings about the importance of kindness and the damage of unkindness to the stability and satisfaction of a marriage has been replicated with straight and gay couples, couples with and without children, rich and poor, as well as violent and non-violent individuals. Professor Andrew Thomas studied what 2700 individuals from five countries (three Western and two Eastern) felt was the most important trait in a long-term partner. The answer was kindness. The second most important trait for males was physically attractive females, and for females financial well off males.[3] And while these findings focused on romantic pairings, I believe Gottman's findings are just as relevant to relationships with friends, family members, co-workers, and others.

What does kindness look like in Gottman's study? In its simplest form, it means that when one partner initiated a connection, the other partner would respond in a supportive, caring and interested fashion. That could mean giving positive feedback by asking to hear more, agreeing, making an encouraging comment, or offering interesting relevant information. For example, if one partner mentioned an interesting passage in a book, the other partner might ask a follow-up question, or ask to hear the passage read out loud.

Other examples of kindness documented by Gottman's research include:

- Giving the other person the benefit of the doubt (for example, when one partner is late, the other assumes it must be for a good reason, rather than taking it personally).

- Being more considerate or giving than usual when the other person is having a hard time (when one partner is feeling discouraged and overwhelmed, the other might offer to carry out some of their responsibilities).

- Expressing interest (the partners learn about what's happening in each other's worlds. They ask questions that show they are interested in each other's day-to-day lives).

- Sharing joy (when one person accomplishes something, the other takes time to celebrate it with them).

- Being gentle in conflict (kind partners avoid criticism or blame, and instead focus on their own feelings/needs).

In Gottman's study, couples who were still together after six years responded to each other with kindness almost 90 percent of the time. Being kind does not mean couples will never disagree or argue. The key is to be positive while arguing. The ratio of negativity to positivity in failed marriages was 1 to 0.8—basically, for every negative interaction, there was not quite one positive interaction. In contrast, for successful marriages, the ratio was 1 to 5.3.[4] For every negative interaction there were 5 positive interactions.

Here are some ways to be kind during conflict: Instead of blaming by saying, You never help around the house," focus on what you need by stating, "The house needs cleaning and I would really appreciate some help." By focusing on your "ask," you replace blaming others with taking responsibility for your own needs. Avoid statements that begin "You never…" or "You always…" Remain positive in conflict by listening to your partner—or family, friends, or work colleagues—without criticizing, becoming defensive, shutting down, or acting superior. Handle conflict by acknowledging your partner's ideas and feelings, while also showing mutual respect, interest, and openness.

It is interesting to note that responding in a kind, supportive manner to a partner's good news may be more important than being supportive in response to a partner's bad news. Shelly Gable, a professor of psychological and brain sciences at the University of California, Santa Barbara, led a research team that found, in general, couples responded to each other's good news in four different ways: passive-destructive, active-destructive, passive-constructive, and active-constructive. The active-constructive response, which involves enthusiasm, eye contact, and authenticity, was the only one that they found contributed to a healthy relationship.[5]

Because kindness is so central to a loving marriage, it should not come as a surprise that it is also critical in selecting a spouse or long-term partner. In *Love Factually: 10 Proven Steps from I Wish to I Do*, Duana Welch, a doctor of psychology who uses social science to study love and romance, lays out in clear detail how a person can systematically and successfully search out and vet a loving partner. What are the non-negotiables? She writes, "If I had to summarize over 60 years of excellent relationship research in just one sentence, that sentence would be: If you can find and be with someone kind and respectful, your relationship will probably work; and if you can't, it won't."[6]

Whether or not romance is on the table, the kind habits essential in finding a suitable partner and for having a loving marriage, like asking to hear more, offering genuine agreement, or making an encouraging comment, are likely to enrich all our relationships—with partners, with friends, family, colleagues, and even pets.

How to use this book

Throughout this book I'll give you a number of exercises, labeled "try it now," to help you develop mindful kindness. Some of these exercises you can do on your own, through reflection or practices like meditation or mindful breathing. Other exercises will require you to write about your thoughts or experiences. Use your practice journal and write the page number of each exercise, to make them easier to reference later. You may not feel you have time to complete every exercise. In that case, do the ones that feel most relevant to you.

try it now

Think about conversations that felt unsatisfactory because you could tell that you were not genuinely connecting with the other person. Next, think about which one of these kindness conversation skills would enrich your conversations in the future: giving feedback in the form of asking to hear more, agreeing verbally with what you are hearing, making an encouraging comment, offering interesting relevant information, or responding in a kind, supportive manner to good news. In your practice journal, write about how you will use that skill in the future.

Sonja Lyubomirsky, a professor of psychology at the University of California, Riverside, and author of *The How of Happiness*, writes: "People who are striving to improve their own happiness may be tempted to treat themselves to a spa day, a shopping trip, or a sumptuous dessert. The results of the current study suggest, however, that when happiness seekers are tempted to treat themselves, they might be more successful if they opt to treat someone else instead."[7] By treating someone else instead, you might be contributing to a close caring relationship, which is at the heart of happiness.

try it now

In your practice journal, make a list of people with whom you would like to have a closer, more caring relationship.

In addition to being critical to the health of our relationships, kindness also contributes a great deal to the health of our bodies. In one study, Barbara Fredrickson, a professor of psychology at the University of North Carolina at Chapel Hill, identified 84 healthy adults between 35 and 64 years of age as belonging to one of two groups: people oriented toward kindness toward others, versus people focused on their own pleasure. While both groups scored equally high on measures of happiness, and equally low on depression measures, significant differences were found at the physiological level. The less-kind pleasure seekers had physiological characteristics similar to people experiencing stressors like loneliness, grief, or financial difficulty. The more-kind, other-oriented people did not exhibit these same adverse physiological characteristics.[8]

Another surprising finding came when researchers at Concordia University and Indiana University looked at how kindness affects wound healing. After creating small cuts on the arms of couples, they found that the wounds literally healed faster in women who were in a kinder relationship.[9] Yanping Li, a research scientist at the Harvard T. H. Chan School of public health reported on how we benefit from kind habits we practice on ourselves: eating a healthy diet, exercising regularly, keeping a healthy body weight, not drinking too much alcohol, and refraining from smoking added about 14 years of life expectancy for women and 12 years for men.[10] Psychiatrist Kelli Harding has written the most comprehensive and compelling book on the power of kindness from a medical perspective, The Rabbit Effect: Live Longer, Happier, and Healthier with the Groundbreaking Science of Kindness.[11]

Science is not alone in recognizing the importance of kindness: so do all the world's religions, by teaching some form of the golden rule. In this book, when I use the word "kindness" I am also referring to the closely related qualities of compassion, forgiveness, empathy, and gratitude, along with acts of generosity, altruism, and cooperation.

try it now

Think about one kind act you did or saw today, and two things you are grateful for today. Write these in your journal, preceded by the number of this page.

Kindness elicits positive feelings. Take a moment now to remember a kindness you have given or received, and the feeling that accompanied that act of kindness. Experience that feeling.

That positive feeling comes from feel-good chemicals (neurotransmitters) your body produces as a kind of reward for giving and receiving kindness.

In contrast, recall a memory of a time when you were unkind, for example, by being selfish, insensitive, insulting, condescending, or even cruel. Experience that feeling.

That unpleasant feeling comes from different neurotransmitters punishing us for an unkind act. And possibly, that unkind act is part of an unkind habit.

Unkind Habits

Unkind habits not only make us unhappy, they are also linked to unkind actions that make our life more difficult, and keep us from becoming happier by getting in the way of close relationships.

UNKIND HABIT
A regular behavior or tendency etched in our brain that is cruel, inconsiderate, or causes harm to oneself or others, whether intentional or unintentional, and whether it involves thinking or action.

There are two types of unkind habits: mental and action. Mental unkind habits make you unhappy. Unkind action habits affect others as well as yourself. For example, our unkind mental habit of feeling unappreciated at work might be caused by our unkind action habits of cutting corners and slacking off. On the other hand, feeling unappreciated at work might stem from negative self-talk, telling ourselves that we're not up to the job—a different kind of unkind mental habit. To help you determine the extent that unkind mental habits are affecting your life, we've prepared the following questions about common unkind mental habits.

Are you agitated or disturbed because you **habitually**:

- Complain to yourself about things you don't like?

- Think about how you are not making good use of your time and are failing to make important changes in your life?

- Feel discouraged and depressed?

- Beat yourself up about your mistakes and missed opportunities?

- Experience anxiety?

- Worry about things you can do nothing about?

- Dwell on what might go wrong in the future?

- Have difficulty knowing how to communicate with your loved ones and friends?

- Feel lonely?

- Feel shame or guilt?

- Are angry at home, at work, or in other places?

- Are dissatisfied and lack a sense of purpose?

- Feel resentful toward people you judge because of your prejudices?

- Feel like a failure?

- Feel unappreciated at work or at home?

try it now

First make an X next to each unkind habit that you are motivated to change, then pick the one you would most like to address. Create a section of 10-15 sheets at the back of your practice journal and label it **Unkindness**. In that section, write this page number, then describe how the unkind mental habit you selected plays out in your life and why you are motivated to change it.

FROM THE OTHER SIDE

Throughout this book, I'll bring you stories "From the Other Side"—letters from some of the prisoners I've mentored in kindness, Buddhism, mindfulness, and meditation. These letters are compiled in my book *Saint Badass: Personal Transcendence in Tucker Max Hell*. Men like Tad have experienced much unkindness in their lives, both in the abuse they've endured, and in their own crimes. I asked Tad about an unkind habit he wanted to break and how he succeeded in doing so. He replied:

My hatred toward my stepfather. This was my greatest unkind habit. What made it "deadly" was the fact that I realized just how toxic it was for me. Eating me from the inside out. This man is a monster. The true meaning of evil, if one believes in such. The shit he did to me and my brothers and sisters is unforgettable. But I've, through years of practice, learned to forgive him. How? Every time I was reminded of the past, I would tell myself, "His past abuse is my strength today." My intention was to stop the self-destruction from within that caused external pain. Not just for myself, but those I would intentionally hurt. Just so they would "feel" my pain and hatred! The realization of this need for change was the beginning... Through each step on this journey, new doors are being opened to other unkind habits to overcome.

Being Mindful to Be Kind

In a simplistic sense, our happiness depends on close, caring relationships that stem from having many kind habits and few unkind habits. And what helps a person build kind habits and leave unkind habits behind? One powerful tool is mindfulness. Mindfulness practice is defined in a variety of ways. For the purposes of this book, think of it in terms of two parts:

- directing one's attention to our intention in the present moment;

- learning to ignore distracting thoughts, particularly judgmental thoughts that distract us from our intention.

Thoughts, feelings, and sensations of sight, sound, touch, and smell are constantly entering our minds. It's natural for the mind to notice these stimuli. After all, the job of the eyes is to see, and the job of the nose is to smell. In the same way, the mind's job is to notice things. The mind's response to these stimuli ranges from mindful (allowing them to arise and pass, and thus letting them go), to unmindful (treating them as a launching pad for a sequence of distracting thoughts and emotions). For example, our intention might be to chop vegetables, but as we chop, we might start thinking about the guests who will be coming over for dinner. Or we may look out the window and notice that it is raining. This is perfectly natural. If we are mindful, we can effortlessly direct our attention away from the rain and return to our intention: chopping vegetables. Continuing our mindful chopping puts our mind at rest. By keeping our attention on our intention of chopping vegetables, mindfulness can help us limit distracting, unhelpful, and sometimes destructive thoughts and emotions that we add to our life.

So if we're mindfully chopping vegetables, it doesn't matter if we notice the rain: we can quickly and effortlessly return our attention to chopping.

But if we are being unmindful, we might add unhappy thoughts to what we have noticed: "I don't like the rain. I'll probably get wet when I go to the store. When I get wet I usually catch a cold." These added thoughts agitate our mind, cause us to pay less attention to our intention—the chopping—and can contribute to our unhappiness—and maybe even distract us long enough for the knife to slip and cut a finger.

Worrying about catching a cold that hasn't happened yet offers us no benefit at all, but noticing the rain might benefit us if we remember to carry an umbrella later.

Here is another example: When you're using a chainsaw to carry out your intention to cut down trees, and doing it mindfully, you attend to the sight, smell, sound, and feel of what you are doing. Maybe most importantly, you attend to how you are holding the saw and where the saw blade will cut, for safety's sake. You also attend to your mistakes. If you don't cut through the tree trunk completely, and the trunk is pinching the saw blade so you cannot move it, you notice the mistake. It's not helpful or necessary to think, "I hate this chainsaw, the blade is dull," or "Why can't I do this right? I'll never get this job done!" When being mindful, you have the opportunity to shift your attention away from these negative thoughts and emotions, and attend to your intention: how to properly operate the chainsaw. You need to change how you are sawing and can do so without giving yourself over to these unhappy thoughts.

Mindfulness does more than shift our attention away from unhappy thoughts back to our intention. It is an essential tool in breaking our unkind habits, in developing kind habits, and in enjoying life. Mindfulness increases both our awareness of and sensitivity to our kind and unkind habits and their consequences. For example, if we have an unkind habit of becoming upset and angry over the news, mindfulness makes us more aware of the habit, and more sensitive to the bad feelings it causes in us. This awareness sets the stage to weaken that habit. It might motivate us to make a change—like limiting the amount of time we spend each day listening to the talking heads on cable TV or on the Internet.

On the positive side, leaving negative thoughts behind enables us to attend to the needs of those around us (and to our genuine needs as well!). Once we fully understand another person's needs, we know how to be kind to that person and can act on that awareness. Our time is better spent becoming increasingly sensitive to the needs of others, rather than focusing solely on ourselves or indulging our unhappy thoughts, lamenting the past, or dreading the future.

Paying close attention to our friends' needs is key to having close caring relationships. Let's say we have a kind habit of paying close attention when we're having a conversation, giving feedback in the form of asking to hear more, nodding in agreement, making an encouraging comment, or offering interesting relevant information. Being aware and sensitive helps us notice the effect this attention has on others. We feel their gratitude and enthusiasm, and these positive feelings encourage us to repeat the habit again and again.

Also mindfulness comes with its own slate of proven benefits, both for our physical health (through reduced stress and lower blood pressure) and for mental health (including reduced anxiety, less misery dwelling on the past and less worrying about the future). In this book, you will learn how to use meditation and mindfulness to pay attention to the world around you. With this clarity, you can easily see ways to be less unkind and more kind to yourself and to others. Finally, when our mind is free from negativity, it can rest. Just as resting your body refreshes you, so too does resting your mind. A resting mind is a happy mind, and ready to be kind!

Mindlessness Hinders Kind Habits

As you might expect, mindlessness has nearly the opposite effect. Mindlessness means we are less aware of our unkind habits and their consequences. For example, we might feel discouraged, angry or frustrated much of the time and unaware of the unkind habits that contribute to this feeling, such as over-doing it with food, alcohol, screen time and TV, and at the same time not getting enough healthy food, exercise, sleep or constructive engagement with others. In addition, we are less able to develop kind habits because when we are kind, we're not noticing the effect that kindness has on others and ourselves. For example, we might not even notice the way the person we're talking to relaxes, smiles, and leans in when we turn our attention back to them after glancing around the room. When we miss this important feedback, it makes it much harder to learn a positive habit, like paying attention to a conversation.

Not being mindful can have dire consequences. Consider the deadly train crash that occurred on September 12, 2008, in Chatsworth, California. An investigation later revealed that the train's engineer was sending and receiving text messages in the seconds before he ran through a red light, crashing into a freight train. Twenty-five people were killed and 135 were injured, making it the deadliest railway accident in the United States in 15 years. Since then, engineers have been banned from using their cell phones while at work. Closer to home is the finding that in 2011, at least 23 percent of all car crashes involved cell phones, which translates to 1.3 million accidents. The damage inflicted by mindlessness is one reason I would call it unkind.

In this book, I'll give you lots of tools to help you cultivate mindfulness, and decrease the time you are mindless. Some of the exercises I'll give you will focus on breath practice. In these exercises, you will direct all your attention to your breathing. Focusing on your breathing with all your attention will help your mind rest, because there is no attention left over for upsetting or worrying thoughts.

try it now

Find a quiet place where you will not be interrupted. As you take deep, slow breaths, start counting each breath silently as you exhale. Count up to five breaths, then start again at "one." It sounds easy, but you will likely find that your mind wanders. Perhaps you'll notice that you're feeling a little hungry. You might start thinking about what you'd like to eat, and make a mental note to stop at the store on the way home. Before you know it, you've lost count of your breaths. If this happens, don't worry! Thoughts arise naturally in the mind. Just go back to "one" and start counting again. Practice this exercise for 2 to 3 minutes, and gradually extend your time if you feel up to it.

Being Kindful

I like to use the word *kindful* to describe how we can combine being kind with being mindful. If mindfulness is how we can "be" in the world, kindness is what we can "do" in the world.

KINDFUL
Combining a kind and mindful state of being

Being kindful frees people from the need for distractions that can lead to over-indulging in eating, alcohol, Internet/social media, video games, or TV. Spending less time with distractions gives us more time to be kind to others, and to reap the benefits of that kindness. When we combine mindfulness and kindness into kindfulness, we benefit, and the receivers of our kindfulness also benefit. This book describes the value—to us and to society—of fusing kindness and mindfulness in all aspects of our lives.

I want to show you why you should make being kindful one of your primary purposes in life. While love is a feeling, kind habits translate that feeling into action. Most important is the hands-on advice for adopting kindfulness and meditation in a way that will better your life and the lives of those around you. In fact, many individuals with strong religious beliefs, including Christians, Jewish people, Buddhists and Muslims, have told me how kindfulness strongly supports their religion's beliefs and practices. Let's begin a purposeful, step-by-step journey to become more mindfully kind!

The Power of Kindness

While I have practiced mindfulness for more than 40 years, the idea that mindfulness and kindness might be intertwined didn't sink in until I started corresponding with Roy Tester in 2009. Roy is an inmate at the Tucker Unit, the notorious Arkansas maximum-security prison depicted in the Robert Redford movie "Brubaker," often called Tucker Max.

Roy first wrote to me because he was looking for someone to answer his questions about Buddhism. As a lay minister at the Eugene Buddhist priory, I agreed to answer his questions. To say that Roy had a traumatic life is an understatement. Throughout his childhood, he experienced repeated sexual and physical abuse at the hands of his father and his father's friend, while his mother did nothing to protect him. After years of suffering and a descent into drugs and criminality, Roy murdered both parents, and was sentenced to life in prison without parole.

It was in prison that Roy discovered Buddhism and began searching for a teacher to answer his questions—which eventually led him to me. Through our correspondence, I learned more about Roy, and encouraged him to undertake "kindness projects," even providing him with modest amounts of money to support this practice, which he used to buy food and supplies for prisoners in need. He gradually came to recognize that practicing kindness and mindfulness was essential to forgiving himself and attaining some degree of happiness even within the harsh environment of Tucker Max. Being kind contributed to caring relationships, the key to happiness.

I'm telling you about Roy to demonstrate that the practice of mindful kindness can benefit everyone, ranging from those who have a privileged life of education, personal freedom, and family support, like me, to Roy and my other prison friends who are serving long sentences, and in many cases have lost everything as a consequence of their violent crimes.

While they were learning about mindful kindness within prison, these men faced many crises, including a disabling illness, a brain tumor, a prison gang attack, family betrayal, medical abuse, and harsh punishments for minor rule violations. I watched, amazed, as each man in his own way overcame these setbacks through mindfulness and the practice of kindness. I came to see these men—who spanned faith traditions from Buddhism to Christianity to Islam, to no religion at all—not only as fellow human beings and students, but also my peers and teachers.

Corresponding with these prisoners showed me how the practice of mindful kindness can bring light, transformation, and a sense of purpose even in the darkest of places. If Roy and the rest of these men can change their lives through the practice of mindful kindness, truly anyone can.

try it now

Think about a time when you acted with kindness toward a stranger, as well as a time when a stranger acted with kindness toward you. In your practice journal, write about what happened, and about how you felt about each episode.

Gratitude

One of the most powerful aspects of kindness is gratitude, which involves being aware and thankful for all the positive things we have in life. Gratitude is enhanced by awareness; for example, being aware of the miraculous functions of our bodies and the work of the nerves, tendons, ligaments, bones, and blood vessels that give us the ability to hold a pen. The stronger and more frequent our feelings of gratitude, the stronger and more frequent our impulses to act with kindness. Multiple studies, such as one by psychology researchers Monica Bartlett and David DeSteno, have shown that feelings of gratitude foster the intention to be kind and increase the help given to others, even strangers.[12] University of Oregon neuroscientist Christina Karns reported that writing in a gratitude journal activated the "pure altruism" portion of the brain.[13] According to Robert Emmons, a professor of psychology at the University of California, Davis, and Robin Stern, director of the Yale Center for Emotional Intelligence, "Grateful people experience higher levels of positive emotions such as joy, enthusiasm, love, happiness, and optimism, and gratitude as a discipline protects us from the destructive impulses of envy, resentment, greed, and bitterness. People who experience gratitude can cope more effectively with everyday stress, show increased resilience in the face of trauma-induced stress, recover more quickly from illness, and enjoy more robust physical health."[14]

If you seldom actually feel grateful, try this activity: visualize something or someone that's very important to you—like your partner, child, parent, friend or even the car that takes you places, the home that shelters you, or the computer that makes it possible for you to work. Imagine an event that takes away this important something. Feel the sorrow and pain. Then remind yourself that you still have it. Feel the gratitude.

How Love Wins

The title of this book is *How Love Wins*. How does love win? The idea is simple. Life presents us with choices every day. To the extent that we choose to love, love wins. When we choose to love, what we do and say demonstrates that we care about others and ourselves. When we choose to love, mindful kindness wins over our unkind habits and self-centeredness. A deeper connection with others wins over isolation and alienation. Love wins by giving purpose and meaning to our lives through a cycle of giving and receiving kindness. Our gratitude grows.

This book is dedicated to helping you become more mindfully kind, a practice which can support you in becoming a better, more fulfilled person in both your secular and spiritual life. Whatever brought you to this book and prompted your choice to develop mindful kindness in yourself, doing so will provide a wide range of benefits, especially if you make mindful kindness a central purpose of your life. You will experience more moments of feeling safe and happy, more joy and gratitude, and fewer feelings of inadequacy, selfishness, indifference, and anger.

The steps that follow provide many examples and numerous exercises to help you develop and practice mindful kindness toward yourself, a partner, child, parent, friend, co-worker, community member, or even a stranger. Over time, as your daily choices build a foundation of mindfulness, you will weaken unkind habits, strengthen kind habits, and experience how love wins.

Tad, an artist, describes how he showed kindness to a friend in prison and encouraged this friend to share kindness with others in turn:

A friend of mine was going home from prison and wanted me to draw his two girls and two sons some pictures. It took me two and a half weeks of drawing. The last one was a Roman Aqueduct in France and the Sydney Opera House in Australia; that took me 18 hours to draw and four hours to shade. Then I added the North and South Constellations at the top and bottom. On the front I drew the seven continents and five oceans. Basically, not only were they nice drawings, but they were educational. When I was asked by my friend how much he owed me, I said, "Nothing. It's for your children. When you get out, stay out, and if you can help someone one day, do so." He was amazed. Even his own Homeboy had charged him.

Twelve Steps for Change

In this book, I introduce twelve steps that will help you rebuild your habits for a more mindfully kind life. In making these changes keep in mind that this is not a "self help" book, but rather an "us help" book. Why? We can rebuild our lives only with the help of those around us. And our rebuilding often contributes to their rebuilding. Also, while the concept of a twelve-step program is a well-established ladder to lasting change, my 12 steps are different because they are based on teaching methodologies developed in the education field, grounded in research on how people learn best. These methodologies include:

- Introducing key ideas, and supporting these ideas with examples and exercises you can do on your own.

- Keeping things simple, starting with something easy, and building on each success to take on a bigger challenge.

- Practicing each new principle, step, or habit until you achieve some level of self-determined mastery.

- Engaging in review of material already presented, returning again and again to practice concepts learned earlier in the book, incorporating them as you build new habits.

- Developing your independence, so that you can apply these new skills on your own, without regular outside help.

Throughout this book, you will find exercises and instruction designed to help you understand the ideas you are learning and how to put them into practice. These exercises are ideal for doing in a group setting or with a partner, sponsor, or therapist. Sharing in this way can add depth and richness to your experience, and it can also help keep you accountable for following through on the exercises and your goals.

Wrapping Up

We all have times in our life that are difficult. Sometimes they are caused by our own actions, and sometimes by circumstances out of our control. The purpose of this book is not only to prepare you for these difficult times, but also to help you live a healthier, happier life, in part by learning more kind habits that foster closer connections in your personal life and in your community as a whole. Seeing our actions as a simple collection of habits gives us the mindset that we can change our lives. That means new, kind habits can be learned, and unkind habits can be unlearned. Gratitude contributes to our resolve to change our habits. And if you are a person of faith, your faith also contributes to your resolve.

try it later

With "try it now" exercises, you can stop and write your answers immediately. With "try it later," you'll be taking time to reflect and write at a later time. Start with these two exercises:

1. Set aside another 10-15 sheets at the back of your practice journal, and label them **Mindfulness/Meditation**. For the next five days (or more) practice counting your breaths, mindfully, for 2 to 3 minutes a day, or longer. In your

journal, describe what went well and what did not go so well. Also, write about how you feel after the exercise. Are you relaxed? Are you frustrated?

2. Set aside a third set of 10-15 sheets at the back of your practice journal, and label them **Kindness/Gratitude**. Each day, list two things you are grateful for—which can be for things as simple as a moment of contentment, a close connection with a friend or pet, appreciation of something seen or heard, or an unkindness left undone. Then describe one kindness you gave or received. Continue this practice for five days (or longer).

Face Your Unkind Habits

I t's been said that nobody likes change except a wet baby, and no wonder. Change is difficult. It's uncomfortable. And because of this, we're not likely to make the great effort needed to achieve lasting change unless we're really motivated. And we're not likely to be really motivated unless we admit that something is wrong.

Good news! You're already there. The fact that you are reading this book means that you recognize there's something important about your life that needs to change. You're ready to take the first step: looking honestly at yourself and recognizing and admitting the habits that are holding you back from a kinder and more mindful life. In this step, we'll practice doing just that.

Recognize the habits that are holding you back from a kinder life.

FAILING "KINDNESS 101"

by David R. Newman

The downtown corner was busy as usual around noon that warm Thursday. Having the library on one corner and the bus depot across the street assured the usual mix of literary, itinerant, and homeless passersby and ploppers-down.

That's probably why I didn't pay much attention to the little old lady right near the crosswalk, perched on the seat of her four-wheel walker, her legs, sticking out from her skirt, looking as though, unaided, they could not carry her too far.

I was just walking by, on my way to an appointment, when she called out "can you help me?" to the two thirtyish looking women who had just navigated the street and were crossing her path. At first, they ignored her, so did I, thinking oh, a homeless lady asking for a handout. But for some reason they paused, and I paused, as she continued, "I am a bit disoriented, can you tell me which way to go to get to 10th and High?"

They hemmed and hawed, and I chimed in, "It's about four blocks that way," and pointed toward the east. The two women went on their way. And so did I for about 100 feet, until something dawned on me. I know where she must be going, I thought. It's the older-adult continuing education center, a place I often visit. And then I realized something else: all she had to do to get there was roll her walker on the bus sitting at the depot right across the street, go one stop, and she would be right there.

I looked back and saw that the woman was still where she had been, sitting on her walker. Then I continued on to my appointment, arriving with plenty of time to spare.

Not until much later, while reflecting on the incident, did it dawn on me how easy it would have been to go back, guide her to the bus, hop on with her, get off and give her a hand to the building, and then go on to my appointment which was in the same general direction.

Not until still later did I look in the education center's schedule for the week to see what might be happening around that time on that Thursday. It was a meeting of the poetry writing study group. And then I wondered this: sitting there on her walker, a bit confused amid the urban swirl, what verse might have been in her head? Perhaps it was about a lack of kindness among those who, when asked for help, responded with nothing more than cursory efficiency, and then moved on.

What Are Unkind Habits?

You may think that you recognize unkindness when you see it. After all, every major religion offers clear guidelines on what it means to be kind and unkind: the Christian ten commandments, the Jewish mitzvahs, the Buddhist precepts, and the Quran commandments. But unkind habits are not just an occasional cruel statement or hard slap on the arm. Unkind habits are patterns of hurtful behavior that we repeat over and over, on a regular basis. Few would doubt that Roy's abusive treatment by his father and mother was an example of his parents' extreme unkind habits. But what about the subtle ways we speak unkindly in day-to-day life?

In the early days of my marriage, if I was looking for something and couldn't find it, I would immediately ask my wife where it was, as if she had put it somewhere. It was a passive-aggressive way of blaming her, and she felt it. When I learned to change this unkind habit and take more responsibility for my own lost things, our relationship improved—and I usually found the object I was looking for much more quickly!

Unkind Physical Habits Directed At Others

Blaming my wife, Linda, when I could not find something was an unkind physical habit. There are many examples of unkind physical habits that target others—angry outbursts, pouting, blaming, gossiping; being controlling, impatient, arrogant, irresponsible, untrustworthy, and selfish; acting with greed; and ignoring the needs of others.

An unkind physical habit might be concrete—like trying to smash the skateboard of an obnoxious teenager. Unkind physical habits can also be verbal, for example, telling someone, "I wish you would get out of my life." Or we might complain frequently to a co-worker about our boss's management style, complain about our partner to a friend, complain to other tenants about the landlord, and complain about our parents to our partner. While it can feel nice to blow off steam, consider how verbalizing these complaints can be unkind to others and us. Bitterly complaining about a politician to your spouse on a daily basis might irritate or depress your spouse. In addition, such complaining fosters your own feelings of being disturbed.

Although our unkind habits are usually visible to those around us, we often overlook them in ourselves. To see them more clearly, take a moment to think about all the people you come in contact with over the course of your daily life: your parents, your partner, your friends, children, other family members, co-workers, fellow organization members, acquaintances, strangers, and those in marginalized groups such as the homeless, criminals, and the poor. Honestly reflect on whether you have unkind physical habits that occasionally make life more difficult for some of these people, or even caused them physical or emotional pain.

Let's look more closely at how unkind physical habits undermine close, caring relationships. Psychologist John Gottman and his research team studied the probability of newlyweds staying together. The researchers collected data that allowed them to identify four unkind habits they found to be toxic to relationships: criticism, contempt, defensiveness, and stonewalling (withdrawing or shutting down a discussion).[15] Couples who eventually divorced engaged positively with each other only one-third of the time; in contrast, the couples whose relationships happily endured engaged positively 86 percent of the time.[16]

Gottman's research team found that in what he called "disasters of relationship," unsuccessful couples disregard the kind acts of their significant others and instead respond with an unkindness. For example, if the wife said, "Ellen gave me some pea seeds that are working really well for her," the husband might reply, "It will take more than new seeds for you to grow anything."[15] In contrast, with "masters of relationship," the husband might respond with encouragement, or ask his wife to tell him more about her garden.

Another telltale sign of "disaster" couples is a lack of interest in the successes of their partner. If one person mentioned something about being honored for volunteer work, the partner would ignore the comment, or display a lack of interest by deadpanning "good for you" while continuing to read the newspaper.

The harm caused by the unkind habits of criticism, contempt, defensiveness, and stonewalling are not limited to marriage. They can also prevent or end friendships, poison relationships with parents, turn siblings against each other, and create a toxic work environment. Of course, this type of harm can come from other unkind habits, such as those involving anger, anxiety, cruelty, fear, jealousy, laziness, addictions of various types, arrogance, narcissism, untrustworthiness, selfishness, malicious gossip, and overeating.

Unkind habits such as overeating can lead to heartbreak. For example, my daughter Leah, a physicians assistant, was treating a patient named Lena. Lena was overweight, as was her 8-year-old son, who was just diagnosed with a fatty liver, indicating diabetes. Recognizing how she had allowed her son to become obese, Lena said with sorrow and horror to my daughter, "I'm killing my own son."

try it now

You already have a five-sheet section in the back of your practice journal labeled **Unkindness**. In that section, describe one of your unkind habits and how it negatively affects a person close to you, such as your partner, child, close friend, parent, co-worker or even your pet. Consider asking the person close to you to identify an unkind habit they would like you to break. Describe how you feel and how the other party feels when you carry out this unkind habit.

Write a check mark in front of your answer because you will return to it later. Writing about our own unkind habits can be stressful. Take off some of the stress with mindfulness while counting your breaths, to give your mind a rest.

A note on using this book:

When reflecting on your own unkind habits, be careful about dredging up experiences from your past that are associated with dark and destructive memories and emotions. If an exercise does bring up these extreme negative feelings, take several moments to allow yourself to become calm before going on to another activity. Using mindful breathing at this point may be helpful. If your distress is not relieved, consider getting help from a therapist, spiritual teacher or friend.

In particular, some people dealing with trauma may find that mindfulness, meditation, building kind habits and weakening unkind habits trigger unhelpful emotions. For a fuller explanation of why these practices may not be helpful for some trauma victims, refer to *The Pocket Guide to the Polyvagal Theory: The Transformative Power of Feeling Safe*, by Stephen Porges.

Unkind Physical Habits Directed at Yourself

While unkind habits almost always affect both ourselves and others, some unkind physical habits—like substance abuse, unhealthy eating, or procrastination—are primarily directed toward ourselves. These habits can lead to real unhappiness in our lives. We might lose sleep at night berating ourselves for a mistake, deliver poor results at work because we've wasted hours scrolling through social media, or lose ourselves in video games at the expense of developing a real-world social life. Being self-absorbed with the consequences of our unkind physical habits also makes us less aware of the harm we cause and less aware of opportunities to act with kindness, which stands in the way of having close caring relationships.

try it now

In the **Unkindness** section of your practice journal, list one or two of the unkind physical habits that you direct at yourself. Reflect on how they make you feel and how they are affecting your life and the lives of those around you. Being honest with yourself about your unkind habits can be challenging. If you are uncertain about the unkind habits you direct at yourself, ask someone close to you. Write a check mark in front of your answers because you will return to them later.

Mind-Wandering Habit

MIND-WANDERING
The state of mind that drifts away from one's intention, and instead attends to a sequence of distracting or upsetting thoughts.

Our discussion up to this point has described unkind physical habits directed toward yourself and toward others. Now we are going to look at our mental habits—habits that take place internally with our thoughts and emotions—beginning with mind-wandering.

Everyone knows what it feels like to let their mind wander. In fact, sometimes letting your thoughts drift along with the clouds can feel quite pleasant. You can get involved in thoughts about life's small and often daily distractions, both pleasant and unpleasant. I call this, "low-keyed mind-wandering." Because we are human, thoughts will arise. Having thoughts is not a problem. Quietly grumbling about the mess in the kitchen while washing dishes; realizing, in the middle of your drive to work, that you forgot your lunch at home; or daydreaming about an upcoming vacation while writing a report are all forms of low-keyed mind-wandering. These thoughts may be distractions, but they don't necessarily lead to unkindness. Sometimes low-keyed mind-wandering helps us remember important tasks, or boosts our creativity with a sudden brainstorm.

But it's important to recognize that when our attention wanders from what we're doing, we're being unmindful, and this condition can result in us being unkind to ourselves or others. For example, think about when you're talking with a friend who is upset. You might only have a few minutes to catch up with their news after not seeing each other for a long time. Listening with your full attention makes your friend feel special, heard, and important, and it strengthens your relationship. But if you're mind-wandering—distracted, for example, by thoughts about your latest money worries, or daydreaming about the romantic date you have planned for that evening—your friend will likely notice and feel that you are disconnected, even if you continue to smile and nod. In fact, your mind-wandering means you are being unkind, even though you do not recognize it. If mind-wandering keeps you from feeling empathy for your friend's distress, you will not see any need to truly connect.

There are times when the harm caused by mind-wandering habits becomes obvious, such as the train engineer you read about in the Introduction. Or think of a kayaker paddling through a long stretch of difficult rapids. She directs her attention to the current, the whitewater, the exposed boulders in front of her, and the sound of the approaching waterfall. Suddenly a rowdy group of fishermen appears on the shore. She cannot let herself become distracted by them and let her mind wander. One moment of inattention to the river could be disastrous.

Mind-wandering can be harmful, even dangerous.

try it now

Sit for mindful breathing, and count your breaths as you have practiced. When a distracting thought arises, notice it, then return to counting. Do this for two to three minutes. Then write about the experience.

Unkind Mental Habits

While low-keyed mind-wandering is often harmless, negative mind-wandering is different. It is an unkind mental habit that does more than just take us away from our current intention—it also causes unhappiness. Studies have found that the more time spent with negative mind-wandering, the more unhappy people are likely to be. Spending less time with negative mind-wandering/unkind mental habits, which frees people to nurture their relationships, is actually more closely tied to people's happiness than how much money they make.[17]

Some unkind mental habits, such as being overly critical, are easy to recognize. When we look at a difficult person and think to ourselves, "I wish he would get out of my life!" or fantasize about destroying an irksome neighbor's blaring stereo, it's no mystery that we are thinking unkind thoughts. Sometimes it's harder to admit to unkind mental habits that we direct at ourselves such as feeling inadequate. "Why did I eat that whole banana split? I have no self-control." "I'm not surprised he didn't call me back. Who would want to date someone like me?" "I'm just being selfish."

For some of us, unkind self-talk has become so habitual, we don't even recognize it as unkind. And yet, identifying and admitting our unkind mental habits is vitally important, because unkind actions begin with an unkind thought or emotion. For example, worrying is one of my own unkind mental habits. While worry may feel like something that stays on the inside, I've seen firsthand how it can affect others. On one occasion, my wife, Linda, and I were preparing dinner for our Buddhist Priory monk and a visiting monk. While working in the kitchen, my worry about whether we would have the food ready in time replaced my intention of cutting tomatoes correctly and safely. I became distracted, and stopped paying attention to what I was doing with the knife. As the monks pulled up in front of our house, Linda and I pulled out of the driveway; she was taking me to urgent care because I had badly cut my hand. My physical pain was from the cut, but my embarrassment was from how my habit of worrying caused me to be unmindful.

Agitating Unkind Habits

We have looked at unkind physical habits and unkind mental habits. All unkind habits occur at one of two levels of intensity: agitating and disturbing.

Some unkind habits are just disagreeable; we call them agitating habits. The negative thoughts from unkind mental habits distract but do not dominate us. For example, we often complain to ourselves with internal self-talk, a very common type of agitating unkind mental habit. We might, for example, complain to ourselves about the weather, our partner's insensitive behavior, a real or perceived slight by a friend, an inability to find anything to do with our free time—even how badly we slept last night.

While complaining silently to ourselves might leave us feeling agitated, complaining out loud can agitate others as well. Our friends might not mind us occasionally venting our frustrations. But when complaining goes on and on (our unkind physical habit), our friends can become irritated about hearing these complaints over and over again.

Besides, does the constant complaining actually change anything? Of course not. This kind of agitating dialogue is itself unkind—it usually makes us feel worse about the situation, and may lead us to ignore the needs of others or even behave unkindly toward them. Moreover, the habit of complaining is likely to make it harder for us to recognize if our own behavior or actions contributed to the situation we're unhappy about. And being unaware of our unkind habits makes us far less likely to change them.

On the other hand, when we stop complaining, we are happier, because we are not dwelling on our complaints and have more opportunities to be kind in our relationships. If you find it hard to break the habit of complaining, try this: each time you feel the impulse to complain, remember something you are grateful for.

Disturbing Unkind Habits

With more intense unkind mental habits, we can become consumed by dark, negative thoughts and emotions; we are deeply disturbed. In this state, we are often self-absorbed, and may feel cut off from everyone and everything around us, or closed in, as if we are in a tiny room from which we cannot escape. We call these "disturbing unkind habits."

Rage is one example. Imagine if, driving on the freeway, a driver cuts across your lane, forcing you to hit the brakes. Agitation would be a typical response. But if you allow yourself to become deeply disturbed, instead of agitated, you might become enraged, and your mental unkind habit of rage could become an unkind physical habit, such as tailgating the offending driver, repeatedly honking your horn, or even trying to pull alongside the offending driver to yell at him and then speeding ahead to cut him off.

While agitating unkind mental habits are upsetting, disturbing unkind physical habits are destructive, to us and often to those around us.

try it now

If you are aware of a disturbing unkind habit (mental or physical), describe it in the **Unkindness** section of your practice journal. Your unkind habit could be one you identified earlier as being directed at another person or at your self. Write a check mark in front of your answer because you will return to it later.

Triggering Our Habits

TRIGGER

An external occurrence that provokes a habitual behavior.

Often there's an external event that serves as a trigger for a physical or mental habit. An unkind habit might be triggered by something undesirable happening to you, or by getting something you never wanted in the first place—like coming down with a cold just before your birthday, or finding out you have rats in your home. The greater our wish to avoid an uncomfortable or unpleasant thing, the more frustration we will feel when it crosses our path, and the more likely it is that our agitation will lead us to a disturbed mental habit.

Failing to get something we desire can also trigger agitation and frustration. A romantic relationship that doesn't work out, a vacation that has to be canceled—the stronger we desire that attractive something, the more likely we will feel disturbed when we don't get it. Thinking about how terrible our disappointment is and how unhappy we are moves us from agitation to disturbance. We just keep feeding it; it's like being on a diet and eating the first potato chip or spoon of ice cream—we keep on eating more and more.

Allowing ourselves to be swept away by unkind mental habits, whether we're just agitated or feeling deeply disturbed, often triggers unkind physical habits. It's no secret that you're more likely to snap at your kids or let loose on a customer service agent when you've had disappointments or frustrations earlier in the day. Moreover, being engaged with our unkind mental habits takes us away from our intention in the present moment, which prevents us from noticing the needs of others or fully experiencing feelings of safety, contentment, and quiet joy.

A common unkind mental habit for alcoholics, drug users, gamblers, and unfaithful spouses is anticipating the rush from carrying out their habit. This anticipation can be a trigger for the unkind habit. Embezzlers, workaholics, and gamblers might daydream about how they are going to spend the money coming from their habit. Such pleasant thoughts are actually strengthening their unkind habits.

FROM THE OTHER SIDE

Once released from prison, Tad, wrongly convicted of rape, is required to follow the rules for sex offenders for the rest of his life. As he describes his struggle, he is more than agitated; he is disturbed, because it dominates his thoughts.

Some days I get so AGITATED. I don't feel like doing anything! On one hand I'm grateful for my situation because if I'd never had come to prison, I wouldn't have met some really inspiring people that helped change my being. But, on the other hand, I want the truth to come out because it's me that will have to face all the bullshit when I get out and for the rest of my life. My sister, Betty, told me, "I could come live with her until I get on my feet." But I can't!! Why? She has two teenaged daughters. By law, I can't live there. She has no problem with me living there because she knows the whole story. And I look at all the other places, by law, I won't be able to go. No public libraries, etc. Hell—I'm even afraid of getting involved with a woman that has kids. Because I know, by law, what will happen. I could be sent back to prison for loving and taking care of that woman and her kids. And the sad part is I want kids. I've learned what it means to be a great dad and husband. But... I won't be able to experience it nor show a kid(s) and wife what it's like to have that type of environment. Very depressing at times.

Yes, I've even thought about killing myself if I don't get some relief on my case. Maybe then someone would look into it. Maybe!

This is my negative mind-wandering. Sleepless nights. Moments when I just want to give up. I hate how it makes me feel. That is, the "Giving up" part. Some action on my case would bring some relief to my misery.

Unkind Personality Types

Unkind habits can occur in clusters. I have described six clusters in the chart below, which I call unkind personality types. These clusters allow the reader to reflect on whether they have a cluster of related unkind habits.

UNKIND PERSONALITY TYPE
A cluster of unkind habits that consistently occur together

To change an unkind personality type means changing a significant number of habits, which is clearly more difficult than changing a single habit. Even if you do not have an unkind personality type, you might find it helpful to read through this list, to help you identify unkind habits you might want to weaken in the future.

Six Unkind Personality Types

Personality Type	The cluster of unkind habits that make up the personality type.
Antisocial	Unconcern or indifference for the feelings of others; often disregards social expectations and obligations; irritable, at times aggressive; at times acts impulsively, lacks guilt in some situations, and fails to learn from some experiences. Relationships often short lived.
Melodramatic	Self-blame from a limited sense of self-worth; well-being depends on attention and approval from others; may take risks to gain attention and approval; may act overly charming, even seductive, but relationships are many times superficial; disapproval leads to a cycle of more self-blame and more attempts to gain attention and be seductive, followed by disapproval.

Narcissistic	Pronounced sense of self-importance, sense of entitlement, needs to be admired, limited empathy; at times lies and takes advantage of others to get their way; in many situations seen as controlling, intolerant, selfish and insensitive; if ridiculed or obstructed, can respond with anger and occasionally revenge.
Avoidant	Self-blame from believing oneself socially inept, unappealing, or inferior; fears being embarrassed, criticized, or rejected. Restrained in some aspects of intimate relationships; spends too much time monitoring one's own thoughts and feelings and those of others. Develops a cycle: frequent monitoring leads to feeling more inferior, followed by more monitoring.
Obsessive-Compulsive	Overly focused on details, order, lists, organization or schedules; inflexible and at times makes unreasonable demands. Can be doubting, cautious, rigid, controlling, humorless and miserly. At times, anxieties arise from perceived lack of control. Sees people and events as black or white with limited tolerance for complexity.
Dependent	Self-blame from lack of self-confidence and frequent need to be looked after, often needing help; lets others make important decisions; fears abandonment and can go to great lengths to secure and maintain a relationship. Acts subservient and ingratiating to some people seen as protective and powerful, further increasing dependency and setting the stage, in some instances, for abuse and exploitation

try it now

Do you recognize several of your own unkind habits in one of the unkind personality types listed above? If you do, in the **Unkindness** section of your practice journal, list those habits. If you do not identify with an unkind personality type, just list one or two unkind habits that you discovered about yourself after reading about the six types. Write a check mark in front of your answers, because you will return to them later.

Not All Unkind Habits Are Permanent

An addiction, whether you consider it a deeply rooted unkind habit or a disease, is particularly difficult to break, in part because of the addict's preoccupation with feeding their addiction, their self-absorption, and their feelings of isolation. However, positive change is possible and happens for many people. Phil is an example. He was an alcoholic who lost his job, his marriage, and his health. He eventually joined Alcoholics Anonymous, and was able to stay sober for 22 years, until his death. After he passed away, other AA members came forward to talk about how he had saved their lives by taking them in and staying with them around the clock while they dried out.

One recovering alcoholic talked about a time when he had just come out of rehab. Shortly after being released, he went to a car dealership where Phil was a salesman. When the man got out of his late-model pickup and walked up to Phil, he asked about buying a new truck. With mindfulness developed during his many years as an AA sponsor, Phil recognized the man as a fellow alcoholic and answered the stranger's question with this question "Do you know Bill W.?" In AA, this is code for "Are you an alcoholic?" The man replied yes, and Phil said, "You don't need a new truck. Here is what you need." Phil handed the man several tapes about AA, his phone number, and information about the schedule for AA meetings. The man would later turn to Phil in times of need. The man ended his story by saying he would not be alive today if it weren't for Phil. Phil illustrated how love wins with his 22 sober years of mindful kindness. In later steps in this book, we will work on breaking unkind habits and replacing them with kind habits.

Overcoming your own unkind habits, especially ones as deeply ingrained as addiction, and spreading kindness to others is truly how love wins.

Wrapping Up

You have learned that kind habits promote happiness by facilitating caring relationships; on the other hand, unkind habits prevent or destroy these close connections. All the world's religions have rules around unkind habits that guide our moral behavior. In this step, you learned about how unkind habits harm ourselves and others and prevent us from resting our mind and being kind to others. You then identified the unkind physical habits you want to break, or at least weaken. Becoming aware of your unkind habits (mental and physical) and becoming willing to change them is an important step in becoming a kindful practitioner. Find time to practice mindful breathing with counting, because it is the foundation for more advanced mindfulness exercises that come later.

try it now

Most of us have so many unwanted habits, we need to set priorities. As you've worked through this step in your practice journal, you made check marks in four places to identify unkind habits, both mental and physical. Now you are ready to set your priorities. Go back through the **Unkindness** section of your journal and find those check marks. Select one unkind habit you want to break, and then write down the answers to the following questions:

- Describe the unkind habit.

- Is the unkind habit mental or physical?

- If it is an unkind physical habit, is it directed at yourself, your partner, friend, children, other relative, co-worker, fellow organization member, acquaintance, or stranger?

- What triggers this unkind habit?

- What is the effect of your unkindness on you and/or on anybody else who is involved?

time for reflection

Near the end of each day take a few moments to reflect on how these practices are working for you and how they are making you feel:

- Mindful breathing.

- Naming two things you are grateful for.

- Naming one kindness you did, received, observed or read about.

- If you are being less unkind, think about whether this change is causing others to treat you differently. If so, what is the difference and how did it make you feel?

STEP 2
Check Your Foundation

You can't build a house on quicksand—you need a strong base of solid ground. So before we start work on the new habits that will help us live kinder and more mindful lives, let's take a look at what we're building on. There are three major skill groups that form the foundation for new habits. These skills are what give you the mental and physical resources, the resilience, and the tenacity to bring about lasting change in your life:

- **Skills of change:** The ability to determine if the cause of your unkind habit is in your mental or physical world.

- **Skills of action:** The ability to assume the role you need to lead a loving, healthy, and meaningful life (also known as the kindful practitioner, detective, and warrior).

- **Skills of character:** The ability to call up a growth mindset, conscientiousness, patience, and humility.

Skills of Change

The ability to determine if the cause of your unkind habits is in your mental or physical world.

In Step 1, you learned to identify your unkind habits. The skills of change assume you are motivated to weaken them. You can start by determining if an unkind habit is caused by a situation in your physical world, or by the state of your mental world. The ability to make that distinction, and then act on your assessment, forms the first foundational skill group you will need to change your life. Step 1 provided examples of unkind mental habits—like worrying, internal complaining, resentment—which are examples of negative mind-wandering. It also provided examples of unkind physical habits, which occur in our material world. Some are directed at ourselves, such as substance abuse, unhealthy eating, or procrastination. Others are unkind habits directed at others, such as angry outbursts, passive resistance to another's expectations, pouting, blaming, or controlling.

Here's an example of why the distinction between unkind mental and physical habits is important. Let's say you're expecting a raise at work. Your annual employee review comes and goes, but the raise never materializes. Now you're really unhappy. You become negative at the workplace and even at home because of your anger about not being given the raise. While it's true that the failure to get the raise happened in the physical world, the feelings of unhappiness actually are occurring in your mental world. With skills of change, you can decide whether to change your mental world, your physical world, or both. You can take steps in your physical world by making the case for why you should get a raise. You can also take steps in your mental world, to calm yourself through mindfulness. The sections to come will give you tools for both changing your physical world and your mental world.

For many of us, figuring out whether it's our mental world or our physical world that needs to change is very challenging. This is why millions of people have found comfort and guidance in the Serenity Prayer:

> *God grant me the serenity to accept the things I cannot change,*
> *Courage to change the things I can,*
> *And the wisdom to know the difference.*

It's not hard to see how the prayer could be rephrased as a mantra of mindfulness:

> *Use mindfulness to change my mental world;*

Kindness to change my physical world;
And wisdom to know which one to emphasize in the present moment.

When my wife, Linda, used to speak to me with a sharp tone of voice, it was my habit to respond with irritation. Realizing that my response was harmful, I had two major choices: should I change my mental world to try to stop feeling anger, or change my physical world by talking to Linda about her tone? I decided to talk with her about it calmly. She responded by saying she was not aware of how I was being affected and would be more careful with how she spoke to me. She actually thanked me for bringing up my concern and softened her voice. While I didn't act on my anger, recognizing the emotion motivated me to speak up and talk to my wife about something that was bothering me. It actually made our relationship better.

Sometimes you'll find that just changing your mental world can solve your problem. I was on vacation with my wife many years ago, and she decided it would be good for us to go for a morning hike. She took us to a trail that turned out to be hot, rocky, and unforgiving. Forgetting all about mindfulness, I quickly fell into agitated mind-wandering. My annoyance increased as I dwelled on my negative thoughts: thinking about what we should have done instead, how this hike was going to ruin the rest of my day, and why Linda made these kinds of terrible decisions. I was unhappy. Even worse, Linda was unhappy because she felt my unkindness. I complained, blamed her for the glare burning my eyes, and snapped at her. Not being mindful or kind toward Linda or myself, made me even unhappier, and feeling my increased unhappiness led to more unkindness.

Two days later, I found myself hiking with Linda on another path of jagged, unforgiving rock at the same hot time of the day. My physical world was virtually identical to that of the first walk. But my mental world could not have been more different; my mind was at rest, preventing the negative mind-wandering. I noticed the rock's richness and a complex mosaic of shards and broken seashells, changing like a kaleidoscope with reflections from the sun. I took in the calling of cardinals in the nearby trees, goats bleating on the hillside, and the feeling of the trail under my feet. I smiled. I was happy without having to put words to it. Naturally, I was kind to Linda too. I thanked her for finding this trail, and we talked about the beautiful things we were seeing.

So if the trail was nearly the same, why was the experience so different? Put simply, I was walking with mindfulness. This time, we had a short wait before we could set off on the hike. During the wait, I spent a few minutes practicing tai chi. The exercise brought my attention back to my body, engaging my mindfulness. By the time I started down the trail, I was ready to be fully present and take responsibility for what I thought and said, instead of blaming Linda.

Acting on our intention to change our mental world can be very difficult when we are aware of great suffering—such as famine caused by corruption, wars caused by hate, or ignorance that leads to the abuse and neglect of children. We need to change our mental world so that the suffering does not overwhelm us; we can still act with kindness in the physical world and reduce the suffering around us. "Not all of us can do great things. But we can do small things with great love."[18]

try it now

In your practice journal, list two or three personal problems that are currently causing you unhappiness. What part of each problem is occurring in the physical world? What part is in your mental world?

FROM THE OTHER SIDE

Here's how Tad answered the question above about changing his mental world:

Knowing I'm in prison for a crime I didn't commit is tough! I must be brutal and stay away from dwelling on it. It's not a feeling of hatred. It's just hurt. Only a person in my shoes could sympathize with me. That is why I got that little powerful saying written down where I can read it on a regular basis. I've shared it before, but it is worth repeating: "It's a smaller thing to suffer punishment than to have deserved it! The punishment can be removed, but the fault will remain forever!!"

Skills of Action

The ability to assume the role you need to lead a loving, healthy, and meaningful life (also known as the kindful practitioner, detective, and warrior).

Once we decide we need to change our mental and/or physical worlds, it's time to take action by assuming one of three roles: the kindful practitioner, the detective, or the warrior. Each of us is capable of being a kindful practitioner, detective, and warrior. This foundational skill involves knowing which role is required, committing time and effort, and learning how to take on that role. Let's take a closer look at each of these skills of action.

Kindful Practitioner

The kindful practitioner describes our primary role. Kindful practitioners make efforts many times every day to treat themselves and others with mindful kindness. And the kindful practitioner does not expect anything in return for serving others. For example, the kind habit of deep listening to a friend, without interrupting to judge or offer advice, is a way to serve, allowing our friend to vent about their troubles and enabling us to better learn how to act with kindness towards them. This authentic conversation and other activities such as mindfully listening to music, exercise, sex, and meditation reward us with positive feelings, caused by feel-good chemicals released in our body. These feelings renew us, which gives us energy and strengthens our resolve to be kindful practitioners.

I think of being kind to others as serving them. The "Renew-and-Serve" Cycle means that we are follow a pattern, alternating between renewing ourselves and serving others.

RENEW-AND-SERVE CYCLE
A pattern of alternately "renewing" by taking care of oneself, and "serving" by being kind to others.

Let's consider two examples of how the Renew-and-Serve Cycle plays out in different relationships.

Parents

Your cranky baby is increasingly irritating you at bed time. You ask your husband to watch the baby as you take a five-minute meditation break after dinner (renew). You then have the calmness to cuddle your baby and play with her (serve).

The kindful practitioner acts with mindful kindness in spite of many distractions.

Partners

Your husband has had a difficult and frustrating day at work and calls to ask to take a half hour walk before coming home (renew). As a kindful practitioner, you encourage him to take the walk, while you start preparing dinner. After coming home, your husband takes over dinner preparation (serve). After dinner, your husband enjoys some time with your daughter (renew) and then comes in to do the dishes (serve).

Renew-and-Serve Cycle for Partners

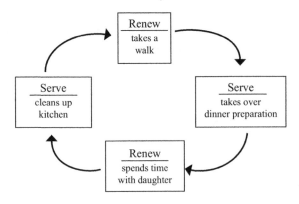

Warning! Some people find themselves playing the role of kindful practitioner so convincingly that they become a doormat.

DOORMAT
Someone who repeatedly sacrifices their own needs in order to serve others.

Many people, especially women, have been socialized to be doormats by too often putting others' needs above their own, and in doing so not taking adequate care of themselves. Making too many of these sacrifices suggests the person is not setting boundaries—failing to say "no" to unreasonable or excessive requests. If you recognize this happening—that you are allowing someone to take advantage of you—it is important to see it as an unkind habit toward yourself. This is something you can work to change by going through the steps in this book. Conversely, many men have been socialized to feel that kindness is a feminine trait. If you recognize this in yourself—a hesitation to act with kindness, because you see it as less "manly"—develop your kindness by continuing through the remaining steps in this book.

FROM THE OTHER SIDE
Tad describes helping other prisoners as a kindful practitioner:

I find their strengths and their weaknesses. I set up situations to help build on their strengths and opportunities to weaken any weakness that hinders them. Example would be Chris. Great people person. Big heart. But he will let people walk on him as you cautioned on the dangers of the kindful practitioner. So...I help him weaken that area. How? I stay on his ass. I will tell him, "Don't sell yourself short. Be courageous. But stay professional." Yes. I do this to help. But, you and I both know, I do it for practice too! Practice to help myself become a skillful compassionate person.

Being a kindful practitioner requires that we use mindfulness to strengthen and build kind habits, while weakening unkind habits. As the graphic below shows, practicing strong compassion and mindfulness help build kind habits. On the other hand, extensive unmindfulness works against building kind habits.

Our Purpose: Being a Kindful Practioner with The Renew-and-Serve Cycle

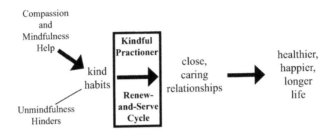

Living life as a kindful practitioner, following the Renew-and-Serve Cycle, can be the purpose that fosters close caring relationships and contributes to a healthier, happier, and longer life.

PURPOSE
A central motivating force that guides our life decisions, influences our behavior, shapes our goals, offers a sense of direction, and creates meaning.

Having mindful kindness as a purpose does not stand in the way of our career aspirations or limit our options for forming relationships. On the contrary, the research summarized by the Fostering Purpose Project suggests that being a kindful practitioner supports every aspect of our personal and professional lives. The benefits of having a sense of purpose are wide ranging, from improved life satisfaction, to better health (including less stress and pain), longevity, resilience, and competence.[19]

But what sustains us in having mindful kindness as our purpose? A number of feel-good chemicals are released in our body when we act with kindness, and even when we observe kindness. In addition, kindness improves our relationships, which again releases feel-good chemicals. Finally, the kindful practitioner benefits from the kindness-happiness loop: kindness begets happiness, and being happy induces us to be more kind, which is particularly fruitful in developing close caring relationships.

The researcher Lara Aknin agrees: "The practical implications of this positive feedback loop could be that engaging in one kind deed (e.g., taking your mom to lunch) would make you happier, and the happier you feel, the more likely you are to do another kind act."[20]

We also renew by weakening our unkind habits, which reduces our negative mind-wandering and unhappiness. For example, I have had an unkind habit of showing my irritation. Because I am often around Linda, I feel guilty and unhappy after making Linda the recipient of my irritation. I renew by reducing the frequency and intensity of my feelings of irritation, and by not being irritable around Linda. I am being kind to myself, as well as to her, which is implementing the Renew-and-Serve Cycle. This Cycle also can be strong medicine when we are suffering physical illness or mental unrest, by giving some relief from the grip of those negative feelings. A good friend described how she broke out of her anger by giving her earbuds to a stranger in the airport. The man was listening to loud music, which was irritating everyone nearby. As soon as she gave him her ear buds, her anger lifted. She told me her revelation: "to change your mind, be kind."

try it now

Turn to the section in the back of your journal titled **Kindness/ Gratitude**. Assume that being a kindful practitioner will be one of your major purposes. Write down your thoughts about how being a kindful practitioner (using the Renew-and-Serve Cycle) could contribute to the purpose of your life, as well as your happiness and the happiness of those close to you.

The Detective

While we want to be the kindful practitioner as often as possible, we take on the role of detective or warrior only when the need arises. When you need to figure out a solution to a problem in the physical world, you can call up your detective role. Not everything has to be resolved by changing your mental world and accepting the status quo in your physical life. In the case of the employee who was frustrated about being passed over for a raise, the employee does not have to just live with things as they are.

He can investigate other options, like talking to his boss, or looking for another job.

We can also take on the role of the detective when our negative mind-wandering is caused by the unkind habit of another person. For example, a wife might often feel frustrated and discouraged because of the unkind way her partner communicates or because he refuses even to discuss problems and deal with them. Taking on the role of the detective, the wife might seek recommendations for a counselor to help repair the relationship. If the partner refuses to go to counseling, the wife can end the relationship or decide to use mindfulness to focus her attention on the many other things she loves about her partner, with the goal of staying with him.

Finding answers or solving problems can be an act of kindness to yourself and others, and is essential in sticking to our purpose of being a kindful practitioner. Even better, detectives don't waste time worrying. So instead of worrying if your mole is cancerous, if your child's acting out in school will lead to expulsion, or why you don't have more friends, take on the role of the detective. Have a doctor look at your mole. Ask the school for an assessment by a behavioral consultant. Practice what you learn in this book to build more close, caring relationships.

The diligent detective gathers information
needed to solve a problem in the physical world.

When the Problem Needs a Detective

When the doctor told my friend Jack, who was a scientist, that he had prostate cancer, fear wasn't just an emotion, it was a physical sensation that tightened his entire body. But after the initial shock wore off, his training as a researcher kicked into gear. His inner detective was on the case.

Jack poured all his fear and anxiety into learning more about his disease. Some of what he learned made him even more alarmed, but some was useful. He learned that while surgery and radiation treatment, as recommended by his urologist, was the standard of care for early-stage cancers like his, a few specialists were recommending a different course of action: active surveillance, which reduced the potential for serious side effects. More research not only helped him find a better doctor, he also learned that a popular supplement he was taking was known to exacerbate prostate cancer. With this information in hand, Jack shifted into the role of a kindful practitioner. He confidently moved forward in managing his own care with a new doctor, changing his regimen of supplements, and eating a healthier diet. Unfortunately, many men diagnosed with low-risk prostate cancer at the same time as Jack received treatments with serious side effects. Today, most specialists put low risk patients on active surveillance.

Wise Warrior

The warrior, who stands strong in the face of adversity, is also critical for us to carry out our purpose of being a kindful practitioner. With mindfulness, the warrior never loses focus, and is mindful and kind under the most difficult circumstances. When you falter, your inner warrior helps you get back up. Think about how you find the courage to act with integrity and refrain from lashing out when you feel attacked, or the inner strength it takes to accept a bitter loss and carry on. In these moments, being able to call up the warrior to lead you forward is a foundational life skill.

For some, the warrior sounds like willpower. But many people find that willpower alone is not enough to confront difficult change. This is why many 12-step programs encourage people in recovery to turn themselves over to a higher power. If willpower is not working for you, your higher power might come from faith in God, a spiritual path, a medical doctor in a treatment center, a counselor, or an inspirational person. Regardless of your choice of a higher power, there are times when it is best to let the warrior give you the strength to let go of listening only to your own advice and accept help.

The wise warrior faces adversity, in spite
of fear and feelings of inadequacy.

Calling Upon Your Warrior

My mother, Olive, had always inspired me with her kindness, but near the end of her life, I was deeply moved to witness her ability to call upon her inner warrior. Even though she suffered with debilitating pain and depression as she approached death, she continued to give more thought to caring for others than she did to her own discomfort. When a longtime friend, Denver, came to say goodbye, she referred to him as my brother, symbolically making him part of our family. That same day, she told Masha, her caregiver, "I don't know why we were meant to become such close friends at this time, but I will miss you when I'm gone. I'm going to wait for you inside heaven's gates until you come. Then we will be together again." Masha later told me, with tears in her eyes, that it was the nicest thing anyone had ever said to her.

In the final days of my mother's life, I called her every day. Each time we spoke, she would tell me that things couldn't be any better. When we finally learned death was near, Linda and I quickly packed and found plane reservations, managing to get to her bedside the next day. Unsure if she could even hear me, I took her hand, saying, "I made it." She looked up, smiled, and said, "I did too." Mom's warrior stood by her until the end, a source of strength, courage, and even humor that lifted up the people whom she loved the most.

try it now

In your practice journal, write about situations in which you have benefited or would benefit from taking on the detective role, the warrior role, and the kindful practitioner role. Which is your strongest role of the three? Which is your weakest? Why?

Skills of Character

The ability to call up a growth mindset, conscientiousness, patience, and humility

You've learned about skills of change, the ability to determine if your unkind habit is in your mental or physical world; and skills of action, the ability to assume the role of kindful practitioner, detective, and warrior. Our third and final set of foundational skills provides critical support in seeing meaningful change through to completion. This set includes developing a growth mindset, conscientiousness, patience, and humility. Not being fully developed in one of these areas can explain in part why we get frustrated again and again when we find it hard to build kind habits or weaken unkind habits. I call them "skills of character," because they represent the ability to recall, in a difficult moment, the core values that make us who we are. That's not to say that people with skills of character execute things perfectly all the time. All of us have moments when we drop the ball or lose our patience. But having skills of character (including the ones described here, and more) means being able to call upon that higher self frequently and reliably when a situation demands it.

Growth Mindset

Everyone occasionally acts in an unkind manner. However, having unkind habits is something else entirely. That's because with a habit, you repeat your unkind behavior over and over again. There are two different views on what makes a habit. Some people see habits as learned behaviors that we can change. Others treat habits as something "fixed," a pattern that is an ingrained and unchanging part of one's personality. In other words, they believe it is impossible to weaken their unkind habits and build kind habits.

But if we want to become more kind, it's vitally important that we believe that we really can change. If we believe that our pattern of engaging in angry outbursts is a fixed characteristic that we can never change, why make an effort? On the other hand, if we approach this behavior as just another habit that can be changed through hard work, we can become motivated to practice mindfulness and kindness every day. In short, to change habits, it is helpful to have a mindset that accepts change as not only possible, but necessary.

Carol Dweck, a psychologist at Stanford University, has researched mindsets for decades. She argues that some people have what she calls "fixed" mindsets about certain aspects of their lives. With a fixed mindset they believe they do not have a choice—they believe they cannot change. On the other hand, people with a "growth" mindset not only believe they can change, they see themselves as a kind of work-in-progress for whom change and challenge are a necessary part of life.[21]

The exercises in this book will help you develop a growth mindset by using mindfulness to build kind habits (Steps 3 and 4) and to break unkind habits (Step 6). Because many of the exercises are challenging, take enough time and put in enough effort to complete them. Your tenacity and success will contribute to a growth mindset. On the other hand, rushing through the exercises and then feeling you failed will contribute to a fixed mindset.

Conscientiousness

It is not enough to believe change is possible. We also have to "Get it done!" Conscientiousness means being responsible and reliable by getting things done through self-control.[22] It includes habits like thoughtfulness, impulse control, and goal-directed behaviors. Those high in conscientiousness tend to be organized, good planners, and mindful of details. This skill is vital to making lasting change in the effort to build kind habits. Without conscientiousness, our thoughtful, organized plans can just dissipate, and we may think about being kind, but not follow through. Even worse, we can develop unkind habits, such as being irresponsible, thoughtless, careless, and unorganized, and then blame others for our failure.

Patience

To accomplish lasting change, you must have the ability to tolerate delays, problems, or struggle without habitually becoming annoyed, anxious, or giving up. Patience helps us to "stay the course" with our kindful practice. Even after we practice redirecting our attention away from negative mind-wandering thousands of times, we will need to continue this practice for the rest of our lives. Being patient is an essential way to be kind to yourself, especially during difficult times when we are learning to live with our unhappiness rather than making it go away. In contrast, the unkind habit of impatience often leads to anger, ridicule and even violence, causing havoc with our attempts to change our habits.

Humility

The final essential skill of character is humility. Researchers Don Davis at Georgia State University and Joshua Hook at the University of North Texas define humility as having an accurate, realistic view of ourselves and being aware of the needs of others. Mindfulness frees us from following distracting thoughts, which means we are more able to attend to the needs of others and to recognize the effects of both our kind and unkind habits. This clarity shows us where we have room for improvement. Humility also helps us limit ourselves to manageable goals, which makes it more likely we will reach the goals we do set. Studies have found that humility strengthens social bonds, reduces stress in competitive situations, and improves health. On the other hand, arrogance impedes efforts to change by weakening social bonds, increasing stress, and jeopardizing our health.

try it now

Which one of the four skills of character—growth mindset, conscientiousness, patience, and humility—do you believe is the strongest in you? How does it help support your specific goals of becoming more kind? Which skill is the weakest?

Your life circumstances and the strength of your four skills of character determine how you respond to the difficulties you will inevitably face as you embark on changing your habits. But what if you've realized that you're lacking in patience or that you've been stuck in a fixed mindset all this time? Don't give up! You will strengthen these skills of character as you work through the challenges you face on the journey ahead. For example, if you have not been conscientious about noting the triggers for your unkind habit of anger, practicing mindfulness during an argument with your partner will not only help you weaken that habit, it will strengthen your conscientiousness. With effort, discipline, and patience as you work towards changing your habits, you will slowly build conscientiousness and a growth mindset.

Committing Yourself

In our culture, and in cultures around the world, when people make a serious commitment, they formalize that commitment with a vow. Think of a vow as making an important intention public. We say marriage vows when we publicly pledge our lives to a partner, and swear to tell the truth when we testify in court. All the major religions also have vows, such as the catechism of the Catholic church, or a Buddhist refuge ceremony.

And so, as you commit yourself to making kindfulness a central purpose of your life, and to following through on your kindful intentions, I invite you to take what I call the Kindful Vow. This vow embraces a widening circle of relationships, beginning with ourselves and our partners, and expanding to include family members, friends, colleagues, strangers, pets, and the Earth. The skills described in this step—skills of change, action, and character—are how love wins, by giving you the strength needed to keep your Kindful Vow.

The Kindful Vow for How Love Wins

> *I intend to be mindfully kind to myself.*
> *I intend to be mindfully kind in all my relationships.*
> *I intend to expand the reach of my kindfulness.*

The vow has three commitments. Let's take a closer look at each of them:

I intend to be mindfully kind to myself.

It's easy to "treat yourself" by splurging on greasy comfort food or indulging in a shopping spree. But is that the same thing as being mindfully kind to yourself? Of course not. When you make this commitment, you are pledging to practice self-care that's grounded in the kind habits that are so important for the Renew-and-Serve Cycle of the kindful practitioner—exercise, healthy eating of moderate portions, and rest. At the same time, it means that you will practice moderation around less healthy habits like alcohol use, sugar consumption, and overspending. With this commitment, you agree to look honestly at yourself and what you really need in any given situation, rather than indulging in self-centered thoughts like worry, regret and self-reproach, or self-centered distractions such as binge drinking, overeating, or drugs.

I intend to be mindfully kind in all my relationships.

The Golden Rule tells us to treat others the way we would want to be treated. But the truth is, different people actually want different things. The pledge to be mindfully kind in your relationships is about agreeing to focus on the other person. The starting point is refraining from treating them unkindly. Then, make it a priority to learn what they truly need from you, and focus on that. The key to this commitment is in a special kind of listening: listening with the intention to understand. When you stop interrupting or thinking about what you want to say, you will start to hear the answers to important questions: Is the other person happy and experiencing comfort and joy at this moment? Do they need help with work, with family, or with other friends? Is there a way I can bring greater happiness or well-being to this person?

I intend to expand the reach of my kindfulness.

As challenging as it can be to treat those closest to us with kindfulness, think about how easy it is to forget about the people outside our inner circle. This commitment is about pledging to include people of different races, political commitments, religions, genders, sexual orientations, education levels, economic status, and nationalities in your commitment to kindness. And what about criminals, the homeless, the disabled, and even people you consider your enemies? Most deserving of our kindfulness: children who are hungry, sick without medical care, homeless, abused, and lacking a caring adult to foster kindfulness and personal responsibility. Harry Walters, the historian and Navajo leader, explains that when a Navajo person asks how you are doing, it includes not just you, but also your family and community. To the Navajo, a person is doing well to the extent the person's family and community are doing well. This is what it means to expand the reach of your kindfulness.

THE KINDFUL VOW AT THE TIME OF DEATH

Linda's best friend, Margy, was in hospice care, approaching death. Margy was one of the most kindful people we knew, and she continued to practice the three tenets of the Kindful Vow for How Love Wins, even at this difficult time of her life. Her letter to Linda describes her experience:

After a recent stay in the hospital (where I endured a rather traumatic event involving a cranky and inept aide), I was glad to arrive at Creekside Hospice for a relaxing three-day stay. The facility was lovely, like a luxury hotel, and the staff was very friendly and accommodating. I was finally able to get a good night's sleep and was feeling quite normal.

One day the Creekside Hospice chaplain came by and asked if she could visit with me. I didn't feel particularly in need of spiritual guidance, but it occurred to me that chaplains, who only want to be of help, are often rebuffed by patients who can't be bothered. Everyone needs opportunities to perform their job, so I agreed to have a chat with her. I explained at the outset that although I had been raised a Presbyterian and still believed in God, I had recently found comfort in the teachings of Buddha and tried to follow those teachings as a way of living. I also told her that I was by nature a cheerful person and that I was completely accepting of my terminal diagnosis and only wished to enjoy what life I had left. I may have said all this because I didn't want any mournful expression of sympathy from a stranger. But that was not the case. Beverly seemed relieved that I had started the conversation and took up the challenge of meeting me on my terms. We had a very pleasant conversation, especially about the difficulty of forgiveness, and fell to providing each other with favorite quotations. My favorite quote is, "Hanging onto resentment is like eating rat poison and waiting for the rat to die." Hers were more of a biblical nature but nonetheless true and helpful. I think we both felt satisfaction with the entire encounter.

The next day I had two visitors. (I think the staff was telling everyone that I was friendly and willing to talk.) Carl was a gentleman who as a healthy senior wanted to give back in some way and so was volunteering simply to chat with patients if they wanted company. He arrived at the same time as Jay and his therapy dog, a Golden Retriever named Bandit. I had expressly asked for the therapy dog but saw no reason why we all couldn't chat because, again, Carl was trying to be helpful and only needed someone to accept his help. As I had with the chaplain, I told Carl and Jay that I was accepting of my diagnosis and always tried to be upbeat and cheerful, so again there was no pity provided, a relief for everyone. We three had a lively conversation and when he got up to leave, Carl said, "Margaret, I'm going to remember you. Look at you. You're all smiles. I hope I'll be like that."

Jay stayed for a while longer. The nurses had told me that whenever Jay came to the hospice everyone fell all over the dog and paid little attention to him. He seemed to want to talk longer so, although I was getting tired, I encouraged the conversation while he told me how he had lost his wife to cancer. After Jay left I thought about how beneficial all three visitors had been to me when I permitted them to help me. I also felt good about the kindness I had shown them in taking the time and allowing them to give their gifts. I think there is a great deal of kindness in the world and that one must only be open to the idea.

Wrapping Up

Earlier in this book, you learned about the benefits of both kindness and mindfulness, identified some of your unkind habits (mental and physical) and selected the unkind habits you want to change. In this step, you've learned about the types of skills (change, action and character) that will support you as you make those changes and form the foundation for your new, more kindful selves.

try it now

Having come this far, are you ready to take the Kindful Vow? Maybe you are ready to take only one part of the vow—to be more kindful to yourself. Or maybe you want to take the vow for only a week or month. You can take the vow alone, with an important person in your life, or as part of a group.

In the **Kindness/Gratitude** section of your practice journal, write down the commitments you are willing to make, then add a few words about what you will do to carry out those intentions:

I will be more kindful to myself by...
I will be more kindful in my friendships by...
I will extend the reach of my kindfulness by...

When you're satisfied with your new commitments, you're ready to take the Kindful Vow by repeating out loud what you have written.

time for reflection

Reflect on how you feel when you name two things you are grateful for and one kindness you did or received. How do you feel after continuing to count your breaths? Many people find it very difficult to shift their attention from their distracting thoughts to counting their breaths. Do you need to put more energy into your mindful breathing?

STEP 3

Set Your Kindness Goals

You've identified unkind habits you want to change, and learned about your foundation of core skills that will support you in that effort. Now it's time to assemble the materials you will use to build positive new habits.

I first learned about the unusual forms kindness can take when I was ten years old. One night, driving through the Smoky Mountains, the fog was so dense we could not see the road in front of us. At a truck stop, we parked our car along with many others and waited for the fog to lift. Finally, a boy in the car in front of us leaned out the window and shined a flashlight down on the centerline of the highway so the driver in his car could steer to stay on the road. When their car pulled out, a wagon train of cars followed, each barely able to see the red taillights of the car in front. The thick fog on the mountain is rather like the confusion in our mind that keeps us from seeing an opportunity for kindness along the centerline of our lives. Mindfulness is like the flashlight that allows us to move safely through the fog and bring the cars down the mountain.

Seven Kindness Practices: Internal and External

Kindness is the quality of being friendly, giving, and considerate. I'm going to describe seven practices that are ways of acting with kindness. Four are internal, or mental: forgiveness, gratitude, empathy, and compassion. The remaining three are external, or physical: altruism, generosity, and cooperation. Although most of these seven words are familiar to us, let's take a closer look at their nuances.

Internal (Mental) Experiences of Kindness

Forgiveness is a conscious, deliberate decision to release feelings of resentment or anger toward a person or group that has harmed you, regardless of whether they actually "deserve" to be forgiven or not. Saying that you forgive someone is only the first step; forgiveness is complete when you no longer feel vengeful, angry, or resentful emotions on the inside. You can direct forgiveness toward others or yourself. When forgiving yourself, take responsibility for your actions and make amends, if possible, while keeping in mind that releasing yourself from shame is a complicated, lengthy process.

Gratitude is a feeling of thankfulness and appreciation for things in your life that directly or indirectly bring you joy. Gratitude is more than saying words about being thankful. Gratitude is complete when you experience the joy in your heart. Gratitude expressed to others is an act of kindness.

Empathy means not only having the capacity to understand another person's feelings, but also experiencing or sharing in those feelings ourselves.

Compassion means giving our attention to another's suffering and, to a limited extent, experiencing their suffering. In some cases, compassion includes a feeling of wanting to help ease that suffering.[ii]

try it later: giving thanks

The major religions have a tradition of giving thanks before eating, which is a simple way to practice gratitude three times a day. Regardless of your religious affiliation, try expressing thanks at each meal. Alternatively, pick three other times during the day

---

ii Compassion is not the same as empathy or altruism, though the concepts are related. While empathy refers more generally to our ability to take the perspective of and feel the emotions of another person, compassion is when those feelings and thoughts include the desire to help. Altruism, in turn, is more than a feeling. It is kind, selfless action.

to express your gratitude, for example, naming something you are grateful for as you wash your hands, or as you put loose change in a "gratitude" jar. A gratitude app on your cell phone can help with reminders and track your progress. In the **Kindness/Gratitude** section in the back of your practice journal, describe how you will express gratitude three times a day. For the next three days, write about your experience expressing gratitude.

External (Physical) Acts of Kindness

The internal, mental experiences of kindness motivate us to act with kindness in the external or physical world.

Altruism is the practice of selfless concern for the well-being of others. Numerous studies have shown that people experience greater happiness when they spend their time or money helping others, rather than when they spend it on themselves.

Generosity means giving more than is expected, given the amount of resources the donor has available.

Cooperation is the process of working together toward a shared goal. This could include listening to others; showing respect for other points of view; and working for the success of the group as a whole, rather than your individual achievement.

The seven elements of kindness work together in many different ways.

These seven kindness practices support each other, and they all work together to foster both kindness and our own happiness through our close caring relationships. For example, practicing empathy helps us understand how the other person feels and what they need, directing our altruism in a way that can actually help. And extending compassion to a friend who's depressed allows us to support them without sharing their depressed feelings. (If we do not shift from empathy to compassion, experiencing the other person's depression for too long a time can take a toll on our own mental well-being, making us less able to act with kindness.)

Put simply, acts of kindness (including generosity, altruism, and cooperation) accompanied by feelings of empathy, compassion, forgiveness, and gratitude strengthen our sense of connection in our relationships. Conversely, our unkind acts diminish these feelings, making us feel isolated and cut off from others, unless we are connected to others who share the same unkind habits.[iii]

NOTE:

Some people, especially women, spend considerable time and energy being kind to others, while neglecting self-care. This is an unkind habit. Make an extra effort to take time for self-care (for example, instead of catching up with chores, get a haircut or a massage, have an early night, watch a movie, or take a weekend getaway). Rather than feeling guilty if you do something for yourself that seems extravagant, remind yourself that being kind to yourself also helps you be more kind to others in the long run. Otherwise, you might end up in an unmindful-unkind cycle.

---

try it now

In the **Kindness/Gratitude** section of your practice journal, describe your strongest kind habit and how it makes you feel when you carry out that habit.

---

iii To learn more about the research on these seven practices of kindness (and much more), go to the Greater Good website at UC Berkeley (http://greatergood.berkeley.edu/big_ideas)

The Unmindful-Unkind Cycle

In the unmindful-unkind cycle, being unmindful and unkind work together in a negative feedback loop. Being unmindful means we are less aware of opportunities to be kind and less likely to act with kindness. Being less kind means we do not reap the benefits of kindness—benefits that would normally motivate us to be mindful. Gottman called couples who lived the unmindful-unkind cycle "disasters of relationships." Of course, this cycle can also be disastrous to other kinds of relationships as well.

Many people caught in the unmindful-unkind cycle feel oppressed and closed in by their miserable negative mind-wandering. They substitute aggression, drugs, alcohol, and other unkind habits for the natural "feel good" chemicals that come from kindness. These individuals feel satisfaction not by being kind, but by indulging in unkind habits with their peers. Their growing negative mind-wandering often leads to unkind acts toward people outside their peer group.

The Mindful-Kind Cycle

The alternative to the unmindful-unkind cycle is the mindful-kind cycle. We've already discussed the powerful ways kindness can improve our relationships and benefit the health and happiness of the giver as much as or even more than the receiver. Research has shown that acting with kindness floods our brain with powerful chemicals like oxytocin that not only make us feel good but also reduce feelings of stress and protect us from stress-related ailments. Other benefits include the appreciation and reciprocity we often receive from others when we treat them with kindness. In combination, these effects give us even more to feel grateful for.

We've also seen how the practice of mindfulness gives our minds a rest, which in turn reduces negative mind-wandering, helps us notice opportunities to be kind, and gives us a greater inclination to be kind. Let's take a moment to remind ourselves of how mindfulness and kindness work together in a positive feedback loop. If mindfulness helps us increase our kindness, the benefits we reap from those acts of kindness reaffirm our decision to be kind, and our gratitude and our motivation to practice mindfulness increase. Then the cycle repeats, beginning with more mindfulness and ending with more gratitude. The cycle builds on itself and gets stronger and stronger each time. Gottman called couples who lived the mindful-kind cycle "masters of relationships."[23]

The mindful-kind cycle is not only central to a healthy, loving relationship with your partner, but also to caring relationships with children, parents, friends, colleagues, and pets. Even if you are struggling to learn mindful breathing, you will still benefit yourself and others by acting with kindness. The mindful-kind cycle helps us savor the heartfelt kindnesses we give and experience in the world.

FROM THE OTHER SIDE

Roy taught mindful kindness to Tad, who is teaching mindful kindness to two other prisoners, Chris and Tex. Here, Tad describes the mindful-kind cycle:

Chris, me, and another guy in this barracks named Tex are pretty close. I will deliberately take myself out of certain situations so I won't be recognized for doing a kind act, e.g., I know Tex is out of coffee. I'll send him some and tell him, "It's from Chris." Tex will send me something (when he can). And I'll send it to Chris and tell him, "It's from Tex." Some would say, "I'm purposely lying." But, I don't see it like that. These two guys have life in prison. They're never getting out. Me...I'll soon be gone. I just want to help build a solid bond between two people. That's my intention! So—after I'm gone, they will continue to be there for each other.

---

try it now

In your practice journal, describe a time when you found yourself in a mindful-kind cycle and how it made you feel. Also describe a time you have been in an unmindful-unkind cycle and how it made you feel.

~

Savoring Heartfelt Kindness

All kind acts have value. But some have a greater impact than others. Think about how the experience of dropping off a can of beans for a food drive is different from delivering a hot meal and a hug to a grieving friend. Heartfelt kindness has a deeper and more lasting impact not only for the recipient but also for the giver. So what makes an act of kindness heartfelt? I look for three criteria: the recipient's need is great, the giver fulfills that need, and the kindness "transaction" happens on a personal level, ideally face-to-face.

For example, Mother Teresa's days were filled with this kind of kindnesses. She found a woman lying in the gutter in front of a Calcutta hospital. So sick, the woman did not respond to the rats and cockroaches eating her feet. When Mother Teresa took her to the hospital, a nurse refused to admit her; there were no empty beds and besides, the woman was about to die. Mother Teresa stayed with the woman on the street until she died. Heart sickened by the lack of kindness at the time of death, Mother Teresa converted an abandoned building into what we would now call a hospice house for the destitute.

FROM THE OTHER SIDE

I've learned about heartfelt kindness through my work with prisoners, since every time one of my prison friends acts with kindness, it almost always involves a personal connection as well as a significant need. Roy wrote:

So grateful, so proud of the ones showing kindness. It's kind of hard to adequately explain. Like this morning, a new guard just started working for ADC and it was her first night at work. She dropped my breakfast into my cell before I could get to it. Oatmeal and syrup went everywhere and that included on me, from the waist down. She was almost in tears and I said, "man, please relax because the world ain't gonna end over small shit like you dropping a tray and painting me with oatmeal and syrup." I said it with a smile on my face. The Sgt. over the shift came over and thanked me for being kool about the "accident" and not clicking or snapping on her new officer.

Of course, helping people with their material needs, such as by writing a check to a relief fund, or donating items to a charity auction, helps others. But as we move forward building more kindful lives, let's aspire to strengthen the habits that will give both ourselves and others more opportunities to experience the sort of kindness that is truly from the heart.

try it now

Think about an act of heartfelt kindness you've experienced, either as the giver, the receiver, or as a witness. In the **Kindness/Gratitude** section of your practice journal, describe what happened, including the significant need, the nature of the relationship, the impact on the people involved, and how it made you feel.

Our Basic Instincts

I used to think that the drive to survive, as well as the drives to reproduce and to succeed[iv] were innate human characteristics, whereas kindness was something you had to learn—that people had no inherent urge to be kind. But a growing body of scientific research indicates that this belief is not true. As it turns out, kindness appears to be as innate to humans as the instinct to pursue sex and food. Scientists now believe that early humans evolved kindness in order to live in groups, something that was essential for them to survive, reproduce, and succeed. Even Charles Darwin wrote that the trait of benevolence is probably inherited.[24]

INSTINCT
An innate, fixed response to a specific situation.

---

iv There are many theories about human instinct. I am working from Professor Robert Winston, MD's book and BBC program: *Human Instinct: How our primeval impulses shape our modern world*. Winston, R. (2002) NY: NY. Bantam Press.
The four episodes on the BBC program were to survive, reproduce, succeed, and act with kindness. (https://www.bbc.co.uk/programmes/b00pfrv4/episodes/guide)

In his book *Born to be Good*, Dacher Keltner, professor of psychology at the University of California at Berkeley, and director of the Berkeley Social Interaction Lab, theorizes that to survive, early humans had to cooperate in highly social, cohesive, cooperative, and altruistic groups, and these traits continue as part of our hereditary makeup today. In our modern world, the feel-good chemicals released in our bodies when we practice kindness, along with the social rewards we enjoy for being kind, continue to reinforce these positive behaviors.

The instincts to reproduce, to survive, or to succeed trigger much of our mind-wandering: for example, when you see an attractive person, your reproductive instinct might kick in, triggering daydreams of a passionate (if illicit) affair. Anger provoked by a tailgater on the freeway could be linked to your survival instinct. Or your instinct to succeed could trigger jealousy over a colleague's accomplishments at work, or feelings of greed for a lucrative deal.

Thoughts and emotions elicited by our instincts are spontaneous. They often arise suddenly and unexpectedly, and can pass just as suddenly. These emotional feelings and thoughts are not a problem in and of themselves. But if the feelings are unkind, and we feed them and act on them every time they arise, they can turn into unkind habits; if, for example, you pursue every attractive stranger, it can lead to serial adultery. If you indulge and dwell on your anger every time someone follows your car too closely, you can develop the habit of road rage. And wallowing in your jealousy of others at work can lead to habitual resentment.

Unfortunately, we are wired to give twice as much attention to our negative thoughts and feelings as to positive ones. This probably comes from the survival instinct.[25] Imagine a hunter-gatherer thousands of years ago who had traveled to a meadow where she found edible plants, then foraged at a lake where a saber tooth tiger almost killed her. She is likely to remember more details about the tiger at the lake than the meadow, because the memory of the lake is more essential for her survival. Being wired to remember negative events explains our tendency to get caught up in what is "threatening."

Even though we attend more to what is negative, we can still choose to strengthen responses coming from our kindness instinct. Instead of responding with aggressive road rage when a car is following us closely, we can choose to tap the brakes to signal concern, or switch to another lane and let the aggressive driver pass. When we meet an attractive stranger, we can shift our intention to an interesting conversation rather than seduction. At work, instead of being jealous and undermining others' success, we can work cooperatively.

Science has found that one powerful way to increase kindness and healthy habits is through meditation. Meditation seems to release our kindness instinct, which makes positive changes *even when we don't intend to do so*. In one study, participants were told they would be taught meditation to reduce stress and improve their performance. In fact, the researcher, Yi-Yuan Tang, a neuroscientist at Texas Tech University, was secretly studying meditation's effect on smoking. Sure enough, he found that even among people who were not actively trying to cut back on smoking, those who had learned meditation smoked less, while those not learning meditation did not.[26] In another study, researcher Daniel Lim of Northeastern University found that people trained in meditation were almost three times more likely to offer their seat to a stranger on crutches than those who did not receive meditation training.[27]

In summary:

- Many of our thoughts and emotions arise as a result of our instincts.

- Our instincts often compete with each other for dominance. This competition can take the form of a struggle between kind and unkind habits.

- Be patient and forgiving with yourself when you fail to be mindfully kind in the face of the negative thoughts and emotions that arise from our instincts. Although they are natural, do not feed or act on them. If you do, they can become unkind habits.

try it now

Turn to the **Unkindness** section of your practice journal. Write about an instinct that seems to contribute to one of your unkind habits, whether it has to do with success, reproduction, or survival. How do you feel after you carry out that unkind habit?

Kindness Begins With You

Now that we've reflected on the nature of kindness, and taken stock of the ways in which we're already kind in our daily lives, it's time to start the work of building new habits. I use the word building, because we must start at the foundation and work our way up, stacking kindness upon kindness. In fact, you are the foundation; kindness begins with you. If you find it hard to be kind to yourself, you will likely find it hard to be kind to others. Why? The self-absorbed and isolated feelings and habits that block you from showing kindness to yourself—whether it's insecurity, regret, need for praise, or jealousy—are also likely to block kindness to others.

Moreover, if you do not take care of your immediate needs, you will be less able to serve others. If you are hungry, tired, or upset, you may need to eat, exercise, rest, or engage mindfulness and meditate before you are ready to be of service. Finally, if you do not set the intention and make the effort to build kind habits for yourself, you will have a hard time developing habits to be kind to others. Start being more kind to yourself by engaging in and building up kind habits in areas like nutrition, exercise, sports, nature, sleep, social relationships, physical intimacy, music, art, dance, crafts, and relaxation. It is important to note that kindness outside of close relationships—for example, to acquaintances or even strangers— also boosts your happiness and sense of well-being.[28]

An important type of kind habit is one that we find pleasurable or gratifying. I call these pleasant kind habits.

PLEASANT KIND HABITS
Kind habits that bring joy, appreciation, and enrichment to your life, help sustain you during dark times, and buffer you against addictive behavior.

Not all kind habits are pleasant, and not all pleasant habits are kind. For some people, exercise is not a pleasant kind habit; it is a chore to be avoided. Others might find it gratifying and pleasurable. On the other hand, when a gambling addict plays cards it may be pleasant, but it is not a kind habit. Think about some of the following kind habits. Which ones are pleasant for you?

- Being mindful

- Acting with kindness

- Exercising and being physically active

- Eating reasonable amounts of healthy food

- Getting enough rest

- Sharing loving intimacy with your partner

- Interacting with friends and family in a kind manner

- Pursuing your spiritual practices

- Being in nature

- Singing

- Playing a musical instrument

- Making arts and crafts

Pleasant kind habits do more than bring enjoyment. They are often more powerful than other kind habits in energizing us and fortifying our intention to be a kindful practitioner. Psychologist Bruce K. Alexander of Simon Fraser University found that when rats were offered plain water or water with morphine, they chose plain water when they were in a large, well-lit cage with toys, ample food, and the company of other rats for play and reproduction.[29] On the other hand, when the rats were in a small, dark, empty cage, with no opportunity to engage pleasant kind habits like play and socializing, they tended to choose the water with morphine, often drinking so much that they died. Alexander and his colleagues hypothesized that having a battery of pleasant kind habits (which also contribute to creating or maintaining close, caring relationships) can help keep us from an addiction. And of course, the more pleasant kind habits we have, the more likely we are to engage the Renew-and-Serve Cycle.

An often under-appreciated type of pleasant kind habit is spending time in nature. For example, Shinrin-yoku, or "forest bathing"[30] is the Japanese practice of spending time with trees to improve your health. Dr. Qing Li, a medical doctor at Tokyo's Nippon Medical School, reported these preliminary findings: sleeping longer (an average increase by 15 percent after a two-hour forest walk), a boost to the immune system and cardiovascular health, better parasympathetic response (rest-and-recover), increased energy levels by more than 30 percent, and reduced stress, anxiety, depression, and anger.[31] Just living in greener areas produces a range of health benefits.[32] These benefits may come from the essential tree oils found in forest air, such as phytoncides (pine trees and cypress tend to be the richest). Yale neurology professor Richard H. Mattson's research article on how plants improve various surgery outcomes, such as reduced pain, reduced use of pain medication and faster recovery, also references nature/plant benefits to physical, emotional, psychological, and emotional health.[33]

try it later

Make a list of your pleasant kind habits in the **Kindness/ Gratitude** section of your journal. Each day for a week or more, write about three times your pleasant kind habits brought you joy or happiness.

Being kind to yourself is a great place to start. But don't wait too long be kind to others! Even as you're focusing on yourself, also start paying attention to those around you. Act with kindness, even if it's only a small kindness. After all, as I've learned from the stories of men I know in prison, small acts of kindness can sometimes have a bigger impact than we expect. And even if an act of kindness is small, it still brings a little brightness into someone's life, and into your life as well. So smile, hold the door open for someone, let the other car merge in front of you, give even a small amount to a charity, do a chore that your partner usually does, or get a treat for your pet.

Small acts of kindness are valuable and an excellent place to start. For ideas about more advanced ways to act with kindness, you can visit feedkindness.com/resources—a website that offers kindness resources related to self-care, couples, parenting, co-workers, and community participation.

try it later: universal kindness

Pick three small acts of universal kindness, meaning they can apply to anyone—like smiling, making eye contact, or a small act of service such as holding a door. Practice these kindnesses with both strangers and people close to you for the next three days. In the **Kindness/Gratitude** section of your practice journal, write about how this practice affected both you and the person who received the kindness.

Even as you're practicing spreading kindness in the world, remember that being kind is not the same as being nice. If a relative asks you for a loan, making the loan would be nice. But if you know the relative will use the money to feed a gambling addiction, it might actually be kinder to decline.

Receiving Kindness

My wife was waiting in line at a coffee shop recently. When she finally made her order and reached for her wallet, the man behind her in line stopped her and asked if he could pay for her coffee. When she protested, he explained that he liked to buy coffee for other people because it helped him take his mind off his own worries. Linda realized that accepting the coffee would actually be an act of kindness toward this stranger.

In fact, one of the most important acts of kindness we can make is to accept kindness from others. This gives others the opportunity to experience the warm feelings that come from a generous act. It's also an act of kindness toward yourself to accept help from others, especially when life is hard. By practicing mindfulness, we focus less on ourselves and are more able to recognize when others are being kind to us; we can help them by accepting that kindness.

This is not to say that you can never say "no." Sometimes, people do use the appearance of kindness as a way to control others, make them feel beholden, or intrude on their personal time or space. It is entirely appropriate to set boundaries with people you do not trust. But if you are always refusing kindness because accepting help makes you feel vulnerable, take a moment to think about the effect this is having on the other person. Refusing kindness denies the other person the positive feedback that comes from helping others. Over time, it may even cause the other person to stop bothering with kindness at all.

Sometimes, learning about the importance of accepting kindness can be painful. A man I knew named Derek got a job as an assistant to a skilled metal worker, who allowed him to sleep in an unused space in his workshop, rent-free. When Derek received his first paycheck, he said he could not accept it because the free rent was worth more than the pay. His boss said, "You can't only give. You must learn to receive or else other people will not be able to give." He then told Derek to move out and find a new place to live. In looking back at the incident, Derek wrote me, "They were good people. I doubt I would remember the lesson if they just said you have to give and you have to receive. I remembered it because of the intense way they did it."

try it now

Recall a time you refused to accept an act of kindness from someone, without considering your intent and the consequences for yourself and the other person. Write about this experience in your practice journal.

~

Kindness Inventory

Kindness to Yourself and Kindness to Others

When I take inventory of the ways I am kind to myself, I think about habits that include seeking out and learning from mentors for my work and spiritual practice, eating a mostly healthy diet, exercising regularly, hiking, practicing tai chi, enjoying nature, singing, getting rest, limiting stress by meditating, and practicing mindfulness in many different settings.

In my inventory for being kind to others, I'd list: maintaining positive social relationships with friends and family, physical and emotional intimacy with Linda, writing to my prisoner friends, taking steps to protect the environment, and helping others in need. One of the most important habits I developed was to learn skills and set aside time to engage in activities that meant a great deal to Linda. I've tried downhill and cross-country skiing, running, river rafting, backpacking, and swimming in mountain lakes, as part of my effort to connect with my wife doing activities she loves. When I asked Linda for her input, she told me that my sense of humor and jokes have been a kindness in our relationship, because they lightened her spirits when she was feeling down and helped her contribute to a pleasant atmosphere for us both—a habit I would not have thought of as being kind.

Kind Habits Self-Assessment and Increasing Your Kindness to Others

1. Kindness to Yourself – How important is it to:

- spend more time in activities that engage you and are enjoyable?

- spend more time in enjoyable interactions with those close to you?

- have more time and energy to get your work done?

- eat and drink in a more healthy fashion and avoid cigarettes, chewing tobacco, and excessive alcohol?

- be more courteous when you are driving, shopping, and talking on the phone?

- engage in more healthy activities, such as regular exercise and adequate sleep?

- do a better job managing your stress effectively—for example, through mindfulness and meditation?

- be more forgiving of yourself and others?

- find a mentor with expertise to help you build important habits in your areas of interest (not limited to kindness)?

2. Kindness with Friends and Family – How important is it to:

- interact more respectfully and kindly with all members of your family and close friends?

- help family and friends without being asked?

- help others weaken an unkind habit?

- encourage others as they work toward a goal?

- respond with positivity when others say something to you?

- make the effort to engage in activities that your partner highly values, which might involve learning new skills?

3. Kindness at Work – How important is it to:

- interact more respectfully and kindly with your colleagues?

- encourage the good work of others more often?

- be more helpful to your colleagues—for example, in strengthening their kind habits?

- focus on the success of your group as much as, or more than, your individual success?

- help a colleague weaken an unkind habit?

4. The Reach of Your Kindness – How important is it to:

- interact respectfully and kindly with homeless people and others in need?

- give direct support to those in need—for example money, food, gloves or other warm clothing to a homeless person in cold weather?

- give time or money to charities inside or outside the US that help those in need, including disaster victims?

- help children and families in need?

try it now

Make a check mark by the one or two most important kind habits you would like to work on. In the **Kindness/Gratitude** section of your journal, write the name of each habit you selected to work on and describe why you want to build that habit.

Ideas for Increasing Your Kindness to Others

In addition to taking inventory of your kind habits, it's important to also think of kind activities you would like to engage in. As you read through this section, think about the one or two activities you are motivated to do more often.

- Give money or volunteer. For example, you can help children who are hungry, sick without medical care, homeless, abused, or lacking a caring adult to foster kindfulness and personal responsibility.

- Learn new ways to be kind by watching others and helping them with their acts of kindness. Also learn new ways to be kind from books, articles, social media, and movies.

- Pick a certain person—someone close to you, such as a friend or family member—to be the focus of your kindness. While your long-term goal may be to be kind to everyone, starting with one person is a manageable first step to start developing the tools and habits to practice kindness on a grander scale. A second step is to keep track of what is important to friends and family members. When you see them, ask how things are going with what matters to them.

- Deliver small kindnesses; they matter. These can be random acts of simple, straightforward kindness. A wealth of ideas can be found on the website Randomactsofkindness.org. Here are some specific ideas:

  1. Send a positive note to a friend—a thank you, compliment, congratulations, birthday or a card recognizing another special day.

  2. Give small gifts for no reason.

  3. Invite friends to join activities with you.

  4. Touch and hug to show that you care (if you know this kind of touch is welcome).

5. Speak in positive terms. Even raising a problem can be done with kindness.

6. Say "thank you" as often as you can.

7. Give genuine compliments as often as you can.

8. Do favors for others (without becoming a doormat).

- Join or create a kindful club. This supportive group of friends can include book discussions, updates (providing accountability) on how members are doing with their kindness and mindfulness, and sharing what people have learned. The kindness club I participate in includes a few close friends who meet once a month at one of our houses, meditate for 20 minutes, and have tea while we discuss what we have been working on in the areas of kindness and mindfulness.

- Join a spiritual or religious group for support of your kindful intentions and for fellowship.

- Invest time and effort in developing new kindfulness skills, such as reading books on relationships or parenting, or taking classes.

try it now

Make a check mark by the one or two ideas for kind activities you want to do more often. In the **Kindness/Gratitude** section of your journal, write the name of each activity you selected and describe why you want to engage more often in those activities.

Constructive Communication: Responding with Vulnerability, Respect, and Interest

One way to build the mindful-kind cycle (and prevent the unmindful-unkind cycle) is to build a habit of constructive communication (verbal and non-verbal) based on vulnerability, respect, and interest in the other person. Many books are devoted to constructive communication, so it is only touched upon briefly here. If you feel you need to significantly improve your communication skills, take on the mind of the detective and find evidence-based resources on communication. As a family, Linda, our daughters, and I have worked to develop the habit of constructive communication: listening to one another with genuine interest, responding honestly and constructively, using a respectful tone of voice, and being vulnerable by openly sharing our successes and failures. The four of us also make it a habit to discuss kindness itself, and share how we use meditation and mindfulness in our daily lives. Each of us has times of stress and discouragement; we also have times of happiness and contentment.

Our family's kind habits, for which we are deeply grateful, have helped us support one another through both good times and hard times. For example, I recently admitted being caught up in worry about the fact that my continuing hip and shoulder pain was keeping me awake at night. In turn, our younger daughter talked about her challenges with sleep, and how she is dealing with them—for example, by not staying in bed if she's awake for more than 15 or 20 minutes. I agreed to try that myself, which helped.

In the introduction of this book, you read about constructive communication skills, like giving the other person the benefit of the doubt, being more considerate or giving than usual when the other person is having a hard time, sharing joy, and being gentle in conflict. An important way to show that you care about someone is to be interested and curious about them. As we've already discussed, you can show you care by asking to hear more, agreeing, making an encouraging comment, or offering interesting relevant information.

Another way to express care is to ask "caring questions" in a respectful manner about what is important in their lives. For example, you might ask about their recent move to a new house, the medical problem of a friend in common, or about their child's recent science award. There are several types of caring questions. We recently had a memorial at our church for the sister of a friend. The altar was beautiful, and the display included a picture of the woman who had passed away. I noted our friend did not have a camera, so I asked a caring question: "Would you like me to take pictures of the altar and send them to you?" She responded that she would greatly appreciate receiving some pictures. The key is to be mindful so that you can recognize an opportunity to ask a caring question. This isn't something you can fake; it's important that you really care and act with genuine compassion.

When you first meet someone, you don't know enough about the person to ask a caring question. The first step is to start a constructive conversation. Many people struggle to get to know someone new or start a conversation with an acquaintance. Try these questions:

1. Which of your activities do you value the most?

2. What activities are valuable because they are fun? How are they fun?

3. How much of your day do you spend on activities that are fun? Which of those activities do you spend more time on?

4. What activities are valuable because you feel they are worthwhile? In what ways are they worthwhile?

5. What activities are valuable because you feel responsible for doing them? How do you feel about those responsibilities?

6. Which new activities would you like to spend time on? Are you thinking of being able to start doing any of those activities?

7. How do you deal with activities you need to spend time on when you don't see them as valuable?

Once you know someone, you can ask the most common caring question, "How are you doing?" in a manner that shows you are seeking a genuine answer, and not just making polite conversation.

It's also possible to communicate without words, as when a couple is holding hands. Pavel Goldstein, a pain researcher at the Cognitive and Affective Neuroscience Lab at the University of Colorado at Boulder, studied how the touch of a loved one affected perceptions of pain. In a study of 23 couples, he found that when one partner was in pain, the pain decreased when the other partner held their hand.[34] Moreover, hand-holding partners tended to synchronize their heartbeats and respiration rate. The synchrony was higher when the pain-free partner also expressed empathy. Physiological synchrony has been found in groups (when watching emotional movies) and in interpersonal action, such as singing together.

Communication can also prevent misunderstandings. A friend of mine was upset because she was told her young house guest had complained about not being treated as an adult. My friend spent more than two weeks worrying about the situation, believing that she had offended her guest in some way. When she finally asked the young woman why she felt she was not being treated as an adult, the house guest replied she was being treated very well. My friend's two weeks of worry could have been avoided by becoming vulnerable and asking the young house guest right away about her concerns.

Tara Brach, founder of the Insight Meditation Community of Washington, D.C., described a more serious example of communication failure. A woman who was a narcissist never listened closely to others, always wanting to be the center of attention. This lack of listening drove away her daughters, friends and even her husband. Late in life, after admitting her loneliness, one of her daughters, with genuine interest, respect, and vulnerability, explained to her mother that she was lonely because she never listened to anyone, which sent the message that she did not care about the person talking to her. The mother broke down, recognizing the truth about her narcissism and the years of loneliness it had caused. She began to listen, and gradually regained connections with her loved ones. We cannot know if the mother would have changed decades earlier if someone had spoken out about how her behavior was affecting the people around her. It may benefit us not to delay in becoming vulnerable and communicating about the beliefs that cause us and others misery.

try it now

In the **Kindness/Gratitude** section of your practice journal, write about a time when you were able to—or wish you had been able to:

- communicate with another person to clarify your relationship or clear up a misunderstanding;

- be more open and vulnerable in a conversation with another person;

- show more interest in and respect for another person.

Making a Kindness Plan

I think it's worthwhile to be deliberate about something as important as kindness. That's why I made a plan for how I would be more kind, and recommend that you do the same. Pick one of the kind habits you identified in the exercise on pages 74-75. It should be a kind habit you are motivated to work on. You will make a kindness plan for that habit.

try it now

Turn to the **Kindness/Gratitude** section in your practice journal and write your answers to the questions listed below:

- What is the kind habit you have chosen to develop?

- Who are you hoping to help by strengthening this habit?

- Who will you ask for support, if anyone? What kind of support will you ask for?

- What detective work will you need to do, if any?

- How, if at all, will you use the mind of the warrior?

- Which skills of character (growth mindset, conscientiousness, patience, and humility) will you need most?

- What action will you take to build the kind habit in your mental world?

- What action will you take in your physical world?

The following day, you can begin to execute your plan. Give yourself some time—whether it's a few days, or a few weeks—to let it unfold. Then take the time to look back and assess how you did. Return to the back of your practice journal, and add your responses to these follow-up questions:

- What happened as you tried to implement your kindness plan?

- What adjustment, if any, did you make?

Expect to make some adjustments as you implement the plan. You can come back to the follow-up questions as often as you need, until you are satisfied that you've done as much as you can to reach the goal for your kindness plan. Then answer this question: *How did you feel as you implemented your kindness plan?*

~

My Kindness Plan

Here's an example of one of my own kindness plans:

- What is the kind habit you have chosen to develop?

  Increase the number of times each day I take a computer break to keep my body from getting sore and to rest my mind.

- Who are you hoping to help by strengthening this habit?

  Myself, by preventing myself from getting a sore back as a result of sitting too long at the computer; and, indirectly, those close to me, by not acting out my irritation from being sore.

- Who will you ask for support, if anyone? What kind of support will you ask for?

  I will ask Linda to ask me if I have set my timer for when to take a break, or ask me if I want to take a break if she notices I have been on my computer for 30 minutes or more.

- What detective work will you need to do, if any?

  Make a list of all the physical therapy, tai chi, hiking, and household activities I can engage in when I take a break.

- How, if at all, will you use the mind of the warrior?

  I will set my intention and make an honest effort to take a break every 30 minutes I am at my computer.

- Which skills of character (growth mindset, conscientiousness, patience, and humility) will you need most?

  I need to be conscientious about taking my breaks and humble about the times I fail.

- What action will you take to build the kind habit in your mental world?

  Review the reasons for why giving my body and mind a rest is important.

- What action will you take in your physical world?

  Set my timer for 30 minutes and be ready to engage in one of my identified activities during the break.

Here are my responses to the follow-up questions:

- What happened as you tried to implement your kindness plan?

  Several times, I did not get up from the computer when the timer went off.

- What adjustment did you make?

  I set my timer for 25 minutes so that if I don't stop immediately I will still stop within the next five minutes.

Wrapping Up

You've now been introduced to mindfulness and kindness, and have learned how to identify your unkind habits. Step 2 explained Skills of Change—the ability to make a shift in your mental or physical world; Skills of Action—the ability to assume the role we need to play to make meaningful changes (kindful practitioner, diligent detective, and wise warrior); and Skills of Character—growth mindset, conscientiousness, patience, and humility. This step focused on kindness—including the different types of kindness, why kindness is important, the ways you are currently kind, more ways you can be kind, how you can receive kindness, the way mindfulness and kindness form a positive cycle, and, finally, how to make your own kindness plan. Acting on your kindness plan is how love wins.

try it later: mindful breathing

Are you ready to change your breathing exercise? From now on, instead of counting your breaths, pay attention to the physical sensations—the movement of your chest and abdomen as you inhale and exhale. We'll call this mindful breathing. Without counting, you may notice more mind-wandering. Don't give in to distractions; just return your attention to the physical sensations of your breathing. Do this new mindful breathing exercise daily for 2 to 3 minutes for several weeks. Write about your experiences in the **Mindfulness/Meditation** section of your practice journal.

checking in

Are you taking the time you need to digest the material and complete the exercises? If not, you might consider spending several days or even a week on a step, setting aside time each evening for reflection. Another approach is to read through the step without reading the exercises, and then go back through the step a second time and do the exercises. Or you can go through the exercises with a friend or as part of a group.

time for reflection

Reflect on whether you are beginning to act with kindness more often. If you are, how is being more kind making you feel?

STEP 4
Meditation

A man named Jeremy convinced me of the importance of meditation. I first met Jeremy when I was a hospice volunteer, regularly visiting individuals who had six months or less to live. At age 35, he was already very sick with advanced ALS, and had had a traumatic life. He ran away from home at age 13 because of his mother's neglect and promiscuity, and lived with friends. In his 20s he devoted himself to a 3-year intensive study of yoga meditation that alienated his devoutly Christian wife. His estranged wife would not allow his 11-year-old daughter to visit him as he was dying.

Jeremy's meditation training and practice had taught him about mindful kindness, and it completely changed the way he approached the fear and pain that came with his illness. By the time I met him, he was almost completely paralyzed. He had no use of his body below his neck; the only movement I saw him make was turning his head to look at me. He operated his computer with voice commands.

And yet, grounded in his meditation, Jeremy constantly focused on how to be kind to those around him, with never a hint of self-pity or discouragement. He radiated contentment, joy, and kindness. He talked about how blessed his life was, about his gratitude, and about the wonderful friends he had at the care facility. Employees at the care facility would sit with Jeremy during their breaks to bask in his joy and interest in their well-being. Another hospice volunteer asked me if she could visit Jeremy to experience his peace and bright light.

Jeremy said he thought of his life as a drop of water in a river. When the river came to a waterfall many drops separated, each reflecting light a little differently, according to its nature. At the bottom of the waterfall, the droplet that represented his life would simply be reunited with the river, and flow on. "Everything is part of me and I am part of everything," he told me once. "It does not make any difference what kind of water drop you are; you could be any shape, any size, or any color. You are all the same as I am, and I am the same as you."

I last saw him on a Saturday afternoon. Later that evening, Jeremy told the nurse he was ready to go to sleep, and asked her to bring his nightly medicine. Then he told her he was going to die that evening—and he did.

Wordless Practices

What happens when we do not meditate and are not mindful? When we notice ourselves getting caught up in negative thoughts, we usually try to "think our way out of feeling bad." For example, if we are overeating chips, we might tell ourselves that we are making ourselves fat and should stop eating the chips. But we keep eating. Then we beat ourselves up for not being able to stop eating the chips. Telling ourselves to stop those negative thoughts is usually not going to work. In fact, telling ourselves to stop often ends up leading to more negative thoughts. Instead of improving things, we now have two sets of negative thoughts making us feel bad: first, that we are making ourselves fat, and second, that we cannot discipline ourselves to stop eating the chips.

Possibly the most effective way to shift our attention away from this kind of unhelpful thinking is to engage in a practice that does not involve words, but instead focuses on attending to physical sensations. This is a wordless practice, because we do not need words when we are attending to our senses. In short, when you realize you are immersed in negative thoughts, do not pile on with more negative thoughts. Instead, shift your attention to your senses. This helps you shift focus to your intention in the present moment and is the foundation for meditation

Sensing-Mindfulness

SENSING-MINDFULNESS
The practice of shifting our attention from our thoughts and emotions to our senses of touch, sight, smell, taste, and hearing in order to focus on our intention in the present moment.

In sensing-mindfulness, we direct our attention exclusively to specific sensations coming from whatever physical activity we are doing, whether it's active—like tai chi, dancing, or playing basketball—or just sitting and breathing. To experience the feeling, try this the next time you are eating: first, eat several bites while you're engaged in another activity, like reading, listening to music, or talking to a friend. Then, eat in silence with closed eyes. Notice the variations in texture and how the food tastes more flavorful when your eyes are closed and your attention is directed toward what you are eating, with no distractions. Of course the food hasn't changed, you're just noticing more.

Distractors diminish the joy of an activity.

With sensing-mindfulness we are calm and can
experience the joy of an activity.

try it later: mindful eating

For the next three days, practice sensing-mindfulness when
you are eating. You can also extend your sensing-mindfulness
to other activities—for example, while brushing your teeth,
folding laundry, or petting your dog. When you notice your mind
wandering, return your attention to the physical sensations of the
activity. For example, if you are brushing your teeth and notice
mind-wandering, return your attention to the feeling of the brush
coming in contact with your gums and teeth.

In the **Mindfulness/Meditation** section of your practice
journal, list the sensations you experienced when you practiced sensing-mindfulness. After your third day of practicing
sensing-mindfulness, note how the practice made you feel, and
whether experiencing those sensations decreased your negative
mind-wandering over the three-day period.

Note: If you have difficulty practicing sensing-mindfulness
with other activities, first spend two minutes with the basic
sensing-mindfulness practice you have already learned: mindful

breathing. Then return to your new activity. You may also need to fortify your intention with the mind of the warrior.

~

Practice sensing-mindfulness often enough, and it will become second nature. Becoming proficient in sensing-mindfulness will give you one of your most potent and versatile tools to weaken unkind habits and to build kind ones.

Using sensing-mindfulness to build kind habits can be more challenging for people who have experienced trauma. It can require extraordinary effort to overcome lifelong challenges like addiction or anger, but those who succeed can become inspirational figures. My friend Cage's early life was full of difficulty and included a long stint in juvenile detention, beginning when he was nine years old. As a young African American adult, he was tormented by racism and struggled with habits like fighting and drinking; he seemed condemned to repeat the same unhealthy patterns over and over again.

But tai chi transformed Cage's life. Learning the slow, precise movements taught him to be more attuned to his body—sensing-mindfulness—and to keep his attention on his intention in the present moment. His growing practice of mindfulness helped him let go of his addiction and anger. Eventually, he became a teacher of tai chi, which strengthened his practice even more, and helped him extend his new self-kindness to others. He also took up meditation to support his practice. Over time, Cage transformed an unmindful-unkind cycle of self-destruction into a positive, mindful-kind cycle.

Meditation

MEDITATION
The practice of focusing your attention for a set length of time
to bring about improved concentration, clarity, and calmness.

Few tools will do more to deepen and extend your capacity for mindfulness than developing a practice of formal meditation.

There are many styles or forms of meditation. Many call for sitting on a chair or cushion, but some people meditate while standing or walking. The actual practice could include:

- Letting thoughts arise and pass;

- Focusing on your natural breathing, on an image, or on an object such as a candle flame;

- Repeating a word or phase in your mind, such as, "May I be well, may you be well;" "Help me, Jesus;" Thank you, Jesus;" "Help me, Buddha;" "Glory to Allah;"

- Controlling your breathing—for example, inhale to a count of four, hold for a count of four, exhale to a count of four, and hold for a count of four.

While mindfulness and meditation are closely linked, they are not the same thing. Formal meditation tends to be practiced for a predetermined period of time, ranging from a few minutes to an hour or more. Mindfulness is an experience that can last for just a second or for extended periods of time. In addition, formal meditation is usually practiced in a place with minimal distractions. Mindfulness can occur under any conditions; we simply direct our attention to whatever our intention might be at that moment.

But meditation and mindfulness work hand in hand. In meditation, the mind is like a muscle, getting stronger with exercise and practice. Meditation offers us an extended opportunity to practice bringing our attention to our intention in the present moment and keeping it there—which is how we use mindfulness in our daily lives. Just as exercise prepares us for physical challenges that arise during the day, meditation prepares us for future mental challenges. Stretching, cardiovascular workouts, and weight training can prevent us from pulling a muscle or becoming too fatigued to do our job. Mindfulness, powered by meditation, can keep us from being swept away by negative mind-wandering and unkindness.

Even if you've never tried a meditation practice before, it will be easy to start. That's because you're already practicing mindful breathing and sensing-mindfulness exercises. It's a short step from there to formal meditation—all we need are a few refinements. In Soto Zen Buddhism, the formal meditation tradition that I practice, we sit in a quiet place with few distractions. If a thought arises naturally, we notice it, but we don't follow it around by thinking about it more and more. We return our attention to our breathing. In other words, we don't engage in mind-wandering distractions.

Let's look more closely at the physical aspects of meditation. First, find a quiet, undisturbed setting in which to practice, and decide on a period of time for your meditation. Start small—many people find five minutes is a good place to begin. Gradually increase the length of your meditation sessions over the coming days and weeks, until you can sit for 20 minutes or longer in the morning (before checking messages or reading the news) and 10 minutes or longer in the evening, creating a "mindfulness sandwich" for your day. As you work to increase the duration of your meditation, take your time and don't bite off more than you can chew. It's better to keep up your practice with shorter meditation sessions than to strive for longer periods and become frustrated or discouraged and stop meditating altogether.

Create a "mindful sandwich" with morning and evening meditation.

If you are following the Soto Zen style of meditation I described above, keep your eyes open when you are meditating. Let your eyelids close slightly so that your vision relaxes and rests on a spot on the wall in front of you at about a 45-degree angle. With eyes-open meditation, the attention you use to look at the wall is not available for mind-wandering. With your eyes open, you are also actively connecting to the real world.

In addition, the transition from eyes-open meditation to daily life is not as great as when you meditate with eyes closed. There is one situation in which I close my eyes during meditation. When something in my field of vision triggers active mind-wandering, I close my eyes briefly. The release from the visual stimulation often brings on a smile. Then I open my eyes and continue my meditation.

When possible, I try to sit facing a plain wall—the fewer distractions in my field of vision, the better. A temperature on the cool side with good ventilation also helps, as does relative quiet. Wearing comfortable clothing and loosening your belt allows you to breathe easily.

Your meditation will start with posture and breathing. Let the breath flow naturally, inhaling and exhaling through your nose with your mouth closed. Your posture is important as well, because correct posture allows both breath and energy to flow freely through the body. Sit up, with an upright attitude, shoulders slightly forward of the hips, and the body centered, not leaning one way or another, looking straight ahead. Don't drop your head, but keep your neck straight, lowering your gaze only by relaxing your eyes.

Meditate with a straight back and the hip higher than the knees.

There are different options for supporting this posture without discomfort. Both a meditation cushion and a meditation bench provide a slope that elevates the hips above the knees, and encourages the natural S curve of one's back. You can use a chair with a wedge-shaped cushion or a folded towel to achieve the same support. After I am seated, I sometimes roll my hips forward to achieve the S curve. I do not sit on the top of the meditation cushion (or bench or wedge-shaped cushion), but rather on the front edge, giving my back the right alignment. Don't slouch! To remind myself to sit erect, I think of a string pulling from the top of my head.

You might be concerned about pain. Of course, some physical pain is inevitable—in meditation, as in life. For minor aches and pains, try to simply let it pass. See if you can sit with the pain and just not move. Severe pain is a different matter. If you have an injury, if a particular position (such as kneeling) causes harm to your body, or if pain is so disturbing that you are unable to meditate, use a more comfortable position. If I have an itch, I usually do not scratch it; the itch eventually goes away. You may not find this easy. Scratch if you feel you must. After scratching you have the opportunity to shift your attention back to your breathing.

What about your hands? I use a traditional mudra, or hand position, from the Zazen style of meditation, resting my hands, palms up, one on top of the other in my lap, with my dominant right hand on the bottom. The fingers of my left hand are on top of the fingers of my right hand and my thumbs touch each other lightly at their tips.

At times I notice that my thumbs are not touching lightly but rather are pressing against each other, a sign of tension. So I readjust the touch so that it is light. If my neck and shoulders are tense, I sometimes put a small pillow or folded towel on my lap to support my hands. Some people use more complicated mudras or simply rest their hands on their knees or thighs.

The traditional hand position (mudra).

Physical sensations can provide another distraction when sitting in meditation, especially if we are meditating with others. Another person's coughing, or the soreness in our back can quickly capture our attention. When this happens, it's easy to start wondering if the coughing will continue, to think about how much we'd like that person to leave the room, or if our back will continue hurting, and on and on. But as soon as we notice we are mind-wandering, we can evoke mindfulness by returning our attention to our breathing. Returning our mindfulness to our breathing is an act of kindness toward ourselves as we practice moving away from mind-wandering, and at the same time we are building our habit of mindfulness.

A more advanced and particularly powerful way to coordinate your breathing and mindfulness is to visualize your breath beginning at your tailbone. As you inhale, your breath rises up your back and passes over the top of your head. Then as you exhale, visualize the breath dropping down the front of your body to your groin, then inhale again, bringing your breath around to your tailbone and beginning the second cycle. Do three of these cycles when you first begin to meditate and every time you realize that you have been mind-wandering.

You may find that you have certain habits that distract you during meditation. I had a habit for many years of breathing loudly and twitching my toes, my fingers, and my eyebrows. Noticing distracting habits and stopping them can become part of your meditation practice. Don't become too discouraged over how long it can take to weaken these habits. Be patient.

Many books and websites provide in-depth instruction on meditation. If you're interested in the Soto Zen Buddhism style of meditation, looking up the websites for the Order of Buddhist Contemplatives,[35] Shasta Abbey Buddhist Monastery,[36] and Throssel Hole Buddhist Abbey[37] are good places to start. If this form of meditation doesn't sound like a good fit for you, take on the role of the detective and investigate other styles. One source describes 23 different meditation techniques, including ones from Buddhism, Hinduism, Christianity, and Sufism.[38] You are most likely to meditate and to continue a meditation practice if you select a form that you personally find both comfortable and beneficial. And, even if you choose to not meditate, you can still practice mindfulness and kindness.

If you do decide to try meditation, whatever style you choose, don't be surprised when mind-wandering arises, just as it does in daily life.

When you notice mind-wandering arise during meditation, think of it as an opportunity to practice kindness to yourself. Be gentle. Notice the mind-wandering, but do not become drawn into negative self-talk about your failure to keep your attention on your breathing. In this way, meditation not only strengthens your ability to move your attention away from these distracting thoughts, but also to practice being kind and gentle toward yourself. Do not get discouraged if you frequently find thoughts entering your mind; stay seated until your meditation period ends, do not get up and walk away. Be the warrior.

FROM THE OTHER SIDE

Roy Tester wrote to me about his experience explaining his meditation practice to those he meets in prison:

I've been meditating a lot lately because the pain from this nerve damage has been red lining almost 24/7. No way was I aware Sgt. Eason was there. I was still in Limbo with meditation, still "in," when I became aware she was at my cell door because of the perfume they apply by the pint it seems, but I still hadn't opened my eyes. She said, "Tester, is you breathing when you do that meditation because I can't tell if you breathing." "Yeah, Sarge, I'm breathing but just real shallow. The deeper I get the less breathing I do." Then she asked, "How many times a week you do it?" I told her every day, at least twice a day, sometimes three and four times a day, and at least twenty minutes at a time, but usually a half hour or more. I told her the longer I meditate, the deeper I get. She said, "Well, shit, then what?" I said I try to get deep enough so I am you and you are me and we're no longer two but one energy, one with everyone and everything. She laughed and said, "Okay, okay, that's enough Buddha for me for today. Here, them nice peoples [Doug] wrote you a thick-ass letter."

WARNING!

For some people, meditation brings painful feelings or memories to the surface. One of my prisoner pen-pals experienced flashbacks of childhood abuse; another friend, who was coping with serious addiction and relationship issues, had bouts of depression when beginning to practice meditation. If your meditation practice causes you psychological or emotional distress and these issues continue or become more serious, consider speaking with a trained therapist or well-qualified meditation teacher.

The Meditative Mind

The idea of meditation—sitting still and quietly, with no intention other than to sit still and quietly—sounds very simple, but the practice can be very challenging. Gradually over time you will be able to meditate with less and less mind-wandering, and with fewer unkind mental habits creeping in. As your practice develops, you may begin to experience a few moments of the meditative mind, a sense of deep calmness, openness, and, at times, joy. In this state of mind, thoughts, emotions, and sensations arise as they always do. The difference is that you simply notice them, and they pass away instantly and automatically, without the need to consciously engage mindful breathing. With this experience comes moments of profound calmness and contentment, a feeling of safety and trust. Both the meditative mind and sensing-mindfulness allow the mind to rest, something science has shown as contributing to our productivity, invigorating our attention, consolidating our memories and supporting our creativity.[39]

Very rarely have I been completely calm during an entire meditation session. Even after you have practiced for some time, you will still almost always experience some mind-wandering in between moments of meditative mind. One moment, the sound of a ticking clock or the soft flow of your breath rises quietly into your consciousness; the next, you're remembering someone you forgot to call and wondering if your forgetfulness will make her angry. Don't let this discourage you. It is critical to understand that even when our minds seem to wander for an entire meditation period, by staying in meditation and not acting on our distracting thoughts, we are still weakening unkind habits. If you feel bored in meditation, resist the temptation to get up and do something else. By continuing your meditation, you are weakening the habit of having to constantly distract or entertain yourself. If you feel angry, but continue to sit and breathe, you are weakening that habit. You can always redirect your attention away from these urges and go back to your breathing.

try it later: meditation

Start a daily meditation practice, gradually increasing how long you meditate. When you meditate, pay attention to both the physical and mental aspects of your practice. For the physical, focus on one change at a time, such as improving your posture, building your tolerance of modest pain, or correcting distracting physical habits. For the mental side of things, as soon as you notice that your attention has wandered, return your mind to your posture and breathing. Use the **Mindfulness/Meditation** section in your journal to make notes on the physical and mental aspects of your meditation, along with the date, and what happens when you start working on them. Each week, write about your experiences after meditating.

From Compassion to Kindness

The forms of kindness described in this book are rooted in compassion. We can define compassion as sympathy for the pain and unhappiness of others, often combined with a desire to help. In some cases, we may take it a step further and actually experience the pain of others, which is empathy. This can forge a powerful connection with the other person. By experiencing another person's pain, we can more accurately grasp how best to be kind to them. But genuine kindness requires taking another step. To be kind we need to not only understand another's unhappiness and desire to relieve it, we must take action to intervene.

It is important to note that whether an act is genuinely kind or not depends on the other person—and what they actually need. Think of the Boy Scout who told his scoutmaster that his kind act for the day had been helping an elderly lady cross the street. The scoutmaster agreed the action had been kind, but added that it seemed a little trivial. The Boy Scout protested, "No, it wasn't easy at all. She didn't want to cross the street!" This boy acted like a "do-gooder," but he was imposing his idea of kindness on another person without taking into account her needs and feelings. This is where mindfulness comes in. Mindfulness reminds us to actually pay attention to the other person and be sure that our intended kindness is actually received as such.

Use mindfulness to keep from imposing your idea of kindness.

Many people who practice kindness by volunteering with those who are less fortunate learn gratitude. Numerous studies have shown that volunteering and altruism offer powerful benefits. But when we look further, we find that people benefit from volunteering only when kindness is based on compassion—as opposed to self-focused reasons like wanting to build up a resume, impress friends, or convert others to your beliefs.

In one study, social psychologist Sara Konrath investigated 50 years of data on more than 10,000 Wisconsin high school students as they aged, and found that the people who volunteered lived longer.[40] But upon closer study, they identified a subgroup of do-gooders who had volunteered for selfish reasons. This group didn't reap the same health benefits as those who volunteered out of pure altruism and, in fact, had the same mortality rate as those who didn't volunteer at all. In short, we are more likely to benefit from acts of kindness when our intention is focused on the well-being of those being served.

This book is about concern for the suffering and misfortune of others, which is compassionate kindness, not selfish kindness. When you see the word kindness in this book, remember that distinction.

FROM THE OTHER SIDE

Tad describes the difference he sees between selfish kindness and kindness out of compassion:

[Our mindfulness practice is] *not for us and it never was. Yes, at first we realize a need, a hunger for something better. But, when wisdom sets in, mindfulness is not for us; it is for my spiritual side that sacrifices to serve others. We show compassion, kindness, good reasoning skills, etc. These are only the fruits of our practice. When I hold on to the feeling of appreciation or gratitude for an act, I miss the true meaning of "ethical living" because the self steps in and holds on to self. In vain living! Seeing these bad habits and correcting them mindfully brings an inner peace, sensual almost, because from my perspective I eliminate remorse and regret. "Pure actions" bring joy and happiness.*

If you recognize that you like to talk most of the time and are not very interested in what other people have to say, what they do or how they feel, you may be lacking in compassion and empathy. Consider engaging in activities such as reading books, listening to music, and watching movies and videos that activate your compassion, empathy and interest in other people. You can find resources and ideas in the back of this book, or look online for inspiration. Remember that a wealth of research makes clear that our well-being depends on close, caring relationships. For this, compassion is necessary.

try it now

In the **Kindness/Gratitude** section of your journal, write down how you have acted with kindness toward someone close to you: your partner, child, friend, parent, or pet. Give one example where you expected to receive something in return for being kind. Give a second example when you offered someone kindness without any selfish expectations; often you will become aware of your expectation only after it is not met and you are disappointed. Write the page number for this exercise in your practice journal.

Strengthening Your Kindness Plan

We've seen how meditation strengthens mindfulness, and how mindfulness helps you be more kind to yourself and others. But what about making kindness a habit? The findings of habit-change specialists, including behavior scientist B. J. Fogg of Stanford University and James Clear, author of *Atomic Habits*, can be organized into five steps for making habits stick:

1. Start with a "tiny habit," something so easy, it's almost impossible to fail—such as exercising for just one minute every day.

2. Set aside a specific time each day for your new habit, and pick a time when it's most likely you'll actually do it.

3. If you have trouble sticking with the habit, try to figure out exactly what is holding you back. Is it fear? Frustration? Is your goal not small enough?

4. Celebrate or reward yourself immediately for every success, even if the reward is as little as telling yourself, "good job!"

5. Expect setbacks and gradual improvement, and develop a plan for what to do when you falter.

try it now

Turn to the kindness plan in your practice journal. If your kindness plan is not going as well as you would like, write about how you will incorporate some of these five habit-building steps into your kindness plan.

If you find yourself frustrated or losing motivation in building a new habit, working with a friend, partner, spouse, counselor, or group may add fun, support, and accountability to your efforts to change. You can discuss your progress and ideas, get a fresh perspective, and make a commitment to check in with each other about following through. If you work with a group, each member of the group can write down their kindness plan at the first meeting, and share their intentions. Follow-up sessions can include progress reports, or the group can support members who decide to change or update their plans. You can use these meetings to practice kindness to yourself and others by celebrating successes and being gentle with perceived failures. Working with a group or someone close to you benefits you, as well as the people you are working with. Using mindfulness to grow kindness by working with others is how love wins.

Sometimes people might take advantage of our willingness to act with kindness. Allowing them to do this harms both us and the other person. Imagine if a colleague asks you to finish his project because he has to leave early. Maybe this person frequently asks you to do some of his work. This pattern may mean the person has the unkind habit of taking advantage of other people's kindness. Also, repeatedly doing his work might cause you to feel resentment, and lead to other types of negative mind-wandering. A kind act on your part could be explaining to your co-worker that you are willing to help but only when there is an unusual need. Your explanation might help the person realize that asking too much of others is unkind.

FROM THE OTHER SIDE

Tad wrote about how he realized that fellow prisoners were taking advantage of him:

I'm loyal to the wrong people. I let some guys in the barracks use me. The whole time I was thinking that I was doing the right thing and helping them but they were lying to me. In the end it cost me $50.00. I don't care about the money, really. It was the fact I put myself out there and got used. Roy and I talked about it and he said I need to quit trying to help people that have no intention of helping themselves. Roy slapped me in the face [with words]. At first I took his words as cruel. He said I needed to take off my Superman cape and quit trying to save everyone. Then I said, "f– it. I'll just give up then." He told me, "Kill yourself then. I got a razor if you need it." I didn't say anything else but got out of the shower and put my head down and tucked my tail between my legs. I went to my cell and lay down on my rack, thinking about what had just happened, asking myself, "Why would Roy say that?" Then I thought about the past and I realized that over the years I've gotten myself into trouble trying to help people who in the end never said thanks or showed appreciation because they were so wrapped up in themselves. They didn't care. Then it hit me. Roy was teaching me something and the only way to get my attention was to say those cruel words. Now all I can do is bow to him three times when I can. He has helped me see compassion from a different side: "Quit putting yourself out there to be used, whether with police or inmates."

---

try it now

Turn again to your kindness plan. Has strengthening your kind habit connected you to others and given you a sense of accomplishment? If so, write about those feelings, and any other positive feelings you have experienced in acting with more kindness.

Wrapping Up

You've learned how mindfulness influences kindness, and have been introduced to sensing-mindfulness and meditation. The most direct and efficient way to boost your mindfulness is through meditation, ideally twice a day, in the morning and the evening. At times, the meditative mind arises. This experience increases your trust and confidence that mindful kindness is a path to how love wins. Attending a full day or multiple-day meditation retreat can be a powerful experience to deepen your trust and confidence in the value of meditation.

try it now

Compare how you might respond to a challenging situation with both kindness and unkindness. Imagine you were involved in an altercation in a parking lot, with another person confronting you for parking too close to their car. How could you respond, either mentally, or in your actions? What about when someone cuts you off in traffic?

checking in

Once in a while, it's a good idea to check back in to see how we're doing with the goals we set in previous steps. Let's take another look at the Kindful Vow:

I will be more kindful to myself by...
I will be more kindful in all my relationships by...
I will expand the reach of my kindfulness by...

Has your understanding of the Kindful Vow changed? How have your actions over the past days or weeks fulfilled—or perhaps failed to fulfill—the vows you made when you took this pledge? Maybe you will decide to be more kindful to yourself by building a new pleasant kind habit. If you decide to revise how you extend the reach of your kindfulness, consider extending kindness to possibly the most deserving group—children in need of food, clothing, and a caring adult.

time for reflection

Near the end of each day, take a few moments to reflect on feelings that have arisen from your practice of mindful breathing; two things that made you happy; and the Renew-and-Serve Cycle.

Take Three Breaths

O n a trip to Myanmar in 2013, Linda and I volunteered to spend two weeks at a Buddhist monastery helping monks improve their English pronunciation. On the lighter side, we had a memorable lesson with the monks' description of their walking meditation practice as "pacing back and forth." Their pronunciation of "pacing" came out as "pissing." So monk after monk would describe walking meditation as "pissing back and forth." Unable to control her laughter, Linda had to excuse herself while I worked with the monks trying to get them to clearly enunciate "pacing."

Even more memorable were the monks' responses when we asked them about what they do when they experience mind-wandering during meditation. They offered many answers, but most were a variation of this: "Note that your mind is 'thinking, thinking,' then return to observing the rising and falling of your abdomen." In the time we were there, Linda and I heard this response at least 200 times. This experience has affected our own meditation practice, so that now when we experience mind-wandering, we too redirect our attention to the physical rising and falling of our abdomen.

Three Mindful Breaths During Meditation

After spending years studying meditation and talking with teachers in the Soto Zen tradition, I adopted a technique to redirect my attention away from distractions and to stop mind-wandering. This technique, which not only works during meditation, but also in daily life, is called the Three-Breath Method.

THREE-BREATH METHOD
The practice of redirecting attention away from mind-wandering by focusing on the air entering and leaving the nostrils and the physical expansion and contraction of the abdomen and chest for three slow, deep breaths.

The Three-Breath Method links sensing-mindfulness to meditation. Here's how. When I breathe in during meditation, I feel the air coming in through my nostrils, and I feel my belly and chest rise slightly. When I breathe out, they sink gently back down and I feel the air passing out through my nostrils again. I direct all of my attention to the physical sensations of this movement. When focusing on these sensations, I do not have any attention left over for mind-wandering. I practice concentrating on the physical sensations of my breathing for three breaths. If my attention drifts away, as it sometimes does, I begin the three breaths again, starting with "one."

Once I finish the third mindful breath, I allow thoughts, emotions, and sensations to arise in my meditation. If I have a thought, I notice it bubble up and then simply allow it to dissipate. I don't get caught up in thinking about it more and more. Sometimes several thoughts might arise in quick succession—I may have the thought, "Eating dinner too late last night gave me serious indigestion," then immediately notice a sore spot on my back, followed by an awareness of a bird singing outside. This is completely natural, and if I allow these thoughts and sensations to pass without getting caught up in them, there's no need to do anything else.

But if I find myself getting caught up in these thoughts—such as by silently rebuking myself for eating that rich meal so late at night—that's negative mind-wandering. When I notice this happening, I can fall back on the Three-Breath Method. By mindfully following my breath and the rise and fall of my abdomen for three slow, deep breaths, I can return to a calm and focused state of mind.

You can use the Three-Breath Method as often as you like during meditation. For example, if you hear birds chirping, then remember that you forgot to call your friend, and then notice negative mind-wandering as you scold yourself for forgetting to call your friend, you can bring your attention back to meditation by taking three mindful breaths.

Use the Three-Breath Method to direct your attention away from negative mind-wandering.

You can use three mindful breaths even when mind-wandering is not negative: if you find yourself wondering what kind of bird might be singing outside your window, then listening for whether you can hear other types of bird calls, next thinking about whether you should put up a bird feeder to attract more birds, you can immediately reset your meditation by taking three mindful breaths.

try it later: three breaths

Use the Three-Breath Method to start your next three meditations. Every time you notice mind-wandering during the session, return to three mindful breaths. In the **Mindfulness/Meditation** section of your practice journal, write about how this tool affected your experience.

Three Mindful Breaths Outside of Meditation

Any time negative mind-wandering arises during the day, you can engage the Three-Breath Method. Making this technique part of your day-to-day mindfulness practice will be easier if you first get comfortable using it during meditation. However, even if you do not meditate, you can start using this technique in your daily life. At the beginning, see if you can use it when you notice mind-wandering in low-stress situations, such as when you're alone in a quiet place, or maybe while walking alone. Some of my prison friends meditate by pacing back and forth in their small cell several miles a day. When mind-wandering arises during their walking meditation, they use the Three-Breath Method.

Alex, a friend who gave me feedback on an earlier version of this book, was having trouble establishing his meditation and mindfulness practice. He decided to try applying the Three-Breath Method at least a dozen times a day. The impact was immediate. He wrote:

Just today I was washing dishes and stopped to do three breaths and immediately turned the radio off and continued with my work in a more mindful manner. The three breaths almost always feel wonderful, not like a chore or something I have to do, just a wave of calmness even when I'm a bit agitated to begin with. The more I do it, the more I feel the benefit, and this is particularly true if I'm doing it at a time when I'm not stressed or upset. It simply feels wonderful and almost always takes me right to the present moment.

Use the Three-Breath Method to bring yourself back
to mindfulness in daily life.

Once you're comfortable using the Three-Breath Method to pull yourself back from distraction in meditation and to bring yourself back to mindfulness in daily life, you can start using it more proactively. You don't need to wait for negative mind-wandering to happen before you take three mindful breaths. The more often you do this before mind-wandering even occurs, the more you will strengthen your mindfulness and accrue the benefits. When more of your day is spent in mindfulness, meditation will get easier; you will find that the distractions are not only less frequent, but also less intense. And when meditation is easier, you'll find yourself doing it more often. But if negative mind-wandering remains, be patient. Your feelings, thoughts, and the situation will change, given time.

FROM THE OTHER SIDE

Tad describes how proactively using the Three-Breath Method benefits him:

This method is awesome for being totally absorbed into a moment, e.g. when I pace the floor of my small cell, listening to my radio, I listen to the lyrics of certain songs, and if the lyrics of that song are: mentally, physically & spiritually stimulating, I will stop walking, close my eyes and allow the music to travel through me, taking in the: lyrics, sound, vibrations, etc. as I breath deeply, taking in every bit of the moment. An awesome song to do this to is: "Humble & Kind" by Tim McGraw.[41]

---

try it now: three breaths in daily life

Look for three opportunities to use the Three-Breath Method in situations outside of meditation. Write about those experiences in the **Mindfulness/Meditation** section of your practice journal.

Being Mindful With Thoughts

MINDFULNESS WITH THOUGHTS
The practice of keeping one's attention on what one intended to think about, without engaging in distraction and mind-wandering.

Mindfulness is helpful for all aspects of our life. Believing that we need mindfulness only for certain activities or in certain parts of our day is a misunderstanding that denies us the opportunity to experience the full range of benefits from this practice. It's important to practice mindfulness with our thinking, in the same way that we engage sensing-mindfulness during physical activities. We may not be aware of all the times we are not mindful in thinking. For example, if we look online to research meditation teachings, but find ourselves perusing sports statistics instead, we're not being mindful. On the other hand, if our search for meditation teachings leads us to a documentary about meditation, and we start watching it, we're still practicing mindful thought, because we're staying focused on our original intention. Being mindful with thoughts means keeping our focus on our purpose—our intended thoughts in the present moment—without becoming caught up in distraction.

One way we are often unmindful with our thoughts is by rationalizing our excuses.

RATIONALIZATION
The act of attempting to explain or justify our behavior or attitude with logical, plausible reasons, even if the reasons are not true or appropriate.

Making rationalizations undermines our willpower. If you're on an exercise program, you need to guard against rationalizing excuses. It's easy to think, "I've got a big deadline coming up, and I don't have time to exercise." But this rationalization is an excuse to abandon your willpower—you have the same 24 hours as everyone else, and you need to manage that time effectively in order to keep up the exercise program you've committed to.

Believing this rationalization and skipping your workouts is an example of being unmindful with your thoughts and unkind to yourself.

Researchers studied the role of rationalizations by comparing the willpower of university students and chimpanzees in delaying gratification. The students and chimps had to decide whether to take two desirable treats immediately or delay gratification and get six treats later. Chimpanzees chose to wait for the six treats about 80% of the time, while university students chose to wait about 20% of the time. Psychologist and author Kelly McGonigal explained the results this way: "When we're on our best behavior, humans' ability to control our impulses puts other species to shame. But all too often, we use our fancy brains to...rationalize bad decisions and promise we'll be better tomorrow."[42]

Chimps don't rationalize their way to impulsive behavior—but humans do!

In fact, poor decisions that we attribute to a lack of willpower can often be traced instead to rationalizations and a lack of mindfulness with our thoughts. From an alcoholic who tells himself it's okay to have a drink because he had a hard day at work, to serving yourself that second slice of cake because you'll stick to your diet tomorrow, to lashing out at someone with anger, we rationalize poor decisions big and small. Mindfulness can help curb this behavior. If you've made the decision to cut back on sweets, mindfulness will help you recognize the thought, "just this once!" as a rationalization. A subtle and harmful rationalization is the idea that because you are having a hard time, it is ok to treat yourself with a couple of bowls of ice cream. When you notice a rationalization, you can always shift your attention back to your intention in the present moment—use the Three-Breath Method if you need help.

Learning not to act on our rationalizations gets easier with the development of the foundational skills of patience, a growth mindset, conscientiousness, and humility. For example, if we are struggling with an alcohol or anger addiction, the skill of patience helps us recognize the impulse to drink or the urge to lash out without chastising ourselves for having those thoughts. Having a growth mindset bolsters our confidence that we are capable of change, and that it's not inevitable that we'll go back to addictive drinking and violence. With conscientiousness, we stay away from places where we are tempted to drink or to fight. Humility helps keep our confidence from turning into the arrogance that might make us believe we can "handle" just one drink, or that we're justified in confronting another person.

try it now: recognizing rationalizations

Think about one of your most common temptations. Practice paying attention to the rationalizations that lead to you giving in to this temptation. The next time you notice yourself beginning to make excuses, use the Three-Breath Method to shift your attention back to your intended activity. In the **Unkindness** section of your practice journal, write about what happens, including how you feel.

～

Being mindful with thoughts offers many other benefits, such as feelings of calm, contentment, and gratitude. By reducing distraction and procrastination, it can help us be more effective and valuable at work. And it can enable us to replace unkind thoughts with kind thoughts.

For me, just looking at people as I walked down the street used to cause judgmental thoughts to flash through my mind. "Too heavy. Too thin. Poorly dressed. Ugly. Attractive. Friendly looking." Now, instead of getting caught up in these rapid-fire, subliminal judgments, I practice being mindful by thinking of positive statements; for example, I might say to myself, "we are the same," as a way of acknowledging that we share the same four instincts. You can pick any phrase that directs your attention away from judgmental thoughts, for example, "be mindfully kind," or something from your religion, such as "Christ's beloved," or "Buddha's beloved."

Unkind thoughts can arise and pass so quickly that we may not be aware of them, unless we closely monitor what our mind is doing. I had a friend in a meditation group who, when I described being constantly judgmental, said he did not have such unkind thoughts about people he would see walking down the street. Six months later, he told me he had been observing himself, and found that, on the contrary, he had been having the exact same experience passing people on the street but had never realized it.

try it now

The next time you sit down to read or write something, notice what happens with your mind. How much of the time were you being mindful of your intention? What distracting thoughts arose? When you noticed you were distracted, were you able to quickly return your attention to your intended task? Were the distractions strong enough that you had to use the Three-Breath Method to return your attention to your intended task? Write about this experience in your practice journal.

Applying Mindfulness to Your Emotions

MINDFUL WITH EMOTIONS
The state of mind in which one is able to experience the emotion of the present moment, without reverting to unthinking, habitual responses, and without getting caught up in distracting thoughts.

Many of the emotions we consider positive, like joy, gratitude, serenity, hope, pride, amusement, and inspiration result from our kind habits—such as the gratitude we receive from others for our altruism or generosity, the gratification we feel from working cooperatively with a team, or our feelings of empathy and compassion from caring for those in a difficult situation. Allowing ourselves to savor positive emotions is healthy, feels good, and often helps strengthen kind habits, making it part of our renewal process.

At the same time, positive emotions carried to an extreme can also cause mind-wandering that interferes with our intention. We might need to shift our attention away from positive feelings when we need to attend to a task at hand, such as completing a report at work, feeding our hungry child, or merging onto a busy highway. When we allow ourselves to become so absorbed in our positive emotions that we become distracted and do not pay attention to an immediate need, we are being unmindful.

Occasionally our happiness makes us manic and giddy. Being in this state doesn't make us more attentive and sensitive to the people around us. In fact, it can lead us to disconnect from others and forget about their needs. And it's important to remember that sometimes these positive feelings can stem from unhealthy habits—like an alcoholic day dreaming about the next drink, or a gambling addict anticipating the next trip to the casino.

For many years, I have been aware of how difficult it was to be mindfully kind when I was in a state of agitation and unhappiness. So I was surprised when I first realized that kindfulness could be difficult even when that agitation comes in the form of happiness. Yet I've seen this play out in my own life: I once accidentally locked Linda out of our house because I was so caught up in my excitement over some encouraging comments I'd received about this book. I learned that it can be as important to take three breaths in response to excitement or happiness but probably not as important as it is when I feel angry or afraid.

But what about when others are happy? We know how to be mindful when others are unhappy—we call this compassion. And yet no single word exists to describe our ability to be mindful of others' happiness. In fact, too often, when we see others enjoying happiness and success, we are not able to share their feeling. And occasionally we react with jealously, envy, or resentment arising from our own unmet desire to be "better" or "special."

EMPATHIC JOY

The emotion that arises when one experiences delight or excitement for the happiness and success of others.

An antidote to unkind habits such as jealously, envy, or resentment is empathic joy. Empathic joy can touch your heart with happiness the same way compassion touches your heart with sorrow. It balances our ability to be mindful with sad emotions with an equal capacity for happiness on behalf of others. To cultivate empathic joy, practice responding to another person's good fortune or achievement with kindness: congratulate them with words about how their achievement benefited others, created something beautiful or useful in the world, or was stimulating or exciting. Empathic joy is a key ingredient in close, caring relationships.

try it now

Think about a time when you reacted with negative feelings toward another person's accomplishment. Write about your feelings in your practice journal. Now think back on that same time with emphatic joy, and write about what happens to your feelings about that person's success.

Negativity

Usually, negative mind-wandering caused by our emotions is more demanding of our attention than positive feelings. Sometimes the negative mind-wandering is only agitating. For example, if your partner asks you to put away the dishes while you are in the middle of brushing your teeth, you may feel irritated. Other times, our instincts might trigger agitation. The survival instinct might be activated when you perceive even a mild threat, real or imagined, such as when someone insults you in front of your friends. The success instinct manifests itself in our judgmental thoughts; for example, when we tear someone down for being poorly dressed, we might actually be building ourselves up as being better dressed. The reproduction instinct might cause us to be put off by another person's looks or actions. In situations causing mild negative emotions, returning to mindfulness is relatively easy. We can use the Three-Breath Method.

If the situation causes a stronger negative emotion, returning to mindfulness will be more challenging, but possible. Neuroscientist Jill Bolte Taylor notes in her book, *My Stroke of Insight,* that there is a physiological response to negative emotions—a surge of chemicals passes through the body and triggers our instinctual "fight, flight, or freeze" survival response.[43] It takes about 90 seconds for those chemicals to pass through the system. This means that if negative emotions stay active for longer than a minute and a half, our unmindful thoughts may be feeding the emotion, or some external event may be re-triggering the emotion.

After the 90 seconds pass, we have an opportunity to use mindfulness to stop recirculating the emotion and instead redirect our attention away from our agitation. For example, a friend of mine reported seeing an acquaintance behave rudely. This disturbed him, but, knowing his physiological reaction would soon pass, he waited instead of responding angrily as was his habit. He was quiet for the next minute and a half, and let himself fully experience the emotions he was feeling. Then he took three mindful breaths. After the third breath, he shifted his attention away from the angry feelings, and his agitation was gone.

Being mindful when confronted with strong, negative emotions that cause misery rather than agitation is a different matter; these strong emotions are much harder to calm. Later, this same friend's partner did something extremely rude. This time, my friend wasn't just disturbed— he was shocked, hurt, and angered. Feeling betrayed by her insulting and insensitive behavior, his response swirled between serious agitation and misery for the next day and a half. Spending time around her kept re-triggering his misery. He was unable to be mindful with these intense emotions being so strong. Caught up in distracting thoughts about his hurt feelings, he couldn't hold back from responding in anger. Taking three breaths helped somewhat, but not enough to free him from his misery. I too find that strong emotions take more than 90 seconds to dissipate. I use sensing-mindfulness to attend to the physical sensations caused by the emotion. Strong emotion causes a tightness in my chest and face. I attend to that tightness without getting into a 'story' about the emotions. I don't think about either the cause of the negative emotion or what I will do about it in the future. Just attending to the physical sensations without a commentary softens the tightness across my chest and in my face.

FROM THE OTHER SIDE

Another of Roy's students, Cody, wrote about how he used the Three-Breath Method to calm himself when guards searched his cell.

Afterwards, this dumb squad came in everyone's cell to check their lights. They were so rude and disrespectful. They threw my books all on the floor around my toilet where water was from the shower. I had a flash of anger run through my mind that I really never had Bro. I wanted to smack that Motherf—er up against the wall and tell him, "Don't take your anger out on me and my stuff. It ain't my fault you got to work." I took three deep breaths and asked them if they would like some candy and they did.

Experience-then-Return Loop

We need to remember that our response to negative emotions—and our ability to return to mindfulness—will always depend on when the triggering event occurred and the intensity of the emotion we experienced.

If the triggering event was only slightly agitating, we can usually just sit quietly with the emotion (without thinking about the agitation) for maybe 10 or 15 seconds before returning to our intention—taking three mindful breaths if we need to. When a slightly agitating emotion resurfaces later, see if it helps to name the emotion. If you feel depressed, try saying to yourself, "I feel depressed." Depending on the emotion, you might say, "I feel angry," or "I feel resentful." After naming the emotion, use the Three-Breath Method. Another option is to name the emotion out loud, possibly telling someone else what you are feeling. Saying how you are feeling to another person can soften the agitation.

EXPERIENCE-THEN-RETURN LOOP
The practice of fully experiencing one's emotions for 90 seconds (without thinking about the triggering event), and then

returning to one's intention with mindfulness, using the Three-Breath Method if need be.

On the other hand, if the event was recent and caused us to be in a state of misery or severe agitation—for example, if we had a bad argument with our partner—we will need to take stronger action to release ourselves from strong emotions, since we are feeling self-absorbed and cut off from our partner. We begin by fully experiencing the physiological effects of the emotion for the full 90 seconds. For example, when I am very angry and yelling, I feel a tightness across my chest and a generalized tenseness. When feeling these emotions, we should not think about how mad we are, whose fault it was, or whether to get revenge or apologize. After the 90 seconds, we use the Three-Breath Method, after which we might engage sensing-mindfulness and then return to our intention. For example, we might be reading a book when we are suddenly overcome by upset feelings about the earlier argument: we can experience the misery for 90 seconds, take three breaths and then engage sensing-mindfulness, possibly feeling the weight of the book in our hand. Next we return to our intention of reading the book.

A strong emotion is likely to quickly reassert itself. When it does, you can repeat the Experience-then-Return Loop. Use it whenever miserable negative mind-wandering and self-absorption arise.

CAUTION!

If the emotion arose a long time ago and still causes negative mind-wandering, it has become an unkind habit. Do not sit with the habitual negative emotion for 90 seconds, because it just feeds the negative unkind habit. Immediately evoke the Three-Breath Method, or in some other way return quickly to mindfulness.

Some of our most powerful experiences of negative mind-wandering arise from fear. Fear not only affects our emotions, it can physically hurt. Our perception of pain stems from two distinct systems in our bodies: one system tracks our physical pain levels, the other taps into our emotions to determine how intensely we are feeling the pain. John Hopkins' neuro-science professor David Linden in his book *Touch: The Science of Hand, Heart, and Mind* describes how fear can dramatically increase our percep-tion of pain.[44] Moreover, professor of psychiatry at University of Texas Southwestern Medical School Hadhukar Trivendi found that depression is an emotion that can intensify pain.[45] Conversely, University of Liverpool professor Christopher A. Brown reported that meditation reduces the perceived unpleasantness of pain.[46]

For me, physical pain is something that triggers a strong emotional response. Nobody likes pain; I struggled with chronic pain on and off for almost ten years. Problems with my back, shoulder, and hips dramatically limited my activities and disrupted my sleep, ultimately leading me to a period of depression. As I was gradually healing, anytime I had pain for more than a few hours, I worried that I might return to that chronic condition and never be free of it. Of course, worry just makes things worse. So now when pain keeps me awake at night, I use the Three-Breath Method to short-circuit the negative mind-wandering about returning to the chronic condition. Being conscientious with my physical therapy has limited the intensity and duration of my pain, so when bouts of pain do return, the Experience-then-Return Loop minimizes my anxiety.

A common response to fear is anger. I was walking in the woods when a cyclist came speeding over the top of a knoll. I heard him coming and was able to leap out of the way just in time to not be injured. Scared and upset, I felt the fight or flight physiological response arise as a feeling of tightness across my chest. A moment later, a second cyclist came along at a more reasonable pace. This time I didn't get out of the way but stood in the middle of the trail to stop him and asked if he was with the cyclist who just passed. After he said yes, I unleashed a tirade. Fueled by adren-aline, I asked him to tell his friend to be more careful and added that in fact this trail was marked as being only for hikers. But after he departed, I couldn't stop thinking about it. I was still angry, but now I was also worried that the first guy would come back to confront me. At first I could not let go of the thoughts and feelings of anger and fear. But after a couple of minutes, as I walked farther along the trail, I activated the Experience-then-Return Loop (experiencing the emotion for 90 seconds, then engaging sensing-mindfulness). Attending to the many shades of green foliage along the trail softened my agitation. My mind took a rest by halting the unmindful-unkind cycle of anger and fear—and allowed me to enjoy the remainder of my walk. Sensing-mindfulness can strengthen the Experience-then-Return Loop by giving us a feeling of spaciousness and connection that cuts through our feeling of being self-absorbed and cut off from others.

try it now

In your practice journal, write about how you could have used the Experience-then-Return Loop with a strong emotion.

A Different Perspective on Negative Emotions

Most of us wish we didn't experience pain, because pain makes us unhappy. But what would happen if we did not have pain? A recent news story described a toddler who was born without the ability to feel pain. While most parents wish to spare their children pain, this boy's mother described it as a "nightmare"—her son would fall down and run into things as a joke, and had severely burned himself by touching a hot stove. So in fact, pain plays an important, and even life-saving, role in our lives.

Unhappiness can act as an emotional pain that plays the same role. Feelings of guilt, shame, and regret over bad decisions we make under the influence of alcohol, for example, can give us the motivation we need to deal with our issues around drinking. While clinical depression can be a debilitating disease, some scientists have reported that mild bouts of depression actually help people shut out the outside world while they deal with the problems causing the depression; one study found that women with mild depression were better at evaluating the costs and benefits of different solutions to marital problems than women without mild depression.[47]

So, unhappiness has its place. For example, anger may signal that we are in danger, but we need to know when to redirect our attention away from it and when to call up the warrior or the detective to deal with the danger. Mindfulness in the role of the detective helps us determine when unhappiness is serving as a motivator and when it has simply become negative mind-wandering. Mindfulness can help us see when our anger over a loss has shifted from grief to obsession, or when unhappiness over a poor decision has stopped being regret and has turned into unrelenting self-blame.

try it now

In your practice journal, write about a time when unhappiness served as a motivator in contrast to a time when it just caused negative mind-wandering. If you wish, draw pictures that symbolize the contrast.

Wrapping Up

The Three-Breath Method for agitation, and the Experience-then-Return Loop for misery are always available, regardless of time or place, to bring mindfulness to your thoughts and emotions. Use them often and they will become habits, coming to your aid without you having to consciously call for them. Think of these methods as tools to help you move from mind-wandering (ranging from low-keyed to miserable) to mindfulness and gratitude. They serve as a spark plug for the mindful-kind cycle, an example of how love wins.

checking in

Review what you wrote for your kindness plan in Step 3. How is it going so far? What has worked and what has not? Think about any changes you might want to make. For example, if your intentions have changed, which sometimes happens as meditation and mindfulness shift your perspective, now is a good time to update your plan. Feel free to add a few notes to what you've already written, or go ahead and start fresh with a new plan to build a new kind habit. Or maybe things are working, and you just need to stick to your plan.

time for reflection

Near the end of each day, take a few moments to reflect on how you feel when you allow your mind to rest as part of the

Renew-and-Serve Cycle. If your mind is not getting enough rest, consider asking yourself if you are engaging both mindfulness and your pleasant kind habits fully enough to renew your energy and contentment.

STEP 6
Get Unkind Habits Out of Your Way

E ven if we're sincere in wanting to build new habits of kindness, we often find ourselves frustrated in our efforts because our old, unkind habits stand in the way. Think about how hard it is to take up running if you're overweight and still smoking a pack of cigarettes a day. In the same way, it's hard to become a better listener if you still have the habit of interrupting. This is why, as you build some kind habits, it's important to also weaken unkind habits.

FROM THE OTHER SIDE

Roy wrote about how chronic, debilitating pain often triggered his habit of anger:

Wasn't really "Lettin' Go" of anger till a few days ago. I noticed the tenseness, the constrictions in my body. I had nearly been consumed by anger at the [health services clinic]. I started to just fkn breathe, slowly but smoothly, visualizing the anger, the tenseness leaving my body, allowing my body to slowly become calmness. I realized I was causing myself a lot of fkn pain and discomfort. Anger was influencing my thinking and intentions, my character.

Came to sit on my bed but saw a tiny tree frog stuck on my window. I got closer and closer so I could "sit" with "Dogen" (that's what I named him) as being part of his sangha. I watched him just "BE," just breathe and be, being in the moment. Moment by moment. All the anger in me was slowly released with every beat of Dogen's heart. I just couldn't fathom how much pain and suffering I was causing myself. I realized I could "Let Go" of my anger and that in turn would lesson my self-inflicted pain and suffering. It's like flippin a light switch. I was feeling my body react in a positive way, a relaxed looseness. Anger is not only a stupid waste of time and energy, it causes pain and suffering; everything about it is negative.

Roy's anger was a habit of extreme unkindness. In fact, you might say that before Roy's transformation, he had an unkind, anti-social personality type. In contrast, some unkind habits seem mild and might even give us temporary comfort, but still serve to harm our relationships, which limit our overall happiness, contentment, and joy. Let's look at Tasha. This young woman recognizes that she's lonely and that loneliness is making her unhappy. She feels inadequate and insecure. She has a goal of being kind to herself by meeting more people and hopefully making some friends. But there's something standing in her way. When she's bored or anxious around other people, Tasha turns to her phone—playing games, checking social media, and generally hiding from the world. Won't it be easier for her to smile and talk to the people around her once she puts the phone away?

Don't let unkind habits stand in your way of building kind habits.

try it now

Turn to the **Unkindness** section of your practice journal and review the unkind habits you have identified. Then write about how some of your unkind habits are standing in the way of the kind habits you want to develop. How do you feel when you engage in these unkind habits?

Changing Our Unkind Habits Is Hard

It's hard to be truly motivated to change unkind habits if we don't allow ourselves to experience the hurt they are causing others and ourselves. We need to really feel the consequences of our actions in order to understand the importance of making a lasting change. Practicing mindfulness gives us the clarity to see the impact we are having on those around us. In the past, when I would express my anger by lashing out, sometimes swearing or slamming a door, I was so focused on myself that I never noticed the look of fear on the faces of my wife and daughters. I now realize that I was using anger to control the behavior of those around me. For example, if I spilled my drink and erupted in anger, Linda would sometimes offer to clean up the mess to mollify me. Once I became more mindful, the shock of seeing how I was hurting and manipulating my family strengthened my motivation to change.

Before we can change an unkind habit, we have to recognize it. Unkind physical habits such as lashing out are often easier to recognize than negative, mind-wandering unkind habits, such as feeling inadequate or anxious. Once we recognize an unkind habit and set the intent to change it, we run up against three challenges: our instincts (survival, reproduction, and success), our personal experiences, and the values of our society.

Many of the men I work with in prison have unkind habits as the result of traumas they experienced early in life. Unkind habits caused by trauma are among the most difficult to change, for several reasons. In Tad's case, his stepfather's abuse triggered his survival instinct, which contributed to him developing the unkind habits of anger and violence.

Tad learned to use violence and anger to get what he wanted—using physical force to protect his mother from his stepfather's attacks.

In contrast to an abusive childhood like Tad's, a nurturing upbringing triggers the kindness instinct, which means the person is less likely to have severe unkind habits.

Even when we have the best of intentions, our society can sometimes make it hard to change unkind habits. We are bombarded by messages every day that encourage values like individualism, materialism, and self-centeredness. Many selfish habits grow out of our belief that getting what we want will make us happy. Despite the hollow promises of the advertising industry about success and sex, the fact is that happiness comes largely from our caring relationships. Egotists focus on their own well-being and less on the welfare of others, which undermines their relationships, ultimately leading to less happiness.

While all humans are wired to be self-centered to some extent, egotists place too much emphasis on habits for the "self," and too few habits that benefit "the group." University of Virginia professor T. Talhelm and his team compared rice farmers and wheat farmers in China. Rice farming, with irrigated paddies, requires farmers to cooperate by redirecting water from one person's field to another's. In the study, wheat and rice farmers were asked to draw pictures of themselves and their neighbors. Wheat farmers do not need to work together—every farmer can tend his or her own field without involving their neighbors. Wheat farmers drew themselves larger than their neighbors, because they perceived their neighbors as being unimportant. In contrast, the rice farmers drew themselves small and their neighbors larger because they saw themselves as part of a larger group that benefited from cooperation. The two types of farmers were also asked how they would punish a neighbor who was a thief. Because the rice farmers were part of a group that wanted to maintain harmony within the group, they sought a more lenient punishment than the wheat farmers.[48]

Focusing so much on themselves, egotists are more likely to be punitive and less likely to notice opportunities to act with kindness. As a result, they do not reap the many benefits that habits of kindness can give. This harms everyone. The harm to self and others caused by egotism is rarely as obvious as addiction to drugs, alcohol, or gambling. However, egotism also seems to contribute to many psychological problems and states of unhappiness. Moreover, when egotism is widespread in society, the resulting divisiveness, lack of civility, and indifference to human suffering can be quite damaging. You need look no further than today's headlines to see examples of this, along with examples of harm caused by trauma-induced unkind habits.

try it now

In the **Unkindness** section of your practice journal, describe how one of your unkind habits may have resulted from one or more of these influences: your instincts, personal experiences, and/or society's values.

The discussion thus far is about unkind habits we already have. Think about how easily one of your unkind habits developed and how hard it is to try to break that habit. The most powerful way to deal with an unkind habit is to not start it.

Weakening Unkind Habits With Mindfulness

I learned anger from my dad, who had PTSD from World War II. Although he never physically hurt his children, his outbursts of rage— unpredictable, and often for something as trivial as missing a shot on the golf course—were a constant source of fear and anxiety for us. I learned that such anger was "normal," and yet, because of my experience growing up, my own anger scared me.

For years continuing into adulthood, I, too, would have angry outbursts and tantrums. I once accidentally knocked over a carton of dog food, spilling the dry dog food all over the floor. Seeing the debris filled me with rage at my own carelessness. I swore and slammed the cabinet door shut. Then I kicked the carton, which of course only made the situation worse—and made me even angrier.

It wasn't until I began practicing mindfulness that my anger habit began to soften. I learned how to recognize the feeling of anger rising in me, and to shift my attention to the Three-Breath Method or to sensing-mindfulness, allowing the stirred-up emotions to settle. The power of this simple tool was driven home to me one day when I once again spilled that dog food and found myself looking down on a mess of my own making. This time, knowing that kicking the carton and spreading the dry dog food would only make things worse, I took a few moments to practice mindful breathing, and as I cleaned up I actually felt relief from not experiencing the stress of a tantrum.

A direct and powerful way of stopping an unkind habit is to recognize the trigger and immediately take three breaths before doing anything else. Knowing to take the three breaths is relatively easy, but actually taking the three breaths can be very challenging. When an alcoholic is offered a drink, the urge to drink is the trigger. The challenge is to take three breaths rather than taking the drink.

A second way to break an unkind habit is to transform it into a kind one. Think of the smoker who transforms the habit of reaching for a cigarette into the habit of reaching for a carrot stick instead. Or if you're in the habit of indulging in gossip, when you feel the impulse to speak unkindly about someone else, you can catch yourself and practice turning your comment into something positive or neutral.

Let's go back to Tasha, who now realizes that anytime she's feeling nervous in a social situation because of her sense of inadequacy, she immediately picks up her phone. Sometimes letting go of an unkind habit—like escaping to your phone—can leave a void. With mindfulness, you can learn to use the trigger for the unkind habit as a reminder to fill that void with something more positive. To break the habit, she can overcome her feelings of inadequacy by writing in her journal about three things she does well each day. She can also plan ahead and pick something else she wants to be doing when she feels this impulse to escape, such as turning to someone near her and starting a conversation, or simply sitting still to "people watch." Whatever it is, mindfulness can help her to recognize when her old habit is being triggered, and to substitute the new habit instead.

Often it's not just one event but a chain of events that triggers our unkind habit. A third way to break an unkind habit is to be aware of feelings, thoughts, and behaviors that occur very early in the chain. We're more successful at weakening habits when we can nip these early behaviors in the bud. For example, if you struggle to control yourself around alcohol, it's hard to resist temptation when you have an open bottle of beer in front of you. Learning to recognize your impulse in the grocery store and stop yourself from putting the beer in your shopping cart (or even avoiding the liquor aisle altogether) makes it so much easier to break the drinking habit.

A fourth way mindfulness can help us make a positive change is by shining a spotlight on the self-centered thoughts that underlie many unkind habits. Arrogance, distraction, needing to control things, competitiveness, and needing to be "special" are at the root of many of the hurtful ways we treat others and, ironically, even ourselves. Learning to recognize arrogance and to feel the harm it causes others motivates us to refrain from arrogance. For example, throughout my life, I realize that I have used my intelligence as a way to become special, to compete, and to control my environment. At times I am arrogant. When Linda and I were first getting to know each other about 50 years ago, I was so controlling that when she said something that I disagreed with in front of other people, I would respond with ridicule or scorn. When I realized how much I was hurting her, I felt pain and shame, and this motivated me to never again ridicule her.

Fortunately, I did not have to rely on my resolve alone. Linda would not tolerate such demeaning treatment. It was clear to me that if I wanted to continue our relationship, I would have to stop that socially embarrassing and controlling behavior, which I did rather quickly by recognizing when I was about to say something hurtful about her. This recognition gave me a moment of freedom before acting on the habit. In that moment of freedom, I actually felt the pain and suffering my ridicule would cause. In addition, I felt the fear of losing her because of my arrogance. Had I not broken that habit, we would not have been married these many years.

Nevertheless, occasionally I still try to impose my preferences on Linda, though, I hope, in a far less damaging way. For example, when she is on the phone giving directions to our house, I sometimes interrupt with different directions. My directions are not "better," they are just mine. In other words, my habit of arrogance has been largely tamed but not completely broken—and I continue to work on it.

Imposing our opinions, preferences, and ways of doing things takes on more force when we think it is something we "need" to do. Such needs cause others to suffer and also strengthens our selfish, unkind habits. Life is much easier when we don't impose our preferences on others. So now, before I say or do something, I use mindfulness to more accurately determine whether I would be imposing my preferences on others or saying something constructive. If I determine that I am about to impose (not merely offer) my opinion or preference, I decide instead to remain silent.

When we don't carry out an unkind habit, we often feel uncomfortable. When a person with alcoholism does not take a drink; the urge to drink is there and it feels uncomfortable. Same for the dieter who stops eating before feeling full, the urge to eat more is there and it feels uncomfortable. When a person full of anger does not lash out, the urge is there and it feels uncomfortable. Same for refraining from telling someone what to do, from wanting to hide from others in your cell phone, and wanting to smoke that cigarette. Mindfulness allows us to recognize that feeling uncomfortable is inevitable and we just need to take our three breaths and be patient with the feeling.

Mindfulness (and being patient when feeling uncomfortable) can be a powerful habit-breaking tool because it can give you the confidence that you can, in fact, change. In the early years of practice at our Buddhist priory, I could be very mindful much of the time when I was there. But being mindful at home and at work was difficult. Away from the priory, low-key and agitated mind-wandering seemed as real and permanent as the five fingers on my hand, something I could not change. Then, one day, several years into my practice I was standing in the shower and noticed that my mind was still; I was not at the priory, yet I was being mindful— just aware of the sensations from showering and nothing else. My mind was at rest! At the time, it seemed as unbelievable as if I had grown a sixth finger. I was stunned and became convinced that I could develop mindfulness and lessen my mind-wandering at work and at home.

Changing the unchangeable shocks us, then empowers us.

FROM THE OTHER SIDE

Due to his experience of childhood sexual abuse, Roy had a deep-held hatred of child molesters. And yet, mindfulness gave him the confidence to act quickly and constructively to break that habit in a dangerous situation:

Much as I used to hate child molesters ["chomos"], one time the [guards] put one in with us. When I realized what was up, every-thing went deathly quiet. Psycho Mike and Hatchet Jack were getting their shanks off the top of the ductwork in the bathroom and I knew they were fixing to pop more holes than a sieve in this little geeky nerd-looking dude and slice him up, so I got off my bed, and went straight at the dude. When I got in his face I said, "You sick chomo maggot piece of shit I'm gonna kill your m-f-ing ass," and slapped him, but cupped my hand right before it connected so it would pop loud and sound like I really hit him harder than what I did and said under my breath, "Run for the door or they're gonna kill you!" And he did just that. I acted like I tripped and couldn't grab him fast enough.

They locked me up for assault but I didn't care because those two killers would have killed him. As much as I hated child molesters, I still didn't want him to die. I even looked proper in the other inmates' eyes because I attacked a chomo. The dude's mom wrote to me and said her son told her what I did. I thought she was going to cuss me out for slapping her son, but she said, "My son said you saved his life." And he explained how I did it. She sent me $50 and a box full of novels. Ain't that something?

try it now

In the **Unkindness** section of your practice journal, describe how you will use one of these practices to weaken one of your unkind habits:

- Notice the trigger and immediately take three breaths.

- Transform the unkind habit into another habit.

- Stop a step early in the chain to prevent you from carrying out the unkind habit.

- Identify a practice you have used successfully to weaken an unkind habit, for example, setting your fork down after each bite so as to eat more mindfully.

- Address your selfish habits of being arrogant, controlling, competitive, or needing to be "special" by answering these questions: What does your selfish unkind habit look like, how does it help you get what you want, what kind of harm has it caused in the past, and how might that harm motivate you to end the habit?

CAUTION!

Just because you're working to let go of unkind habits doesn't mean you shouldn't at times express negative feelings. Everyone gets frustrated sometimes, and if someone treats you in a hurtful or disrespectful way, or asks you for something that's unreasonable, unsafe, or violates your personal boundaries, it's important that you are able to say, "No." With mindfulness, you can say "no" in a calm, matter-of-fact manner, possibly also explaining why you are saying no, without being defensive or accusatory.

Speaking up about your boundaries is a way of being kind to yourself, and respectfully expressing your feelings is actually a kindness to the people you interact with.

Responding to the Unkind Habits of Others

Mindfulness also makes us more aware of the unkind habits of others. When we are the targets of the unkind behavior of another, we have two choices. One is to work on changing our mental world so that we tolerate the other person's unkind habit with minimal resentment. The other is to work on changing our physical world by staying away from that person or by trying to get the other person to break his or her unkind habit.

The choice depends on the severity of the unkind habit. For minor habits, we can just change our mental world. For example, my wife has a well-entrenched, but minor, unkind habit of continuing to point out why I misunderstood something even after I agree with her explanation. Instead of responding with annoyance as she continued to expand on her explanation, I decided to change my mental world. I would politely allow her to restate her explanation one more time.

The stakes are higher when an unkind habit of another person has a major impact on our life. One option is to not be around the person. For example, a casual friend was obsessed with how horrible our government and corporations are. It was all he could talk about, at great length and with great conviction, and it made him increasingly unpleasant to be around. The habit was so ingrained that I changed my physical world by seeing less and less of him. Other people might find themselves bullied by a boss or supervisor at work. In some cases, the problem might be so bad that you decide to look for another job. Other times, you might be able to make changes that improve the relationship or minimize your exposure to the abusive behavior. If you decide the problem warrants attempting to change your physical world, take on the detective role to research different options.

The most straightforward way to get friends to break an unkind habit is to ask them. For good friends, we can try to help them break their unkind habits by telling them how the habit affects us, and asking if they would consider changing the habit. I previously described how, from time to time, Linda would speak to me with a sharp tone of voice. Unaware of the habit, when I spoke with her about how it made me feel, she readily agreed to stop using that tone of voice and asked me to remind her when she did so in the future. I also became more sensitive about interrupting her when she was concentrating, which is when that sharp tone usually came out. But of course, getting a friend to change an unkind habit is rarely this simple.

Tips for Problem-Solving Difficult Situations

You can apply these tips for problem-solving as a kindful practitioner. Taking on that role also helps you decide if you want to pursue other resources to learn more about how to deal with any of these situations.

Anger

Anger can cause stress in any relationship. Sometimes we may find ourselves interacting with a friend or loved one who is angry for reasons that have nothing to do with us. University of Wisconsin-Green Bay psychology professor Ryan Martin suggests five steps for dealing with an angry person:

1. If you did something to cause the anger, apologize. However, if the emotion is out of proportion to your mistake, continue to step 2.

2. Appear calm even if you do not feel calm.

3. Don't make broad generalizations such as "You have never been able to control your anger." Instead say, "Please don't yell at me."

4. If a positive resolution seems unlikely, disengage. Say, "Maybe we can discuss this later?" or "I'm feeling uncomfortable," and walk away.

5. At any time if you feel you are in danger, get away from the person immediately.[49]

A Difficult Family Member

It's often said that we can't choose our family. Sometimes we may find ourselves dealing with a family member who is really difficult. Here are three options for what you can do:

1. Avoid being around the person if possible, otherwise engage in a distracting activity.

2. Confront the person in a constructive manner, articulate your frustration then be clear about what is acceptable (without arguing), and, if possible, practice empathy for the person.

3. Seek perspective and help from other family members. See if another family member has a better relationship with the person and can address the person's problematic behavior.[50]

Estrangement

Some relationships become so strained that we stop talking to the other person altogether. Here are tips for reopening communication:

1. Acknowledge the situation, with a phrase like one of the following:

- Can we talk? I know I've pulled back, and I want to change that.

- I've not been open with you. I'd like to tell you what I'm trying to figure out.

- Would you be willing to listen while I try explain why I have been so remote?

2. Describe what worries you:

- If I keep drifting away from you, I'm afraid we won't ever feel close again.

- I feel alone and it scares me. If we can't figure out how to connect, I worry that I will lose you.

3. Work on communicating more respectfully with your partner (or another significant person in your life) by expressing care and asking caring questions, as described in Step 3. In addition, be sure to take seriously the other person's opinions and preferences, especially when decisions are being made that affect both of you.

Serious Psychological Problems

It is important to have realistic expectations about how much we can help another person with their very damaging, unkind habits. For example, Charles was valedictorian of his high school graduating class, class president, handsome, and athletic. As a young adult, he had a successful career and family life and was a charismatic and humorous public speaker. However, he developed a gambling addiction. By the time Charles reached his early 60s, his mental world was full of guilt and shame. Self-absorption precluded mindfulness, despair and isolation impeded kindness, and unhappiness was extreme. He was broke, unemployed, about to be evicted; his mind was never at rest.

One of his oldest friends, Wayne, and three other friends encouraged him to relocate to the town where they lived, and eventually he moved in with one of them. These friends spent hundreds of hours over almost two years and thousands of dollars to help him. The support failed. Charles moved away again, and not long after he emailed Wayne that he was on the verge of homelessness, depressed, and suicidal. In spite of Wayne's frantic attempts to support and encourage him, Charles ended up taking his own life.

Realize that it is sometimes not possible to help another person to change. However, some people are indeed able to lift themselves up from trauma, using the power of mindful kindness. There will be others whose problems are so deep seated that they require professional help.

FROM THE OTHER SIDE

Because Tad taught his student Chris to be mindful and kind, Chris was able to break his lifelong, controlling habit of gambling:

Gambling is one unkind habit I have to myself. I thought I had it done with in my life. Once you stop practicing mindfulness of your problem, you will slip right back into old habits/ways. To this day, I make it a point to not include myself in betting. I know it's a small thing, but I have got to the point where I didn't even have a stamp to write my son. I will not, through practice & thoughtfulness, allow that to happen again.

A Plan for Weakening Our Unkind Habits

Unkind habits not only harm us and other people but also take up time and effort that could be used for kindness. Think about the amount of time alcoholics lose to their drinking—not just the hours they might spend actually consuming alcohol, but also the time during which they are impaired, and then the time they spend recovering the next day. In the same way, unkind habits like anger can consume our attention for hours at a time, and even leave us "hungover," as we regret later what we might have said or done. How many kind words could we have said to those around us during that time? How many opportunities might we have missed to help someone else? Any process to change an unkind habit has to start with acknowledging that the unkind habit exists, that help is available, and that it is possible for the person desiring to make the change to be successful. A willingness to put trust in a loved one, a therapist, or higher power to help can also be part of the process to weaken the unkind habit.

In Step 3, you learned how a written kindness plan could help you focus your goals and hold yourself accountable in building new habits. So it makes sense that writing out your plan will also help you succeed in weakening unkind habits. Your plan will help you clarify both your intentions and the actions you will take in pursuit of this important work.

If you are uncertain about the unkind habit you want to change, you can review the **Unkind Habits** section of your practice journal. You can also think about the unkind habits that block your skills of character, like a fixed mindset, irresponsibility, arrogance, and impatience.

Think about the actions you will take in both your physical world and your mental world. If your goal is to reduce angry outbursts at your spouse, you may make some mental changes, such as recognizing that your spouse's behavior triggers your anger, and reminding yourself how your anger hurts your spouse. At the same time, you could change your physical world by taking three breaths before responding. Or possibly your goal is to reduce angry outbursts directed toward a co-worker or friend. In both these situations, a good deal of effort will be directed toward weakening these unkind habits in your mental and physical world.

try it now

Make a plan to weaken an unkind behavior. In the **Unkindness** section of your practice journal, write your answers to these questions:

- Why are you making this plan?

- What is the unkind habit, and how does it manifest itself in both your physical world and mental world? How do you feel after you execute the unkind habit?

- Who is harmed by your unkind habit?

- Whom will you ask for support, if anyone?

- What detective work will you need to do, if any?

- How, if at all, will you use the mind of the warrior?

- What foundation skills of character (growth mindset, conscientiousness, patience, and humility) will you need most?

- What action will you take to weaken the unkind habit in your mental world?

- What action will you take in your physical world? Consider this five-step process:

    1. Describe what you will do when you are about to carry out the unkind habit.

    2. Identify when and where you will weaken the unkind habit.

    3. On a sticky note or piece of paper, write: what, when, and where you will weaken the unkind habit. Post this note where you can see it.

    4. Identify the obstacles that could get in your way.

    5. Write down how you will overcome the obstacles.

- Now that you have made the plan, are you willing to implement it?

try it later: follow-up

After you begin putting the plan into action, answer these two follow-up questions in the **Unkindness** section of your practice journal:

- What happened?

- What next?

Although there are only two questions, you will probably spend more time answering them than you did writing the plan itself. That's because we usually don't succeed in breaking a habit on the first try. It often takes many steps, missteps, and corrections before we can change something and make it stick. So for the first three times you take action toward your habit-changing goal, make an honest assessment of what worked and what didn't work, then adjust your plan and write down what you intend to try next. Don't forget to include both your physical world and your mental world when you follow up. Write the title "Weaken Unkind Habit," this page number, and the date for each entry you make.

Bob Dylan sang, "There's no success like failure." Love wins when we admit our failures of mindfulness and kindness in weakening unkind habits, seeking help, and rededicate ourselves to changing our habits.

NOTE:

This plan is intended to help people with a sincere desire to change unkind habits. For help addressing personality disorders or other serious emotional issues, seek the help of a mental-health professional.

Practicing One Habit or Another

When you stop to think about it, we are often practicing a habit, kind or unkind. Snacking on many thick slabs of cheese and crackers during the day and before bed may or may not give you heartburn and insomnia—it does, though, build a habit of including too much fat in your diet. On the other hand, if you're hungry before bed, you can choose to eat half an apple or drink some milk. The point is that much of the time we are deciding whether to practice habits that are kind or habits that are unkind. Being mindful helps us recognize the habits we are strengthening and the ones we are weakening.

Given this step focuses on unkind habits, let's switch to kind habits. It is important to be mindful about which kind habits we are strengthening. For example, are you spending enough time and effort on habits directed at yourself, to take care of yourself so that you can enjoy your well-being and be better able to serve others? You can also ask yourself if you are spending enough time acting with kindness to others.

try it now

Write about how it is going for one kind habit you direct at yourself. Also write about what is going on for one kind habit that involves how you interact with another person.

Wrapping Up

Unkind habits can foster negative mind-wandering, which often leads to agitation or misery. In some situations, the misery can fuel anger toward others and ourselves, and to unkind distractions such as substance abuse. Moreover, these unkind habits often stand in the way of building kind habits. The downward unmindful-unkind cycle is likely to continue until we realize how our unkind habits harm ourselves and others. This is the first step to change. With mindfulness as our foundation, we carry out our plan for weakening unkind habits. As we see and feel the benefits, the urge to carry out that unkind habit will likely diminish of its own accord. As we use mindfulness to dismantle our most harmful unkind habits, we begin to see how love wins by expressing our feelings of love through acts of kindness.

It's time to put what you've learned about unkind habits into practice. There are a number of skills in addition to mindfulness that can help you weaken unkind habits, such as mentally preparing yourself ahead of time for challenging situations, and enlisting support from your loved ones and friends (such as asking a friend if you can call her to talk for a few minutes to distract you when you feel the temptation to drink a beer) and rewarding yourself for small accomplishments.

The moment we recognize the harm we cause with our unkind habit is the moment to vow to be done with it. In the same way, there's no more powerful motivator to continue kind habits than truly feeling the impact our acts of kindness have on others. This is how love wins.

checking in

Turn to the last page of your practice journal and find your answers to these two questions: What are your purposes in life? What is meaningful to you in your life? Underneath those answers, write today's date and write your answers to the same two questions. Compare the answers you wrote when you were reading the Introduction to the answers you wrote just now. What has changed? What has remained the same? How do you feel about these changes?

review: comparing your kind and unkind responses

Think about how you might respond kindly and unkindly (mentally or with an action) when you get a hard-driving sales call from a live person.

Now think about how you might respond kindly and unkindly (mentally or with an action) to someone you are jealous of because of an accomplishment you wish had been yours.

time for reflection

Reflect on your feelings as you have practiced the Renew-and-Serve Cycle. How does it feel when you:

- allow your mind to rest?

- practice a pleasant kind habit?

- serve by acting with kindness?

Finally, during the evenings, take time to revisit positive feelings from the day. For example, recall a time you experienced happiness, gratitude, an appreciation for friendship, an act of kindness, or a positive communication.

STEP 7

Practice Sensing-Mindfulness

When I was in seventh grade, I joined the school choir. I wasn't a natural talent. The teacher kept moving me next to people who sang well in the hopes that I would improve. At the beginning of one class she would move me next to a strong tenor. Several classes later, she would move me next to a different strong tenor. When I had failed to improve even after several moves, I decided it would be simplest for me just to drop choir.

Years later, I realized my problem: I had been so worried about hitting the wrong notes that all my attention was focused on thinking about singing, rather than actually hearing myself or listening to how I fit in with the voices around me. Over the next 40 years, I was in fact able to improve my skill in singing quite a bit (going all the way from atrocious to mediocre) by listening closely to the sound of my own voice as Linda gave me feedback when we sang together at home.

With Linda's help, I was able to simply listen carefully to my own voice as I sang scriptures during services at my Buddhist church. This careful listening without judging the correctness of my singing is an example of sensing-mindfulness, which is the practice of focusing our attention in the present moment on sensations coming from touch, sight, smell, taste, or hearing, without adding any extra thoughts or judgments. We discussed sensing-mindfulness earlier, but now we're going to explore it more fully, and look at how this simple but powerful practice can help you develop mindful kindness.

Anchored in the Present Moment

In previous steps, we learned how to direct our attention to the physical sensations coming both from within our own bodies (such as movement, breathing, pain, relaxation, and tension), and from the outside world (such as touch, sight, smell, taste, and sound). This practice of sensing-mindfulness keeps our attention anchored on our intention in the present moment, improving our ability to stop mind-wandering and any resulting unkind actions. Moreover, sensing-mindfulness is one of the most important ways to renew; it gives our minds a rest by creating a sense of connection. Feeling connected releases us from the self-absorbed pastimes of chasing desires and fleeing fears; we no longer feel cut off from the world around us.

The beauty of this practice is that you can do it anytime, anywhere. If you're watering plants in your garden at the end of the day and finding yourself ruminating on something that happened at work and getting more and more angry about it, you can shift your attention to your senses—observing the shape of a tomato, feeling the weight of the heavy watering can in your hands, enjoying the temperature of the evening air, hearing the sound of the water spattering over the leaves and dripping to the ground. Directing sensing-mindfulness to our external world is pleasant and relaxing as well as a way to shift out of negative mind-wandering. If you have time to develop only one kind habit while reading this book, make it sensing-mindfulness. The benefits will become clearer as you practice from one year to the next.

try it now

You have the power to shift attention to your senses any time you wish to. Let's practice: First take 10 seconds, and focus entirely on what you can hear. Next, for 10 seconds, shift your attention to the things you can feel. Take a bite of food and spend 10 seconds focused on what you can taste. Finally, shift your attention to the sensations in your own body—a pain, tension, or just the feeling of joints in contact with each other. Focus on that sensation for

10 seconds. Write how you feel in the **Mindfulness/Meditation** section of your practice journal—possibly more calm?

∽

Shifting to sensing-mindfulness throughout the day is like taking a water station break while running a marathon. Every so often, runners grab some water to refresh themselves and prevent dehydration and fatigue. Similarly, sensing-mindfulness refreshes us by relaxing our bodies, which brings contentment and calm. In addition, it helps reduce mind-wandering, and can prevent any agitation from escalating to disturbance and unkind acts. And the best part of sensing-mindfulness is that, unlike a marathon runner, you don't need to wait for that water station to come along; you can refresh yourself wherever you are—as you walk through a doorway, notice a painting hanging on the wall, feel your feet on the floor, or just take a breath. You can apply it at any time during the day: when you brush your teeth in the morning, when you are using a hammer at work, when you are eating, or when you are playing cards with friends. Take every opportunity to allow sensing-mindfulness to give your mind a rest.

Practicing sensing-mindfulness offers many benefits beyond relaxing the body and reducing stress. Think about how much your physical agility—balancing on a pair of skis, riding a skateboard, correcting your form to become a faster swimmer—depends on your own body-awareness. In weight training, if you're working on a lats pull-down, sensing-mindfulness is what helps you activate your back muscles instead of your arm muscles to do the exercise correctly. You can choose when to engage your senses. There are times when I could use sensing-mindfulness but do not; when my gym is playing loud music, I listen to an audiobook.

try it later: exercising

What physical activity do you enjoy or would you like to improve, such as shooting hoops, golf, jogging, skate boarding, or yoga? Next time you engage in your chosen activity, practice with sensing-mindfulness. For example, feel the texture and pressure of the basketball against your hands as you shoot; concentrate on the sensation of the road under your feet while jogging; or focus on the stretch of your muscles during yoga. When you notice mind-wandering, direct your attention back to the physical sensations coming from the skill you are practicing. Write about your experiences in the **Mindfulness/Meditation** section of your journal.

∽

Tuning in to your senses can also make exercise—and other activities—more enjoyable, helping them become pleasant kind habits. A 2015 study from the Netherlands found that people who practiced mindfulness while exercising and paid close attention to all aspects of their experience found their workouts more satisfying.[51] Of course, enjoyable things like eating delicious food, and listening to beautiful music are enhanced by sensing-mindfulness. Sexual intimacy with a partner can become many times more pleasurable when both partners are completely present, give each other their undivided attention, and give themselves fully to their experiences. The pleasure and gratification from sexual intimacy is enhanced even more because of the role of kindness—the intent of giving your partner pleasure. Each partner being mindful and kind magnifies the intensity of the sexual experience.

Sensing-mindfulness can also take an ordinary experience and elevate it to something transcendent. My prison friend Tad, a man who is a talented artist, wrote about the wonderful feeling he gets when he draws with mindfulness: "When I'm drawing and really into it, I feel as if I'm not even here at that moment," he wrote. "[It's] as if someone else is directing my hand."

try it later: mindful listening

Find a piece of music you love, and listen to it while reading a book and eating at the same time. Next, listen to the same piece of music, but without reading or eating. Close your eyes, and focus deeply on the music. In the **Mindfulness/Meditation** section of your practice journal, write about how your awareness was affected when you listened with sensing-mindfulness. Was there a feeling of spaciousness and connection?

∽

Tune In to Your Senses

Sensing-mindfulness not only rests our mind, giving us energy, but also creates opportunities for the meditative-mind to arise. Walking alone in nature is an excellent opportunity to practice sensing-mindfulness, because there are so many sights, smells, sounds, and other sensations to draw from. You may not be in the habit of tuning in to all these sensations, but you can learn. Your sensing-mindfulness is like a muscle, and all it takes is practice for it to grow. I'll introduce you to several exercises that will strengthen your capacity for sensing-mindfulness. But while physical exercise often begins with tightening or contracting a muscle in your body, sensing-mindfulness exercise starts with relaxing. When we narrowly focus and concentrate our attention on one thing—like listening to a conversation, watching a stoplight, or looking at a computer screen—we have a tendency to tune out everything else. With most sensing-mindfulness practices, we will learn to relax our attention and take in sensations more broadly.

Tune In with Soft-Eyes, Sharp-Eyes, Soft-Ears, Soft-Contact, and Soft-Taste

During much of the day we are looking straight ahead with a narrow field of vision; generally, we aren't focusing on any one thing in particular because we are mind-wandering. Think about how disengaged your mind is from your senses during these moments—for example, as you are walking to your car after buying groceries, you might be thinking about how hungry you are and how long it will take to fix dinner. Or maybe you are dwelling on a reprimand at work. There is plenty of unfocused attention during which you might slip into negative mind-wandering, which might escalate into stronger emotions, like anger. A practice called soft-eyes is one way to direct our attention to a different way of seeing that takes our attention away from mind-wandering

SOFT-EYES
The practice of relaxing one's focus to take in not only what is in one's direct line of sight, but also in one's peripheral vision.

Several years ago, an Aikido master taught me what he called "soft-eyes"—widening the field of vision so that we are aware of all that is around us. Aikido practitioners use this technique to be aware of challengers approaching from any direction. It takes a lot of attention to maintain this broad, open awareness, so soft-eyes and its feeling of spaciousness also makes it hard for us to engage in mind-wandering. While they may not call it by the same name, lots of activities engage this same practice of wide attention, from training horses, to being a football quarterback.

A good place to practice using soft-eyes as a helpful tool to stop mind-wandering is during meditation. If you notice your attention beginning to drift, simply engage soft-eyes. Shift your attention to your vision, and begin softening and widening your perspective. Without focusing on any one thing, increase your awareness to include a wider area of the wall in front of you, and maybe some objects in your peripheral vision. Shifting to soft-eyes takes your attention away from mind-wandering.

FROM THE OTHER SIDE

Tad, the artist who created the cover for the book *Saint Badass,* wrote:

In here, [soft-eyes] is a must. Always pay attention to your surroundings. Always...Early in my beginning of doing time I witnessed a man being beaten because someone scuffed the guy's shoes by not watching where he was going. Then I saw a man get his throat cut because he stepped in front of another man; in here that is very disrespectful unless one says "Excuse me."

---

try it later: soft-eyes in meditation

Practice soft-eyes. Sit in meditation facing a wall with your gaze directed to the lower part on the wall. Focus on a very small area. Allow your mind to wander so that you are not paying much attention to what you can see in front of you. After five or ten seconds, begin expanding your field of vision, gradually including a larger and larger part of the wall and beyond. How does your mind-wandering change? Write about the experience (including your feelings) in the **Mindfulness/Meditation** section of your practice journal.

Soft-eyes also can also be a valuable tool to support mindfulness outside of meditation. Practice soft-eyes when walking in nature. Walking on an easy trail with few obstacles requires little attention, so soft-eyes can open our awareness to the full range of sensations included in our peripheral vision. I find that looking between 20 and 40 feet ahead of me on a well-groomed trail seems to be the right distance to engage soft-eyes while still feeling grounded and secure that my next step will be "safe." Engaging our peripheral vision in soft-eyes can help us shift into the meditative-mind, a sense of deep calmness, trust and spacious connection, during these easy walks. However, gazing off in the distance, beyond 40 feet, is an invitation to fall. And some walks aren't suited for soft-eyes at all. When a trail is rocky and steep, I don't try to keep a wide field of vision but instead focus carefully on the path directly in front of me.

Use soft-eyes to widen your perspective—but keep your mind on your intention.

try it later: soft-eyes outdoors

Practice sensing-mindfulness with soft-eyes while taking an easy walk or engaging in another simple, repetitive physical activity.

Write about the experience (including your feelings) in the **Mindfulness/Meditation** section of your practice journal. Note if a feeling of spaciousness or connection arises.

SHARP-EYES

The practice of focusing all your attention and vision on a specific point or object.

With soft-eyes, your focus is very broad, and includes your entire field of vision. "Sharp-eyes" is the opposite; it requires you to focus all your attention and vision on a specific object. You can use sharp-eyes during the day as a calming exercise during times of stress.

I engaged sharp-eyes while walking on the University of Oregon campus during a winter break. There were few people around. The sky was blue after several days of gray. My sharp-eyes shifted quickly from image to image: a long blade of grass, the leaf of an oak tree, a smear of mud on the side of a trash can, a blue phone receiver in one of the few remaining phone booths on campus. Each sharp-eyes glance took in the object in question completely. All of my attention was focused on each thing in turn, leaving no room for mind-wandering. Although the objects I was looking at were mundane, the intensity of the meditative-mind made it a glorious, joyful experience.

try it later: sharp-eyes

Pick a quiet place to practice sharp-eyes. When you're comfortable, try engaging sharp-eyes in a variety of places or social situations. Play with alternating sharp-eyes and soft-eyes. In the **Mindfulness/Meditation** section of your practice journal, write about the experience, including what you focused on, and the degree to which you experienced mind-wandering or meditative-mind. Did a sense of spaciousness, a feeling of connection, or other feelings arise when you used sharp-eyes?

SOFT-EARS

The practice of opening one's attention to take in all surrounding sounds, without focusing on any one source.

After practicing soft-eyes for a couple of years, I began to experiment with something I came to call "soft-ears." Soft-ears is the practice of opening one's attention to take in all surrounding sounds, without focusing on any one source. With soft-ears, we widen our range of listening to include the periphery of our audible field, listening to everything at once, rather than focusing on one particular source. You don't hear better because of soft-ears; you just hear differently. Soft-ears removes mental distractions to make sounds more "hearable." For example, using soft-ears while sitting on a bench near a river, we notice the sound of the water running over rocks, a breeze rustling the leaves in the trees, and the singing of birds, without focusing our hearing on any one of the sources. The sounds rise and pass, as in all applications of mindfulness. Or, in a crowd, we might experience the sounds from multiple conversations blending together into a kind of low-keyed buzz. Listening to this buzz, we do not hear and follow any one conversation.

Use soft-ears to open your attention to all
surrounding sounds.

try it later: soft-ears

Experiment with soft-ears in a place where you are on your own, but surrounded by people. Open your attention to all the noises and conversations around you. In the **Mindfulness/Meditation** section of your practice journal, write about your experience, including what you heard, and whether you experienced meditative-mind or mind-wandering. Finally, if soft-ears and other sensing-mindfulness practices give your mind a rest, will it be easier for you to be more kind? Write about your thoughts.

SOFT-CONTACT

The practice of opening one's attention to take in tactile sensations from all the parts of your body, without focusing on any one source.

While "soft-contact" may be a new idea, it is closely related to the more familiar body-scan meditation, a technique to systematically check for tension in all parts of your body. In body-scan meditation, you lie on your back, directing your attention to each body part in turn to notice the presence of tension—and release it. Releasing our physical tensions puts our mind at rest. For a quick body scan, start releasing with your forehead, then eyebrows, cheeks, lips, chin, neck, shoulders, arms, elbows, forearms, wrists, palm of hand, top of hand, each finger, then go to the chest and step by step move your attention to your feet.[52]

The mindfulness practice of soft-contact, which does not require you to be lying down, takes body awareness a step further, and opens your attention to physical sensations both within your body (for example, any tension in your posture during meditation) and coming from the outside world. For example, soft-contact practice helped me notice and release the tightness in my face during meditation and tai chi; it also helped me feel the external sensation of using too much force when typing, which cued me to type more gently.

Think about how many tactile sensations you are experiencing at this moment—the surface of a chair supporting your body, the tension in a foot propped at an odd angle, a lock of hair brushing against your face, the temperature of the air on your skin. At any moment of any day, you can practice soft-contact as a technique to strengthen sensing-mindfulness and allow contentment and gratitude to arise.

try it later: soft-contact

Try practicing soft-contact during different activities throughout the day, from putting on your shoes, to pouring a cup of coffee, to attending to your posture during meditation. Relax any tension in your body as you tune in to these physical sensations. Write about the experience (including your feelings) in the **Mindfulness/Meditation** section of your practice journal.

SOFT-TASTE
The practice of focusing as we eat, keeping all one's attention on the changing texture and taste of food and on the sensations from chewing and swallowing.

With soft-taste, we notice the initial texture and taste of the food we take in. The five tastes are bitter, sweet, sour, salty, and umami (savoriness). As we chew, the taste of the food may change, while the texture usually also changes. For example, a soft caramel might stick to our teeth at first, before melting into our mouth. Biting into a mango or an ear of sweet corn often leaves us with fibers stuck between our teeth. A pureed soup might simply glide down our throat.

In chewing a bite of food, notice which side of your mouth does most of the chewing and where the pressure is on your teeth and jaws. Does the chewing switch from side to side? Listen to sounds the chewing creates. Chew each mouthful of food completely, then swallow. In initially learning to experience soft-taste you might intentionally shift your attention from taste, to texture, to chewing, and to swallowing. Eventually, these various sensations will arise and pass naturally as you eat.

try it later: soft-taste

The following exercise not only supports your mindfulness, but can also help you develop healthy eating habits. Each day for a week, write in the **Mindfulness/Meditation** section of your practice journal what you noticed when you did the following for each of two different foods: Chew a bite completely. Swallow, then put down your eating utensil. Describe the sensations of taste, texture, chewing and swallowing for that mouthful. Wait a moment. Pick up your utensil, take another bite. Chew then swallow. Describe the sensations as you chew that bite. Next turn to a second food and take the steps of chewing, swallowing, putting down your utensil, and then describing those sensations in your practice journal.

Of course, you can also combine multiple senses, such as soft-contact and soft-eyes, especially while carrying out a simple, repetitive physical task. I often find myself experiencing meditative-mind while cutting back the blackberry bushes that overgrow our forested property in Oregon. The task is repetitive, simple, requires little thinking and can be done without talking to anyone—perfect for engaging both soft-eyes and soft-contact.

in depth

Let's expand our practice by going deeper with some exercises that will help us experience and develop our capacity for sensing-mindfulness. Choose one of the following four practices to try: sharp-eyes, soft-ears, soft-contact, or soft-taste. After completing the exercise for that technique, write about the experience in the **Mindfulness/Meditation** section in your practice journal.

From Sensing-Mindfulness to Kindness

Practicing sensing-mindfulness can energize us, help us relax, get better at sports, and enjoy the simple pleasures of life, but that's not why it's in this book. In fact, learning and incorporating sensing-mindfulness in daily life is also a key step toward practicing kindness, both to ourselves and to others. It gives our mind a rest, and reduces the mind-wandering that distracts our attention from the needs and feelings of those around us. And it increases our enjoyment of life, which renews our reserves of energy and happiness, so that we have more to give. By bringing us back to our intention in the present moment, it tempers the feelings of anger or fear that can sometimes cause us to lash out. Along with other types of mindfulness we've learned about, like mindfulness with emotions and thoughts, sensing-mindfulness is a powerful tool that we can use both to benefit ourselves and, by extension, every other person in our lives.

Sensing-mindfulness might be beautifully simple but that doesn't mean it's easy. In my own practice, I didn't begin working with sensing-mindfulness until later in life. After retiring from the University of Oregon, I began practicing sensing-mindfulness on my long walks in the woods. Even with years of training in meditation, my mental world did not make the shift easily. During a 40-minute hike I repeatedly directed my attention away from mind-wandering and settled into sensing-mindfulness with a feeling of spaciousness and connection with the natural environment surrounding me. Then mind-wandering returned and again I would shift into sensing-mindfulness.

Even after years of practice, outside stressors and your own internal state of mind can make sensing-mindfulness maddeningly elusive. In my own life, there was a period when several factors combined to make it very difficult to practice—my brother-in-law was in hospice care and I was fighting a persistent respiratory infection, all while coping with more-than-usual pressures from my work. During this time, those walks in the woods just wouldn't "click." A birdsong was just a birdsong; a shaft of sunlight was just sunlight. I wanted desperately to feel the relief of meditative-mind, but it remained outside my reach.

Later, when my life was back to normal again, it took some effort to get back into practice. I had to set my intention to practice sensing-mindfulness with the mind of the warrior. On my next 40-minute walk, I engaged sensing-mindfulness to the fullest extent. The most salient sensations drew my attention: if a bird was singing, I listened completely; when the forest was still, I would feel the sensations of my breath or the cool air on my skin.

For some, it might be the pressures of caring for children or trying to make ends meet that make certain times difficult to practice sensing-mindfulness. But remember that this practice is always available to you, anytime, anywhere. For example, if your children are fighting, you can engage sensing-mindfulness with soft-contact to feel your feet make contact with the ground as you walk toward them. Whenever you need a break from your negative mind-wandering, give your mind a rest by tuning into the feelings and sensations of the moment, whether you're in a beautiful forest or on a crowded city bus, whether you have an hour for focused practice, or just a few moments in a busy day. You don't need anyone's permission to practice sensing-mindfulness, and it's always completely free. Use it to foster your kindness.

try it later: coping with stress

In the **Mindfulness/Meditation** section of your practice journal, write about a time when outside stressors or your state of mind made it difficult to engage with the world mindfully. Describe how you used sensing-mindfulness, how using it made you feel (did it give your mind a rest?), and how others were affected.

⌒

Wrapping Up

The five types of sensing-mindfulness (soft-eyes, sharp-eyes, soft-ears, soft-contact, and soft-taste), Three-Breath Method, and the Experience-then-Return Loop take us out of our self-centered thoughts and connect us to the world around us. These practices benefit us in two ways. First, they allow us to savor moments of joy and contentment by bringing us to mindfulness. And second, they shift our attention away from negative mind-wandering and unkind physical habits. These two benefits help us dismantle unkind habits and build up kind habits. Practice sensing-mindfulness long enough to make it a habit, and it will come to your aid unbidden. That's how habits work; they are automatic. Sensing-mindfulness assists us in developing physical skills and, combined with kindness, improves our mood, increases our enjoyment, and dramatically intensifies intimacy with our partner. Experiencing life through sensing-mindfulness is a powerful ingredient in how love wins.

try it later

Think about ways you can take a sensing-mindfulness break for one minute or less. For example, try rolling your neck and shoulders, breathing in through your nose and blowing out through your mouth, or feeling the vibration in your lips while you hum a "mmmm" sound. Start by taking a short sensing-mindfulness break at least once a day. If possible, work up to doing it multiple times a day for three days. Write about the experience in the **Mindfulness/Meditation** section of your practice journal, including feelings such as of connection and spaciousness.

checking in

Review what you wrote for your kindness plan from Step 3. How is it going so far? What has worked and what has not? Maybe things are working, and you just need to stick to your plan with patience and conscientiousness. Or, maybe it's not working and you need to revise your plan—or create a new one altogether. Make an honest assessment of your progress and make whatever changes are needed to your plan.

time for reflection

Near the end of each day, take a few moments to reflect (including your feelings) on one or more of the following:

- Your efforts to renew and serve

- Three things that went well that day

- Any positive emotions—for example, from acts of kindness, friendship, contentment, gratitude, and appreciation of things seen and heard

- Any negative emotions—for example, from acting with unkindness, and what you are learning

- Your use of the Three-Breath Method or the Experience-then-Return Loop to calm negative mind-wandering

Mindful Micropractices in Daily Life

L ife tends to go better when we are mindful throughout the day. Each moment we are mindful is a moment in which small pleasures can replace negative mind-wandering and unkind acts. But of course, there will always be stressful events that catch us by surprise, stirring up agitation and sometimes misery. In this step, we'll learn how to prepare for those moments by taking advantage of the small daily activities that give us a constant opportunity to practice mindfulness.

MINDFUL MICROPRACTICE
A familiar, daily activity or chore that is performed as an exercise in mindfulness, from start to finish.

I call these activities "mindful micropractices." Sometimes just stepping outside can be a mindful micropractice. Linda and I have a small dog who often can't be bothered to go all the way out to the yard to do his business. As a result, stepping onto our deck is an exercise in mindfulness. If you don't pay attention to what's under your feet, you're likely to get a nasty surprise on the sole of your shoe!

The way to transform a daily chore into a mindful micropractice is simple: Engage sensing-mindfulness during the entire activity. When you notice you are mind-wandering, return your attention to the activity.

We can think of these micropractices as an extension of sensing-mindfulness, deliberately engaging sensing-mindfulness while we walk the dog, fold laundry, drive, wait in line, turn out lights not being used, or take a shower. The more we intentionally engage mindfulness, the more we:

- reduce our mental "bandwidth" for mind-wandering;

- increase our awareness of life's tiny joys and our intention to act with kindness;

- notice when we are being unkind;

- give our mind a rest.

By doing these micropractices regularly, you give the mind a rest as you cultivate an ongoing sense of calmness and balance, taking care of yourself (renewing) and helping others (serving). Building a reservoir of joy and balance reduces the intensity of stresses that are likely to crop up throughout your day.

I used to think that chores like taking out the garbage, driving my daughters to school, grocery shopping, waiting in line at a deli, and washing dishes were "second-class" activities. If I had to do them, I'd try to squeeze in something more important by multitasking, like making phone calls or thinking about work at the same time. But now I realize that these kinds of chores are a blessing, because they are great opportunities for mindfulness and resting the mind. For example, when grocery shopping, I pay attention to the sensation of my feet coming into contact with the ground, as my hands feel the pressure on the bar of the cart as I push it toward another aisle. When waiting in line at a deli, I listen to the hum of conversations with soft-ears and notice with sharp-eyes specific features of products in the refrigerated deli case.

try it now

In the **Mindfulness/Meditation** section of your practice journal, describe how you could turn some of your daily chores into mindful micropractices.

᠆᠊᠊᠍

Using chores and everyday activities as an opportunity to practice mindfulness and rest the mind offer some powerful benefits. We're likely to have fewer accidents and mistakes because we're paying attention to what we're doing. We experience more time in meditative-mind and less in mind-wandering. Routine activities become more enjoyable, energize us, and give us moments of contentment and gratitude. We have fewer episodes of agitated and disturbed mind-wandering and fewer acts of unkindness to ourselves and others. We make the most of our time—it's not necessary to take an extra hour out of the day to practice mindfulness, as it's something we can do while engaged in activities we would be doing anyway. And we build up a "mindfulness reserve," increasing our capacity for calmness and kindness in times of stress in the same way lifting weights in the gym increases our capacity to build physical strength to lift heavy boxes on moving day.

Transforming Chores and Everyday Activities into Mindful Micropractices

Below, I describe five common, almost universal, activities that can be transformed into mindful micropractices.

Doing Housework

Doing chores around the house is often done in a mindless fashion—daydreaming, listening to audiobooks or simply going through the motions like a robot. We might engage in mind-wandering—for example, we might think about what we are going to do later, feel angry that no one is helping, or focus on how long it's going take to finish. Cleaning and other chores are excellent opportunities for micropractice with sensing-mindfulness. When making the bed, use sensing-mindfulness to rest the mind by focusing on the texture and color of the bedding, the tactile sensations of spreading and tucking in the sheet, and feeling the weight of the pillows as you put them back in place.

Attending to Personal Hygiene

Taking a shower is also often treated as a time for daydreaming or multitasking, while being largely unaware of the very body we are supposed to be washing. Here's how taking a shower can be a mindful micropractice:

engage sensing-mindfulness by focusing on the sensations of beads of water striking our face and eyelids, the relaxing massage delivered to our scalp as we rub in the shampoo, and the feel of our hands on our bodies as we soap up and then rinse. The microractice of showering sloughs off mind-wandering like a snake sloughs off its dead skin.

Brushing our teeth is as fertile ground for multitasking as taking a shower. To make brushing our teeth a micropractice, we close our eyes and direct our sensing-mindfulness to where the toothbrush makes contact with both our teeth and gums. After brushing our teeth with sensing-mindfulness, we can enjoy the feel of the water swishing around our teeth before we spit it out.

Making and Following a Schedule

Many of us find ourselves rushing through our daily lives. Often this happens because we try to squeeze an activity into a schedule that is already full. We think we have extra time to do one more thing. Of course, we don't. Squeezing in another non-urgent activity when we don't have time for it is a form of greed, trying to get more and more done. Rushing because you squeezed in an extra activity is unkind to yourself and the people around you. It causes you stress, and it can inconvenience others when you are late.

Don't stress yourself by trying to squeeze
another activity into an already full schedule.

The cure for rushing is to be mindful and direct our attention away from the urge to do more and more. Instead of beginning a "schedule-breaking" activity, we can remind ourselves of our intention to stick to our schedule and move on to the next activity we have planned. If we find ourselves running late, behind schedule, or feeling rushed, we can take a moment to experience that unpleasant feeling as a motivator to stop rushing. This unpleasant memory can be your trigger to approach scheduling with mindfulness and not to plan more activities than you have time for. You can take three breaths before planning your day, or whenever you are looking at your calendar, to prompt yourself to be honest about how many activities can fit in your schedule.

Organizing Our Surroundings

Many of us grew up believing that neatness was an artificial imposition to be ignored. Practicing mindfulness increases our sensitivity to messes, such as a messy office, dirty pans after a meal, or an unmade bed; these messy distractions contribute to a subtle form of agitation. Converting clutter into order by rinsing dishes after a meal is a mindful micropractice, as is turning off lights when no one is in the room. Of course, cleaning up requires time and effort. But putting off rinsing dirty dishes usually means having to do more work later. If the pans dry overnight with food still on them, the cleanup requires more effort.

Cleaning up clutter is an act of kindness not just to ourselves but also to others we live with, who are much happier when we are conscientious about not creating clutter by cleaning up the kitchen and making the bed.

Moving Quietly Through the World

Many of us are not bothered by all the noise we make; it is as if we don't hear the noise coming from the plates that clatter as we set them down, the doors we slam, and our own loud talking. But noxious noise can be an irritant to others, and practicing mindfulness increases our sensitivity to noise. Out of kindness to ourselves and respect to others who are nearby, we can refrain from causing unnecessary noise. Refraining from being noisy is a mindful micropractice. When you notice a trigger for being noisy, such as talking to a person from across a crowded room, respond in as quiet a manner as possible. Move closer to the person and suggest you go out into the hall to talk. Or, if you are in the kitchen putting away dishes and silverware, use sensing-mindfulness to put down the objects gently so there is no loud banging. Think proactively: Do not turn on the radio, TV, or other devices unless it is going to be the focus of your attention. Silence, or at least being quiet, is often a support for mindfulness and resting the mind and, thus, a kindness for us. Not imposing noise on others is a kindness as well.

FROM THE OTHER SIDE

Tad wrote:

Some in here seem to fear silence because then they have to listen to their own mind and they'd rather get into loud radio/TV, yelling, etc. just to keep their mind distracted.

---

try it later: micropractices

Pick one everyday activity that particularly resonates with you to transform into a mindful micropractice. Over a three day period (or longer), carry out that activity with mindfulness. In the **Mindfulness/Meditation** section in your practice journal, describe what happened (including your feelings) during the three times each day you used mindfulness to transform the activity into a mindful micropractice. In particular, describe how the mindful micropractice had any of the following effects:

- reduced your negative mind-wandering;

- gave you simple pleasures and a greater willingness to act with kindness;

- helped you notice your unkind acts and weaken them;

- rested your mind.

When Daily Chores and Activities Trigger Unkind Habits

Some of our daily chores and activities are triggers for unkind habits; for example, driving can trigger multitasking, washing dishes can trigger resentment, following slow drivers can trigger anger, and washing your face can trigger anxiety about your looks. Waiting is so often an exercise in impatience and frustration. We feel frustration when waiting at a stoplight, in a grocery store line, or for a table at a restaurant. Our agitation is greater when the wait is "needlessly" long—think about how quickly you become frustrated when you see the customer in line in front of you at the grocery store pull out a fat envelope of coupons.

You can identify impatience as an unkind habit to replace with the micropractice of patience. Rather than glare at the person with the coupons, you might engage in a combination of soft-ears, soft-eyes, and soft-touch. With soft-ears you hear the hum of conversation and carts being unloaded and moved along the conveyor belt at the check stand. With soft-eyes you have a broad view of all that is in front of you, not just the checkout line you are standing in. With soft-touch you notice your feet resting on the ground and your arms hanging at your sides or resting on the bar for pushing the cart. (Sometimes I practice a subtle weight-shifting qigong exercise, shifting my weight slightly from my left side to my right side, then forward and back.)

Before long, waiting in line becomes a micropractice that encourages kindness. You might find yourself letting someone in front of you in the checkout line because they only have two items and you have a full cart. Believe it or not, waiting in line with mindfulness, like most other micropractices, is an opportunity to "refuel," to experience contentment, connectedness, and even joy.

You can transform unkind habits into mindful micropractices. Follow these four steps:

1. **Set your intention.** Identify an activity that often triggers an unkind habit. It could be a chore, like wiping down the counters or folding laundry, or just part of your everyday routine, like washing your face.

2. **Diagnose.** Before you get started with this activity, take a minute to think about how the activity triggers your unkind habit.

3. **Practice.** Go ahead with the activity, while engaging sensing-mindfulness. You might find it useful to start with the Three-Breath Method. As you carry out the activity, notice whether any triggers for your unkind habit crop up. When this occurs, you can take three breaths then redirect your attention back to your activity using sensing-mindfulness.

4. **Monitor.** Watch for backsliding.

BACKSLIDING
The lapse in attention that occurs after a period of mindfulness, when an old trigger once again provokes an unkind habit.

While you may be able to perform the activity with mindful focus for a while at first, this level of attention can be hard to maintain. After a while, you may find that the same old triggers are again setting off your unkind habits; you are backsliding. For example, wiping down the counter starts rekindling your resentment over doing household chores. When this happens, find a time of stillness and rehearse how you could respond to the trigger differently. Remember the moment you experienced the trigger, and then visualize a different way you could respond. For example, visualize wiping down the counter and keeping your attention on the feeling of the cloth coming in to contact with the counter, then on noticing what is on the counter you need to move to continue wiping up, and then the damp feeling of the cloth. Finally return to actually doing the micropractice.

Many unkind habits seem to be triggered while people are in transit, either while taking public transportation or while driving back and forth on various errands and activities. One unkind habit is multitasking—talking on the phone, eating, listening to music, daydreaming or stewing about problems, and possibly the most dangerous task of all, texting. I'm no different, but later in my life I realized that driving is a daily chore that presents a great opportunity to develop a mindful micropractice.

Avoid multitasking when doing your chores. Practice
sensing-mindfulness instead.

Here is how I applied the four steps to transform driving into a mindful micropractice. My intention was to drive with mindfulness. When I diagnosed what happened when I drove, I found that multitasking often brought on agitation. Conversely, when I did not multitask, sensing-mindfulness made driving enjoyable and relaxing. To engage sensing-mindfulness, I stopped turning on the radio, and eventually I was able to cut way back on "hands-free" cell phone use and to stop eating in the car. Instead, I began practicing a driving version of soft-eyes: widening my attention to include more of my peripheral vision in addition to what's directly in front of me. If I drifted into mind-wandering while using soft-eyes, I shifted my attention to the feel of the hard plastic of the steering wheel in my hands, the seat against my back, and the sounds of the traffic around me. At all times, the focus of my attention was on driving safely.

After a number of weeks, I was driving with sensing-mindfulness much of the time. Sometimes I would even get into the car with negative mind-wandering, and just the sound of the engine turning over reminded me to engage sensing-mindfulness. However, when I checked in to monitor my practice a few months ago, I realized I was starting to backslide. Feeling overwhelmed by my responsibilities, I had started "saving" time by making frequent phone calls while I was driving. My solution for backsliding, which took a few weeks, was to make fewer phone calls and pull over to the curb if the content of the call was complex and complicated.

try it now

In the **Mindfulness/Meditation** section of your journal, write a plan to transform a daily activity that triggers an unkind habit into a habit of mindfulness. Include all four stages in your plan. Describe how you will rehearse a constructive response to the trigger if you backslide. Describe what happens (including your feelings) when you implement the plan.

FROM THE OTHER SIDE

For my youngest prison friend, Cody, cleaning is a very important micropractice. After three failed back surgeries, Cody struggles with chronic pain. He describes his practice this way:

Get up. Brush my teeth. For some reason it makes me feel more fresh. Then I will put my mp4 player on and clean the barracks. I sweep. Wipe the windows down. Get into like a spaced-out zone and before I know it, I done spent a whole hour cleaning and I ain't had my mind on no pain and a handful of people will say thanks man for keepin it clean around here. Damn. Your back is F-up and you do more work than the barrack's porters. If we focus so much on the pain and the problem and cry and waste that type of energy on it when you can shake it off and do what you Can Do. Small stuff like wipe down clean sinks and windows and get in your zone of nothing but the cleaning, you feel no pain but the moment at hand and focus well.

Wrapping Up

Whether it's brushing the dog, drying dishes, shaving, or turning off unneeded lights, converting a few of our daily tasks into mindful micro-practices is a powerful way to build the habit of sensing-mindfulness. Often we are humbled by our struggles to be mindful with what are seemingly trivial activities and by the backsliding we experience after we have established a micropractice. At other times, the habit of sensing-mindfulness arises of its own accord, giving our mind a rest with contentment and joy. But when there are setbacks, we can engage the Three-Breath Method or Experience-then-Return Loop, and kick-start the mindful-kind cycle with our micropractices. Over time, our capacity to be kind and to weaken our unkind habits grows, which is how love wins.

checking in

Look back at your plan for weakening unkind habits from Step 6. How have you progressed in implementing the plan? What's worked and what hasn't? Do you need to make any changes to the plan? What will you do differently going forward?

time for reflection

Take a few moments to reflect on one or more of these practices that you have found helpful. Also reflect on how they affect the way you feel:

- Sensing-mindfulness

- Recalling gratitude for two things, one kindness—given or received—or two things done well during the day

- Meditation

- Strengthening a kind habit

STEP 9

Kindful Options for Hard Times

Along our kindful path we will encounter times when we are the ones who are in distress. In such times it's important to be aware of how to apply kindfulness practices to our own situation. These practices will not quickly "fix" your unhappiness. You will need to be patient and gentle with yourself. If you become impatient and frustrated along the way, gently and patiently return to the kindful option you are using (or just shift your attention to your breathing).

Meditation can be an anchor during hard times. Linda's life-long friend Nancy was diagnosed with rheumatoid arthritis in mid-life, a condition that eventually left her partially disabled. Innumerable surgeries followed, culminating in the amputation of her left leg below the knee. Later, she couldn't resist smiling as she told us about what happened in her aerobics dance class, when her prosthetic leg fell off mid-workout, causing her to crash to the floor. Without missing a beat, the instructor called out, "Dancer down, dancer down!" Friends helped collect her prosthetic and Nancy reattached it, and the class continued. After spending a couple of days with her and Linda, I asked Nancy how she was able to maintain such a positive attitude in the face of her pain and disability. She said her secret was meditating for half an hour each day. If she misses even one day of meditation, she said, her thoughts turn negative.

But if meditation isn't your thing, you have learned about a number of other practices that are options for dealing with misery, such as using the Three-Breath Method and other forms of sensing-mindfulness (the Experience-then-Return Loop and mindful micropractices), and taking on the role of the detective, warrior and kindful practitioner. Serious trauma might sink us into deep distress or even despair (the complete absence of hope) if we have lost something of great importance—our vision, a loved one, personal freedom, walking without pain, or a feeling of safety and trust after being abused. The grief over these losses strikes us down, making it all too clear that in trauma we feel that we are not safe and/or we are not in control.

FROM THE OTHER SIDE

Roy wrote about the psychological effects of experiencing childhood sexual abuse:

Your own father sharing you with a deer-hunting buddy is crazy shit, Bro. It will kind of screw up your head a bit, especially when dear old mom don't do diddly shit to even curb the violence. Nope, her attitude was pretty much: "Just don't bother me, okay?" How do you let your husband do that kind of crazy shit to your son?

This step reviews some kindful practices, presents several new kindful options, and describes how to use them to cope with feeling deeply disturbed or even despair. Besides using the role of the kindful practitioner in applying these kindful options, the role of the detective helps you decide if you want to pursue additional resources, seek support from a loved one, or get help from a professional.

Keep in mind that meditation and mindfulness, especially sensing-mindfulness, are essential anchors for us. When we are in deep distress, we often lack the willingness and energy to develop the kindful options you will be reading about. That is why we must practice these kindful approaches **before** the hard times arise. When we practice when life is ok, we are strengthening habits that will be needed in times of difficulty and are also increasing our confidence that we can call up these options in hard times. It is in dark times that we put these kindful options to the test. Remember to be patient and gentle with yourself. You will be asked to practice each kindful option as you work through Step 9, so you will be more able to activate the options when times are hard.

It may seem paradoxical, but the kindful options described in this step are stepping-stones to a happier life, as well as tools for dealing with difficult times. In other words, these kindful options are all paths to increased mindfulness. In fact, the kindful options can become kind habits that support us in weakening unkind habits, building other kind habits, solving problems, improving our relationships, managing stress, increasing our awareness of opportunities, acting with kindness, and experiencing more joy and contentment.

KINDFUL OPTIONS FOR HARD TIMES
Specific practices for our physical and mental worlds that help us grapple with feeling deeply disturbed, or feelings of deep distress.

Kindful Options for Our Physical World

The first kindful option for our physical world involves taking the perspective of the detective, to determine if we can change the situation itself as a way to deal with feeling deeply disturbed—for example, by getting help for pain management, by moving away from a toxic environment, or by changing some of our habits. You can look back to the table of unkind personality types in Step 1 (pg 33) to see if any of those unkind habits are disturbing you or causing deep distress. If an unkind habit is causing your unhappiness, return to Steps 1 and 6 to plan how to weaken that unkind habit.

On the other hand, if the thing causing you pain is out of your control—for example, if you have lost a loved one or been diagnosed with a serious disease, or if you have had a disabling accident—your deep distress likely comes from grief and/or pain. Grieving is not an unkind habit to be weakened. Instead, recognize that grief is a process that takes time. Be gentle with yourself and patient while enduring the suffering as you practice your kindful options.

In practicing the kindful options for hard times, you may need to engage the warrior mind to draw your attention away from your deep distress. If you are overwhelmed by emotional pain, your options for engaging in activities may be limited. For example, Tad was in prison, and was still able to refocus his grief and anger by creating art.

try it now

In your practice journal, describe a time when you felt disturbed or in despair—first, from something outside of your control, such as illness, an accident, or loss; and second, from something you have caused through your own unkind habit. Describe any coping techniques that helped you deal with your feelings of disturbance or distress, such as something you read about earlier in this book.

We must recognize that while coping practices and kindful options can often soften our disturbance, they are not likely to totally eliminate it. During these hard times, be patient. The softening may not come quickly or be as powerful as we like. Also be kind to yourself. When suffering deepens, return to your kindful option with gentleness, minimizing your frustration and anger. And of course, our problems can sometimes be so severe that we need professional help from a therapist, spiritual healer, or treatment center. If you need more support, get outside help or intervention.

If you're facing a big challenge or difficult situation on your own, here are other kindful options to try:

Spend Time with Those You Care About

Consider building up the pleasant kind habits that connect you to others, especially loved ones and friends. Shelly, a longtime participant in a water aerobics class, connected to other members of the class through her kindness—for example, bringing a bag of goodies to share with everyone on her birthday. She was having problems with motor coordination and eventually stopped coming to class. Then one day she returned in a wheelchair and was lowered into the pool. She had been diagnosed with ALS and treated herself with kindness by reconnecting with this group of supportive friends. Her return spread joy through the group, to all her friends in the pool. In turn, their joy supported Shelly as she struggled with her ALS.

Make an effort to make intimate connections with your partner (including sexual intimacy), and be close with other family members, especially children and parents, and your pet. Reach out (literally through physical contact) to close friends you trust and can be open with. Try to be physically close to those who you feel are protective toward you and care deeply about you. As much as possible use the closeness to receive feelings of love, care and safety. You might also be able to find these warm connections within your faith community or spiritual group.

Spend time with friends who give you comfort; make appointments to see them, play cards, participate in sports, dance and sing with others, volunteer in multiple ways, and go to performances, movies, and plays. For most of us, spending time with people we care about is one of the most powerful kindful options. But you can also consider calling on the warrior mind to make new friends by joining a support group or in some way spending time with others who are suffering for the same reason you are. Spending time with others suffering in a similar way can provide ideas for coping, encouragement, and a sense of community, a realization that you are not alone.

try it now

List some people you are comfortable spending time with during difficult times. Do you feel you need to have more people who would be available for you to spend time with when times are hard? If your answer is yes, list one or two people you will try to become better friends with.

Engage Yourself in a Positive Solo Activity

Many pleasant kind habits that lessen our disturbance do not require interacting with other people, for example, singing, laughing, smiling, making arts and crafts, following where our curiosity leads us, playing a musical instrument, and spending time in nature. Seek out pleasant events that invigorate your sensing-mindfulness. To tune in to smell and taste, enjoy cooking, eating, and trying new dishes. For the visual, watch a nature documentary, take out photo albums of loved ones and special places, wear bright-colored clothing, and appreciate new spring growth, fall colors, scenic rivers, and mountain landscapes. To engage hearing, listen with your full attention to music and the sounds from nature. Use soft-ears to listen to the hum of multiple conversations. Both pleasant kind habits and pleasant events draw us out of our mind's unhappiness, while creating opportunities for sensing-mindfulness that give our mind a rest along with a sense of contentment.

try it now

In your practice journal, list activities that you find engaging or fun. What activities could you turn to in difficult times?

Deepen Your Mindfulness Practice

A moment of difficulty or personal challenge can be a great opportunity to dig deeper into your mindfulness practice, exploring new levels of experience, while also taking your attention off your troubles. Here are three possibilities:

Intensify your three-breath practice. To intensify your three-breath practice, inhale and exhale very deeply for each breath. Expand your chest to its fullest extension as you inhale, then exhale slowly and completely. If you want, you can simultaneously open your arms and reach outward to further the sense of expansion as you inhale. As you exhale, bring your arms back together in front of you. You might also find it useful to hold your breath between inhaling and exhaling. Count to four as you breathe in, hold for four counts, count to four as you breathe out, and hold again for four counts. After finishing the third breath, shift to the practice described next.

Rotate through sensing-mindfulness practices. First, find a comfortable position—you can be upright, sitting, or lying down. Engage soft-touch for several breaths, approximately 15-20 seconds. Then shift to soft-ears for several breaths, then sharp-eyes, then soft-eyes. For example, as you are riding the bus to work, you might become anxious thinking about the report you have to finish. You can help ease this worry by rotating your senses with soft-touch, sensing the pressure from sitting on the seat, your arms resting on your thighs, and the shifting of your weight as the bus turns. Next, use soft-ears, listening to the buzz of conversations, the road noise from the movement of the bus, the sounds of cars driving alongside, and finally alternating sharp-eyes (focusing on a tear on the seat across from you) and soft-eyes (widening your peripheral vision to take in the scene around you). Continue the rotation until you begin to feel relief.

I love to rotate through my senses while I'm outside in nature, for example, when I'm walking among old-growth fir and cedar trees along the McKenzie River. It's a most pleasant kind habit—alternating between hearing bird calls, seeing the river, and feeling the breeze against my cheek. After practicing this rotation over several weeks, it becomes a habit, something I do automatically as I walk. The bonus of this habit is the smile that arises of its own accord—I am resting in my meditative-mind.

Abandon your fears about the future. A third way to deepen your mindfulness practice is to abandon fears about the future. I am not talking about the immediate fears caused by a frightening medical diagnosis or from facing loneliness after losing your partner. These fears are instinctual and will take time to process. But when it comes to everyday worries and fears about the future, you can deepen your mindfulness practices by learning how to set these fears aside. If you have a history of feeding your fears with "what ifs," try starving them. One way to starve those fears is to tie your breathing to a modification of these words from Rumi's poem "There's Nothing Ahead," as translated by Coleman Barks in *The Essential Rumi*:

"if you can say, There's nothing ahead, there will be nothing there."

As you inhale, say to yourself, "there's no ____" (name the source of the fear—like chronic pain, humiliation at work or retaliation from you partner—that is causing the negative mind-wandering). As you exhale, say to yourself, "Ahead." For example, if you are afraid that you will always have the pain that interrupts your sleep at night:

Inhale …"There's no pain"
Exhale…"Ahead"

If you fear humiliation at work:

Inhale…"There's no humiliation"
Exhale… "Ahead"

Repeat this process until you feel your worries begin to release. If this exercise does not soften your disturbance and distress, add the

Experience-then-Return Loop, in which you experience the negative emotion for 90 seconds and then direct your attention to your original intention.

try it now

Practice tying your breathing to repeating "There's no _____" and "Ahead."

∽

try it later

For the next three days, work on one of the three ways to deepen your mindfulness practice: intensifying the Three-Breath Method, rotating through your sensing-mindfulness practices, or addressing fears about the future. In the **Mindfulness/Meditation** section of your practice journal, write about your experiences.

∽

Kindful Options for Our Mental World

When coping with difficult times, it's also important to be kindful with your mental world. The first option is the simplest. When we feel deeply disturbed, we often believe we will always feel that way. But actually, our feelings are constantly changing. Take a moment and ask yourself how you are feeling right now. Have you felt exactly that same way all day? Did you feel that same way all day yesterday? All week? All year? Of course not; our feelings change. So when we are distressed, we can have confidence that relief, even if for only a short time, will come. One way to stop dwelling on your fears and worries about the future is by cultivating patience to simply wait for your feelings to change. Two other more active options are: shifting your attention to the needs of others, and calling up memories of joy and appreciation that trigger gratitude.

Ask for Help for Those in Need

Pain and disturbance isolate us and make us feel alone. Focusing on the needs of others reminds us that we are not the only ones who are suffering, and brings us back up from the dark well of isolation. And of course, recalling these individuals by name reminds us to be aware of opportunities to act with kindness toward them.

With compassion, take a moment to genuinely wish for help for someone in need, whether it's a friend, a stranger on the bus, or a refugee on the other side of the world. Many spiritual traditions, from Christian prayer to Buddhist merit, involve asking a higher power to send help to people who are struggling. Asking for help for others is a powerful way to draw our attention away from feeling disturbed, at least for some period of time. I ask for help for others at the end of my morning meditation. What might surprise you is that I sometimes ask for help for those I dislike or don't respect. By including them, I am acknowledging our common humanity, our shortcomings as human beings, and my hope that they will bring mindful kindness into their lives.

When asking for help for others, you can take a moment to coordinate your breathing with naming people who are having difficulty. In the Buddhist practice of Tonglen, practitioners say to themselves the name of a person who is suffering as they inhale, then exhale fully to spread a feeling of relaxation through their body. A longtime friend, who is a former monk, said she would feel a knot of anxiety residing in her chest when one of her children was sick, depressed, or stressed in some other way. Once she began the practice of saying the child's name as she inhaled, and spreading relaxation as she exhaled, the anxiety would disperse.

A more intensive approach to asking for help for others begins by mentally naming the person who is suffering, visualizing their body, their pain, and their thoughts, then mentally "sending" peace and kindness to that person. You first imagine yourself inhaling the other person's suffering fully as you visualize the person, and then exhale that suffering away from you. Next you imagine inhaling pure, healing air, and finally exhale to send kindness for the other person, in whatever form best meets the person's needs.

I use this with my aunt Pat, who is ill from a number of conditions, including rheumatoid arthritis, shingles, and COPD. I focus on experiencing her suffering as I inhale. I visualize her deformed toes and fingers from the arthritis. I feel the pain of the shingles around her chest, and imagine her nostrils as she breathes laboriously through her oxygen tube. Next, as I exhale, I think of her face, and mentally remove her pain and worry, sending it far away into space. With my next inhalation, I bring in pure, healing air for my aunt. Finally, I exhale fully, mentally sending her kindness and peace.

Asking for help for others is always a kind practice, one that you can do anytime—not just when you feel deeply disturbed.

try it now

Practice asking for help for those in need.

Call Up Memories of Joy and Appreciation That Trigger Your Gratitude

Sometimes, asking for help for others, rather than drawing our attention away from our own suffering, can serve to magnify our unhappiness. When this happens, we can change our focus and recall moments of joy and appreciation. Thinking about acts of kindnesses can shift our attention to gratitude. We can think of our own kind acts and of the kind acts of others.

One evening, I found myself in sudden abdominal pain. I became even more alarmed when I went to the bathroom and noticed blood in my urine. It wasn't bad enough to go to the emergency room, but I knew if it continued I'd have to see my doctor the next day. Worrying about the pain and what it might mean consumed my thoughts. Neither three mindful breaths nor asking for help for others was able to draw my attention away from my fears. So to lessen my distress, I began to reflect on the kind acts of others, coordinating the memory with my breathing. For example, as I inhaled, I thought of the countless times my wife cared for me when I was sick; then I exhaled fully. For each inhale I thought of other ways she made me feel loved. I thought of my friend Jeremy and how he spent his last days focusing on the well-being of those who visited him in hospice care. I thought of my friend Roy in prison, giving help and support to Tad, and Tad then giving help and support to Chris. I thought of my mother telling Marsha that she would wait for Marsha in heaven.

Reflecting on these kind acts as I inhaled and exhaled gave me a healthy perspective on my own circumstances. The kind actions of those in distress inspired me. Their situations were exceedingly difficult. Yet they had chosen to be kindful—they were being present, set their purpose to being kind, and were not dissuaded by the challenges they faced. This perspective helped me to stop struggling with my own situation that night and to accept that I was simply going to have to call up the warrior and live with it until morning when I could engage the detective role.

There are many types of memories we can call up to bring us feelings of joy and appreciation. You can think of friends and loved ones, including animals, who bring joy, or at least smiles, to your life. You can also do this in coordination with your breath; call a person to mind as you inhale, and say an inner "thank you" as you exhale. Repeat this for each person. You could also try this activity: Smile, then spread the feeling of the smile across your face and then move it down into your chest and abdomen. Then, visualize someone you care a great deal about. See their smile. Let your smile join their smile.

Or, you can just recall memories that bring you joy. My wife, Linda, fondly remembers sliding along the kitchen counters as a child, and even climbing on top of the refrigerator to stay close to her mother as she cooked. If Linda's mother needed something from the refrigerator, Linda simply raised her legs so her mother could open the refrigerator door. Having her mother all to herself made these moments in the kitchen very special, and remembering these times gives Linda joy.

We often forget that animals give us some of our purest experiences of joy and appreciation. Pet owners have many such memories. And there are also unusual times of joy and appreciation with animals. Some of my memories of joy and appreciation involve kindness from animals. For example, when Linda and I were in a small boat watching gray whales in the San Ignacio Lagoon, a mother whale pushed her baby up to the side of our boat, allowing us to touch the baby whale. Another time, at an orangutan reserve in Sumatra, a young female orangutan came over to me and, through a fence, kissed me on the cheek.

You can also evoke feelings of joy and gratitude by recalling special times you've spent engaged in a pleasant kind habit.

try it now

In the **Kindness/Gratitude** section of your journal, review your list of pleasant kind habits. Each habit will provide you with warm memories; for example, if you love to swim in mountain lakes, smile as you remember cooling off in one of your favorite swimming holes.

~

Finally, focusing our attention on heartfelt acts of kindness not only evokes our gratitude, but also reminds us to be humble about our own acts of kindness. When I want to be humbled, I think of a woman in Eugene, who adopts children from Cambodia with severe disabilities. Inspiring examples of kindness by individuals, organizations, and animals are all around us. Noticing such heartfelt kindness shows us how much room we have to grow, how much more we can do to help others. The ways in which our kindness grows will differ from person to person. For example, while I may not feel equipped to adopt disabled children, I am continuing a ten-year mentoring partnership with about a dozen incarcerated men.

try it now

Practice triggering your gratitude by recalling memories of joy and appreciation.

~

Each kindful option gives us a way to respond to disturbance or other strong emotions. Some people find physical kindness options, such as spending time with those they care about and engaging in pleasant activities, work better for them. For others, mental kindness options such as asking for help for others and calling up positive memories are more effective. Also feel free to create your own physical and mental kindness options. Whatever is kind and gives you respite from deep distress and discouragement is good to do.

To be honest, there are times when these kindful options cannot significantly soften our deep unhappiness. When in deep distress, coping with your feelings is the goal, not controlling them. Remember that you have two choices: descending into deeper misery in the form of fear, dread, anger, depression, and self-pity; or learning from your pain.

If you're in such pain that these options give you almost no relief, think of the pain as your teacher. Say to yourself, "Teach me," "let me be at ease," "it is so," or some other phrase that works for you. Of course, if you follow a religious path, you can ask for help from your higher power. As a last resort, you might try the "fake-it-till-you-make-it approach," smiling when you feel sad, laughing when you are in pain, or just being curious about your situation.

Dealing with unhappiness during difficult times teaches us how to be mindfully kind as best we can. Be gentle with yourself. Consider telling yourself that you can take a break and return to the difficult situation when you feel better prepared to deal with it. If deep distress is relentlessly tightening its grip on your mind and body, seek guidance or treatment from a counselor, therapist, medical healer, spiritual advisor, or trusted friend.

Turning Kindful Options Into Kind Habits

These kindful options can help you cope when times are hard, but that doesn't have to be the only time you use them. You can turn them into kind habits that benefit you in your everyday life.

try it later: from kindful options to kind habits

In the **Kindness/Gratitude** section of your journal, make a list of the kindful options you would like to turn into kind habits. These may include:

1. Taking the perspective of the detective or the warrior.
2. Being with those you care about.
3. Spending time in engaging and fun activities.
4. Deepening your mindfulness practices (intensifying the Three-Breath Method, rotating through your senses, and reciting "no ____ ahead.").
5. Asking for help for those in need.
6. Calling up memories of joy and appreciation that trigger your gratitude.

Pick one of the kindful options you listed and, for three days, work on making it a kind habit (or better yet a pleasant kind habit). Write about that experience.

Learning from Hard Times

While we will probably never be grateful for feeling disturbed or distressed, we *can* be grateful for what we learn from those difficult times. Going through such a challenge can give us greater trust in our practice of mindful kindness, increase our empathy and compassion, and make us more willing to forgive others and ourselves. Practicing mindful kindness helps us to better cope with hard times, by showing us our own capacity for kindness, and giving us relief. Such accomplishments gradually build our confidence that the practices will be there for us when hard times come again in the future. For example, if rotating through our sensing-mindfulness practices pulls us out of our disturbance from time to time and allows us to act with kindness, we see that our disturbance is not impenetrable and that our practices work, at least some of the time. Successfully coping with a disturbed state of mind makes our expectations or hopes for relief more realistic; we accept that our distress may soften, but not completely disappear as quickly as we would like.

FROM THE OTHER SIDE

Cody, one of Roy's students, suffers from multiple health issues, as well as chronic pain. Here, he describes how he took on the mind of the warrior and was able to continue his practice of mindful kindness in prison:

The emotions I'm having is Anger, Depression. The pain and suffering. The long nights laying awake in bed. Can't sleep till I been up so long that my body shuts down only to wake right back up to pain. The tears. The feel of neglect. I could tell that it was taking me way off my practice. A practice that has made me a strong person. Only just a few weeks ago, I realize this can make me a stronger person. Stop crying. Take a few deep breaths and bring good out of it cause bad ain't getting me nowhere. Yeah. It hurts. But I got to suck it up. I got myself here. Nobody else. So I started being even more kind to all the medical staff and thinking about others [prisoners]. How to help them in any way I can and in doing this, seeing and hearing joy...I have went over some names of people in my life that have tried to help me and that have help me and how they help me. I send them my best and good health be with them. Then I thought about the ones that have just treated me like I was scum on their shoes...I smiled and wished their family wishes of good health and strength. Then I will take me a few deep breaths.

In applying not only mindful kindness but also the skills of character like patience, humility, a growth mindset, and conscientiousness during times when we truly feel miserable, we can gain confidence that relief will come, even if just for a few minutes at a time. Recently, I find that feeling of relief is lasting longer and longer, because negative mind-wandering has less power over me. That doesn't mean that I will never feel negative mind-wandering again, or that a disturbing event may not trigger it in the future, but I know there will be moments of relief.

We can be grateful for hard times when they increase our empathy and compassion. When I sat with my mother as she died, it opened my heart to others, especially people who were going through a similar experience. Only later did I recognize that these feelings of gratitude, empathy, and compassion also helped me become more kind. I could never be grateful for my mother's death, but I can be grateful for learning more about compassion and empathy as a result of being with her at the end of her life.

It can be much more difficult to feel gratitude for hard times that were caused by another person, such as Roy being abused by his father. But as Mother Teresa said, "Some people come in our life as blessings. Some come in our life as lessons." When other people's actions cause us deep distress, we are more likely to feel rage and seek revenge than to be grateful for what we have learned. But mindful kindness can help us to forgive those who treated us with cruelty, which is another way we gain confidence in our practice. This is what Tad meant when he wrote, "My hatred toward my stepfather. This was my greatest unkind habit...But I've, through years of practice, learned to forgive him...How? Every time I was reminded of the past, I would tell myself, 'His past abuse is my strength today.'...The realization of this need for change was the beginning... Through each step on this journey, new doors are being opened to other unkind habits to overcome."

In writing this book, I reflected on the cruelty others inflicted on me when I was very young. I was bullied as a child, sometimes quite badly. At an outdoor birthday party, two boys pulled me in a wagon over the embers of a dying campfire, then jerked the wagon out from under me so I fell into the still-hot coals. On another occasion, children killed my brand new kitten in front of me. When I was even younger, two children in a tree house dropped a slab of concrete on my head. No child should have to experience this cruelty, and I know that what happened to me was wrong. Looking back now, many decades after these events took place, I can also see how these events planted seeds in me that grew into empathy and compassion, and a deep sense of caring for the suffering of others. Though it can be challenging to respond to another person's cruelty with compassion, doing so can eventually displace the anger and resentment you might feel. Ridding yourself of anger and resentment is a way to be kind to yourself, because anger and resentment serve you no benefit.

try it now

In your practice journal, write about something you learned from a hard time in your life.

Wrapping Up

All of your work in the earlier steps of this book has prepared you to benefit from kindful options. You have learned how these options can become kind habits that help you improve your relationships, manage stress, solve problems, increase your awareness of opportunities to act with kindness, and experience more joy and contentment. In this step, you have also learned how these options can help you cope with difficult times that bring deep distress. When you're facing hard times, you can:

1. Take the perspective of the detective, to look for ways to actually change your situation; or the role of the warrior, to take action in spite of your deep distress.
2. Be with those you care about.
3. Spend time in engaging and fun activities.

4. Deepen your mindfulness practices, by intensifying the Three-Breath Method, rotating through your senses, and reciting "no ____ ahead."

5. Ask for help for those in need.

6. Call up memories of joy and appreciation that trigger your gratitude.

Of course, continuing to be kind to others is a pleasant kind habit that also softens your disturbed state.

Practice these kindful options during your everyday life, before you are in a moment of deep distress. That way, you will be ready with these practices when you truly need them, rather than trying to find a way to learn something new in the midst of a challenging or difficult situation. Employing kindful options consistently turns them into habits that will eventually come to you almost without effort, to enrich your life, and help you cope in times of need. Engaging the kindful options in hard times is how love wins.

try it now: comparing your kind and unkind responses

In your practice journal, write about how you might respond kindly, or unkindly, when you are waiting in a store line that is moving very slowly because a customer has given the clerk several dozen coupons to process. Now write about how you would kindly or unkindly respond when you speak on the phone to a company representative who is not able to help you sufficiently. Think about your responses in both your mental and physical worlds.

checking in

Review what you wrote for your kindful vow and ask yourself how you are following through on each part:

I will be more kindful to myself by...

I will be more kindful in my relationships by...

I will extend the reach of my kindfulness by...

time for reflection

Near the end of each day, take a few moments to reflect on one of the practices you are focusing on, such as:

- Mindful micropractices

- A habit you are working on changing—strengthening a kind habit or weakening an unkind habit

- Meditation

- The Renew-then-Serve Cycle

- Naming things that went well and things you are grateful for

STEP 10
Return to the Present Moment

I used to think of time as a series of stages: I came out of the past, moved into the present, and got ready to enter the future. Over time, I came to realize that there is only one stage—this present moment. My past, which comprises everything that I have done or that has happened to me, is what makes me who I am now, and in that sense it is a part of the present moment. Similarly, everything I expect, anticipate, hope for, or dread about the future is also part of who I am now, and so it is also part of the present moment.

Think of the present moment like gravity. We are always in it. There is no place on Earth where it does not apply. Whether we stay home or travel to the North Pole, gravity exists. In this same way, everywhere we go, we are in the present moment. Awake in the middle of the night or meditating in the morning, we are in the present moment. When the future arrives, we will be in that present moment. The only time we can think about the past or the future is in the present moment. Thus, for all practical purposes, the present is everything—it is all there is. I think of the present moment as being the time to take one cleansing breath. No matter whether we are in pain, regretting the past, or worrying about the future, you can take one cleansing breath to clear your mind.

Awareness that our entire life is the present moment is a powerful antidote to one of our most commonly occurring unkind habits, being unhappy when our preference (disguised as a need) is denied. In other words, when we're not getting what we want, or when we're getting what we do not want. Maybe it's a little thing, like having to do a chore such as cleaning the toilet, something we prefer not to do. In the moment we're doing the cleaning, we can choose to take a cleansing breath and then make the cleaning a mindful micropractice and actually benefit from the experience, by giving our mind a rest and enjoying our sensing-mindfulness. We can also choose to wallow, cleaning resentfully and stewing over our displeasure at the task. Or, we can engage in low-keyed mind-wandering by listening to music or an audiobook. We all have hundreds of preferences—from eating the food we like, to avoiding unpleasant chores, to not spending time with people who make us feel uncomfortable. Dozens of times every day, our preferences are denied, and each time, we must choose how to respond. Maybe we can start with one cleansing breath. In a sense, that breath can cleanse your entire life—because that moment is your entire life.

A few years ago, I came down with a bad flu. I had been feverish for almost a week, coughing up blood, and feeling like a zombie. On top of this, I had planned a trip to visit my sister and her seriously ill husband, who had recently entered hospice care. I was still very weak from my illness, and I was overcome with grief as well. I was telling a friend about my situation, and she reminded me that no matter how difficult the circumstances, we can still be mindful and act with kindness to everyone we come in contact with. In an instant, I saw that she was right. In spite of my unhappiness, I realized that the present moment was my only opportunity to practice kindfulness, so I thanked my friend for her advice, took one cleansing breath, and let my sister know that I was looking forward to my visit.

Recognizing that this is our only moment to practice kindfulness can motivate us to address self-defeating, unkind habits such as complacency, self-pity, laziness, and procrastination. For example, sometimes when I do not sleep well, and feel tired the next day, I wallow in my self pity. I think to myself, "It's so irritating to wake up at 4 am. I'm going to be tired and grouchy all day." And on it goes. So when I become aware of my complaining, I come to this fundamental question: "Will I spend this moment ruminating on the past lack of sleep, and worrying about being grouchy in the future? Or will I live in the present moment being kindful? You can answer the question by taking one cleansing breath.

try it later

For the next three days (or more), take a mindful breath when you are relaxed, stressed, busy, tired, discouraged, or experiencing other emotions. Write about your experiences in the **Meditation/ Mindfulness** section of your journal.

Five Traps That Keep Us From Kindfulness in the Present Moment

Unkind habits can prevent you from practicing mindful kindness in the present moment. I call these unkind habits "mindful kindness traps." I will discuss five traps: thinking about the past or the future, judging your own practice, thinking about kindfulness rather than practicing it, devaluing the present moment, and losing your mental balance. Noticing these traps can help you avoid them, or at least bounce back from them more quickly. The first step in dealing with these traps is deciding whether to take on the role of the warrior or the detective in the present moment. If you're worrying about a project at work, you might ask yourself, "If this moment is my entire life, should I be a detective and figure out how best to finish the project?" Or, realizing that you have done as much as possible on the project, you might instead ask, "If this moment is my entire life, should I be a warrior and change my mental world by stopping my worrying?"

Regardless of the role you choose to take on, you have no choice but to answer this question with respect to the five traps: Will you live your life with mindful kindness or not? Remember, there is only one time for practicing kindfulness: Now.

FROM THE OTHER SIDE

Being in prison is a very real physical trap. Tad wrote about the present moment, using his painting of a rose with thorns as a metaphor:

I started out using Skittles and M&Ms for the colors in the paintings because I was limited in art supplies. But, later I saw a teaching in using candy as paint: "Utilizing what is available around us at all times." What the present moment gives us—be mindful and utilize it, even if it's candy or a small prick from the thorn of a beautiful rose that draws blood. The thorns are there to remind us not to grasp just for the beauty in life, but to be mindful of all that is around us. Don't just desire instant gratification in life, but be mindful of every opportunity we encounter or create.

As a kindful practitioner, and by following the Renew-and-Serve Cycle, you already have a set of practices that can help you to avoid or quickly escape from these traps and return to the present moment: sensing-mindfulness (including rotating through your sensing-mindfulness practices), the Three-Breath Method (including breathing deeper and slower), the Experience-then-Return Loop, and mindful micropractices. Other practices include asking for help for those in need, calling up memories of joy and gratitude, acting with kindness to someone or yourself, getting together with someone you care about, and being engaged/having fun. Let's look more closely at each of the five traps.

Thinking About the Past or the Future

Sometimes thinking about the past or future is productive—for example, when we take on the role of the detective to learn from a mistake or prepare for an upcoming challenge. We might look to the past when we feel hungry at bed time, and think to ourselves, "The last several times I snacked on cheese before going to bed, I had indigestion and felt bloated. Maybe tonight I'll have an apple instead." Or, we can plan for the future, asking ourselves, "What food do we need to buy for the week?" or "What do we need to pack for our trip?" However, much of our thinking about the past and the future does not address practical questions but rather wastes time, diminishes how we value the present moment, and makes us agitated or miserable. When we recognize we are caught up in such thoughts, the simplest remedy might be to share these thoughts with a friend. Merely hearing your thoughts said out loud places them in the context of the larger world, and thus can reduce their seriousness. And it always helps to receive support from a friend.

Getting Trapped Thinking About the Past

We cannot undo the past. Perhaps in a moment of anger you said something hurtful that ended a friendship. Or maybe you were distracted while driving and caused a crash that hurt another person—or even took a life. You can take responsibility for what you did, for example, by apologizing and trying to make amends. But being consumed by regret over what happened can never make it right. And yet our regrets can consume us to the point that we have trouble focusing on what is happening to us now, the actions we are taking, and the decisions we are making.

When we notice that our attention is focused on our regrets, the first thing we can do is evoke the Three-Breath Method and then return to our intention. If regret continues to dominate our thoughts, we may need to put more effort into forgiving ourselves, by trying the kindful options for hard times described in Step 9. In changing your mental world, you might ask for help for others, or call up positive memories. Should your efforts to change your mental world fail, try changing your physical world—for example, by cleaning, spending time on volunteer activities, or calling a friend who is having a hard time. Of course, if you find your life disrupted by feelings of despair caused by worry and regret, consider getting professional help.

Getting Trapped Thinking About the Future

There are two ways to be trapped in the future: anticipating something positive, and dreading something negative. It's natural to think about the nice things in store for us. When a pleasant thought about something we expect to happen enters our mind, we can choose to acknowledge the feeling of anticipation, enjoy the feeling, and then return to our intention. The anticipation becomes problematic when we hold on so long and so intently that we are distracted from our current intentions. Think about what it's like when you're talking with a friend, and spending the duration of your conversation looking forward to the dinner you're planning with someone else later on. The dinner may be lovely or it may be canceled, but either way, you're missing the opportunity to strengthen your ties and enjoy your time with the friend in front of you right now. Attachments to future pleasures can cause even more harm by feeding our unkind habits, such as when an alcoholic anticipates the next drink, an obese person daydreams about eating an ice cream sundae, or someone who struggles with anger management fantasizes about punching the object of their rage.

In addition, eager anticipation of pleasant events can undermine our ability to enjoy the present moment. In her book *When Fear Falls Away*, writer Jan Frazier says, "I used to look forward to Fridays...The reason I don't look forward to them any longer is that I don't look forward to anything. Why do we look forward? It is because whatever we are doing **now** feels like less than **that** will be. Because everything I do...is a genuine pleasure, I do not look forward."

The flip side of anticipating pleasure is worrying about something negative that may occur. When worries about the future arise over and over again, be a detective. Confront the agitating thought and deal with it head-on. Or be the warrior and keep redirecting your attention back to your intention. For example, if you struggle with chronic back pain or a persistent injury, you might worry that it will interfere with your enjoyment of an upcoming trip, or make it difficult for you to participate in an event you were looking forward to. First, take on the role of the detective. Instead of being agitated about the future, are there actions you can take? What about exercises or stretches that can speed recovery? Is there medicine you can pack that will help you feel better? If there's nothing you can do about the pain, your best strategy might be to take on the role of the warrior and be persistent in your mental world, redirecting your focus back to your intention in the present moment—after all, you will have to live with back pain wherever you are, so you might as well prepare to live with it on your upcoming trip.

In addition to confronting your pain, you can confront your worry, for example, by taking a cleansing breath. If that is not enough, coordinate your breathing by inhaling as you say "There is no fear of pain." Next exhale as you say, "ahead." Then, return your attention to a kindfulness practice in the present moment, without distraction.

try it now

Think about something that is causing you to regret the past or worry about the future. In your practice journal, write about how it is affecting your mindfulness practice as a kindful practitioner in the present moment. Next, write about how you could take the role of the detective or warrior to be able to return to being a kindful practitioner.

Judging Our Kindful Practice

Judging our kindful practice as "not working" can lead us to abandon the practice. Instead of helping, we may feel that our practice actually contributes to our frustration and negative mind-wandering. We might think, "I am doing a bad job," "this mindfulness is a waste of time," or, "I'll never get this." These excuses are rationalizations for abandoning our kindful practice. Remember, when you rationalize, you are attempting to explain or justify an unhelpful behavior or attitude with logical-sounding, plausible reasons, even if the reasons are not actually true or appropriate.

Ask yourself: were you privately expecting that your kindfulness practice would result in your being happy all the time? Of course, you know that this would be impossible. Or does your negative mind-wandering come from comparing yourself to others—perhaps someone very advanced, like a mindfulness teacher, or maybe just a friend who has more free time to practice and thus, seems to be getting "results" faster than you are? These comparisons aren't useful. Remind yourself that everybody's practice is different, and their experience doesn't reflect on yours. Be patient with yourself and remember that improvement occurs gradually, and at a different rate for each of us.

Another reason not to let frustration discourage your kindfulness practice is that you might actually have improved more than you realize. In fact, as New York Times columnist David Brooks wrote in his book *The Social Animal*, the conscious mind is often not aware of the progress we are making in our practice.[53] There are hundreds of processes operating in the non-conscious portion of our minds. These non-conscious processes include many that are related to mindfulness, meditation, and kindness. If we place too much emphasis on our conscious rationalizations, we might give up our practice when in fact we are making significant progress at the non-conscious level.

One way to get a better perspective on your progress is to read through your practice journal. Look back on what you wrote about your unkind habits (Steps 1 and 6) and building kind habits (Step 3). How does your state of mind today compare to how it was when you first wrote these observations? Overall, are you experiencing less negative mind-wandering and unkind habits today than you were back then? What about kind actions? If reading your journal doesn't help, you can also ask someone close to you if they've noticed a change in your attitudes, behavior, and relationships.

Finally, even though you may be frustrated that you haven't yet achieved what you imagine to be yogi-like enlightenment, I'm willing to bet that your practice actually does help you feel better—at least in the moment. Ask yourself: When you're having a bad day and you're frustrated with yourself and the world, how do you feel after you've practiced meditation or mindfulness? Do you feel a little calmer, more clear-headed, refreshed? I know I do. Sometimes, we experience really hard times, and this clarity might last only a few minutes, but that's okay. If things are that bad, all the more reason to give yourself those moments of respite, however brief. Keep in mind that our entire life is made up of present moments, and in every one of those moments we can take a cleansing breath.

try it now

Describe the biggest frustrations that cause negative mind-wandering about your kindful practice. Write about how these frustrations make you feel. Finally, write about what you intend do in the future when these frustrations arise again.

Learning vs. Practicing

It took many years for me to understand that reading, discussing, and thinking about mindfulness and kindness could not give me the same experiences and understanding as actually doing kindful acts.

Reading and thinking are not enough. You must practice kindfulness.

Studying kindfulness without actually being kind would be like reading books about dieting without changing what you ate, talking with experts about fitness and never actually doing any exercise, or creating a self-improvement plan but never acting on it. These failures to act can cause you to feel like a failure. The point of mindfulness is to drop the story about how bad you are—**and** drop the story about how great you are going to become. Let go of these stories, and just pay attention to how you can be kindful in the present moment. I finally accepted the fact that I cannot think my way into kindfulness, nor can I think my way out of unkind thoughts and emotions. Kindfulness comes only through moment-by-moment mindful kindness.

While I still enjoy reading and writing about kindness, mindfulness and meditation, I spend far more time practicing mindful kindness and weakening unkind habits. When I'm immersed in writing or study, I try to take a break every half hour or so, and shift out of thinking mindfulness for a few minutes to practice qigong, do my physical therapy exercises, or do some other activity that engages sensing-mindfulness. I use this time to let go of my thoughts about what's on the page and give my mind a rest. I am being kind to myself.

That's not to say reading and study shouldn't be part of your practice. On the contrary, you can read regularly about the importance of weakening unkind habits, whether from a secular perspective or a religious perspective such as the Judeo-Christian Ten Commandments or the Buddhist precepts. Being a kindful practitioner means refraining from unkindness, which also means not breaking the commandments or precepts. Reading and discussing your ideas can also motivate you to stick with your practice, give you solace and guidance in difficult times, stimulate ideas about how to refine your practice, and remind you to be humble from the perspective of how much more there is to understand. Of course, it's also important to make sure that when you talk about mindfulness and kindness with others, you can do so accurately and in a clear fashion.

try it now

Are you reading or thinking about kindfulness more than you are actually practicing it? If so, write in your practice journal about how you might increase your practice of kindfulness.

Devaluing the Present Moment

When we feel the present moment is boring, lackluster, or unimportant, we often seek some form of distraction. For example, I have about 20 physical therapy exercises I do every day. To make the exercises more enjoyable, I listen to an audiobook while doing them.

Creating excitement in the face of boredom is a different matter; we may revert to an unkind habit, often times directed at ourselves. When we feel we need excitement, we might be tempted to turn to drugs, alcohol, gambling, video games, or conflict—verbal or physical. The moment we seek distraction is often when we also stop paying attention to the well-being of others. Sometimes our desire for stimulation leads us to recruit others to join us in our high risk, unkind acts.

At other times, we do not intentionally seek to enlist others to join our unkindness. Rather we are just oblivious to the well-being of others. For example, when we interact with others, we sometimes need to be a detective to determine whether we are feeding their problems or supporting them in their efforts to do better. We can ask ourselves, "What do I need to know about his person?" Seeking to add some spark to the evening, you might offer a friend a glass of wine—not thinking about the fact that he's trying to stop drinking. This is a way of devaluing the present moment, of failing to appreciate the consequences, importance, and impact of what you are doing right now.

On the other hand, there is always the possibility that a seemingly lackluster moment might provide an opportunity to act with kindness. When we remember that the present moment is our entire life, we are more likely to treat our moments of boredom mindfully, and possibly relax and even feel contentment. In my own life, finding myself in disagreement with something Linda said, I would sometimes interrupt to "correct" her. But a few years ago, I reflected upon how our entire relationship exists in the present moment. As she was explaining something, this realization prompted me to ask myself the question: "What do I want our relationship to be?" Of course, I wanted it to be a relationship of respectful listening, not arguing and interrupting. After she finished making her point, I realized that my "correction" would have been inappropriate and was best left unsaid. I am fortunate that with the mind of the warrior I kept my mouth shut instead of interrupting my wife. Now I frequently learn from her, which brings me joy and more respect for her. Fulfilling relationships with deep caring cannot exist without mutual respect.

FROM THE OTHER SIDE

Tad wrote about how he experienced the present moment when "nothing" was going on:

I got an email from you with "Activity in the Heart of Samantabhadra" [a Buddhist scripture about the bringing to fruition the seed of Great Love to be found within us all]. *After I read it, tears started to fall. It is amazing how the "pull" is so great with us. What made you decide to pick this teaching and send it to me? All of this has shown me how blinding the discriminating mind can be. I've found the meditation hall within me. You wrote to me recently: "Hope you are able to practice in the face of all the discouraging news." Now I see clearly, even in my moments of "nothing" that practice is still going on. Bad days or good days, it's still practice. Yes, I was "lost" but the dharma showed me I'm right where I need to be in my present moment.*

---

try it now

Write about a time you were bored, and distracted yourself in an unkind way. Then write about a time you were bored and managed to be mindful, increasing your appreciation of the moment.

Losing Our Mental Balance

Our mind often falls into negative mind-wandering, losing our mental balance, so to speak. A student of Morihei Ueshiba, the founder of the martial art Aikido, once told me that Ueshiba's goal was not to always keep his balance, but rather to learn to come back to balance quickly. In fact, scientists analyzing human movement have determined that people don't actually keep their balance as they walk, but go through a cycle of falling forward and rebalancing with every step.

The challenge is to return to mindfulness quickly, in the present moment, just like you return to balance on your feet. Like a baby learning to walk, practice makes "perfect." By practicing sensing-mindfulness and micropractices in daily activities—for example, while driving, cleaning, dressing, showering, and brushing your teeth—you will find yourself able to maintain your balance for longer and longer periods of time, and to rebalance yourself to mindfulness more quickly when you falter. Learning to make frequent, quick transitions back to mindfulness is one of the most important skills you can use to break the traps that prevent mindful kindness.

Returning to mindfulness is easier when we are grounded in our connections to others, through relationships we have forged through kindness. Our responsibilities toward others can pull us back to our center. For example, I may be complaining to myself about having too much to do, when I pick up a letter in which a prison friend describes the prison's refusal to give him the medicine he needs. My responsibility to write him back with support and encouragement pulls me out of my negative mind-wandering about how busy I am. His medication is a significant problem; my busyness is not.

try it now

A way to practice returning to balance (mentally and physically) is slow-walking meditation with sensing-mindfulness. Walk for a minute, slowly extending one foot after the other, focusing your attention on the movement and sensation of rebalancing from foot to foot: when you step forward, first feel the heel coming in contact with the ground, next the bottom of the foot, then the front of the foot, and finally feel the front of your foot propelling you forward. In the **Mindfulness/Meditation** section of your practice journal, write about or reflect upon what happened (including your feelings) with both your mental and physical balance.

"In a Moment, Life is Gone"

I was writing at a table overlooking the McKenzie River when I heard a loud splash. My head jerked up and I saw an osprey lifting up from the river into the air, holding a fish in its talons. Watching the osprey carrying away the fish reminded me of the Buddhist teaching, "In a moment, life is gone." That moment had come for the fish, as it will for all of us. Perhaps never had I felt more keenly the idea that our entire life exists in the present moment. Each moment is unique, and no moment can be changed. When we think of our lives this way, it prompts us to ask the question: "Who should I be at this moment? Do I want to give my attention to the past, the future, to cravings and unpleasantness? Or, do I want to fully live and experience my life in the one moment I have to live it?" Having the habit of returning our attention to our intention in the present moment strengthens our sense of purpose and confidence as we pursue a life of kindfulness.

Thinking about how we, like the fish, do not know when our last moment will come, I was inspired to write a poem:

The Last Time
One time when you brush your teeth, it will be the last time.
One time when you flush the toilet, it will be the last time.
One time when you stop at a red light, it will be the last time.
One time when you give someone a kiss, it will be the last time.

When will be the last time you turn off your bedroom light?
When will be the last time you walk down stairs?
When...

Am I grateful that I can brush my teeth?
Am I grateful that I can flush the toilet?
Am I grateful that I...

Pure brushing
Pure flushing
Pure stopping
Pure...

try it later

In the **Mindfulness/Meditation** section of your practice journal, describe what happened (including your feelings) when you tried to make the most of the present moment by stopping what you were doing and asking yourself, "In this moment, what is it good for me to do?"

Wrapping Up

Recognizing the ultimate importance of the present moment sensitizes us to the value of avoiding or quickly exiting traps such as those we've discussed: thinking about the past or future, judging our practice, thinking about kindfulness rather than practicing it, devaluing the present moment, and losing our mental balance. Minimizing the moments we spend engaged in these traps maximizes the moments we can spend practicing kindfulness and being aware of consequences of our kind and unkind habits. This awareness motivates us to build kindful habits with our thoughts, emotions, and sensations. When we recognize our laziness about acting on our intention in the present moment, we can remind ourselves to pay attention by asking, "Who should I be at this moment: kindful practitioner, warrior, or detective?" When times are really hard, we engage the Kindful Options. All these efforts are captured in the Kindful Vow, which guides us as we learn how love wins:

> *I intend to be mindfully kind to myself.*
> *I intend to be mindfully kind in all my relationships.*
> *I intend to expand the reach of my kindfulness.*

try it later

If you knew you were going to die in the next moment, what are you aware of in this moment that you have left undone in your life? Write about what you are going to do to bring closure to one thing in your life that is undone, possibly by writing a letter of gratitude or a letter of apology. Are there any areas of your life that you have already begun taking steps to resolve? If so, write about that as well. How did taking that action make you feel?

checking in

Go to the **Unkindness** section of your practice journal and find your plan for an unkind habit. What progress have you made in weakening the unkind habit? Write about how things are going so far, as well as any changes you need to make to improve. Or maybe you've decided to change the plan, and are working on weakening a different unkind habit. Write about what you are doing and about the progress you are making.

time for reflection

Near the end of each day, take a few moments to reflect on the practices you are focusing on to rest your mind, such as:

- Micropractices

- Pleasant kind habits

- Sensing-mindfulness

- Savoring positive emotions

- Remembering things you have done well

Reflect on how these practices affect your feelings.

STEP 11
Expand Your Circle of Kindfulness

In the Introduction, I explained that this is an "us-help" book, not a self-help book. Until now, the focus has been on your own well-being, using mindfulness to build kind habits and weaken unkind habits. Although kindness is one of our four basic instincts, the reach of our kindness has often been limited to those we consider similar to ourselves. In fact, our history shows many examples of discrimination against groups we consider "others." Looking back over US history, we see discrimination against men without property, against women, and against people of color. When the US was first settled, only white men who owned property could vote. All other humans were denied that right, and many other rights and opportunities as well. This type of discrimination increased the likelihood of success for white, property-owning men, because they had fewer other individuals to compete against.

But when heroes risk their lives to save the life of a stranger, we see compelling evidence of the power of our kindness instinct to care for others, not just those who are like us. So how do we build on that instinct? I believe that one of the most important questions facing humankind is: Can we expand the group of people we treat as "us" by creating a kindness circle that includes those considered to be "others"—people of different races, different religions, different educational levels, different genders, different sexual orientations, different nationalities, different political beliefs, and different economic levels? And what about criminals, the homeless, those with mental illness, and even the Earth itself? As you expand your circle of kindfulness, you typically do form close, caring relationships, but you do learn to care for "others," which contributes to your own well-being and happiness.

Our State of Mind Determines the Reach of Our Kindfulness

Our ability to act with kindness toward those who are different from us—both individually and as a member of a larger group—depends in part on our state of mind. For example, when we are feeling grateful, we are more likely to feel less threatened and more open to extending the reach of our kindness. Of course, when we feel miserable, cut off, and completely focused on ourselves, we have less capacity for kindness. Before we can extend the reach of our kindness, we need to have a realistic under-standing of our own state of mind, and learn how to spend more of our day in mindfulness rather than a disturbed state.

The lives of my prisoner friends, Roy and Tad, were filled with trauma. Before they could focus on the third part of the kindful vow—extending the reach of their kindfulness—they needed to direct their mindfulness toward the first two parts: being intentionally kind to themselves, and being mindfully kind in all relationships. As we have already learned, mindfulness enables us to act with kindness and to notice when we are not acting with kindness. Once Roy and Tad had dealt sufficiently with their trauma to be able to be kind to themselves and those close to them, they were ready to reach out further.

FROM THE OTHER SIDE

Tad, Roy and others in our partnership expanded their circle of kindfulness to include prison staff, which seemed to benefit them in an unexpected way. As the guards and nurses experienced kind treatment from these prisoners, it became easier for the prison staff to be less aggressive and to respond with pro-social emotions like kindness, compassion, and gratitude.

I witnessed this firsthand, when Linda and I flew from Oregon to Arkansas to visit Roy, who was suffering from health problems. While we were talking to Roy in the visiting area through 4-inch thick bullet-proof glass, a burly, tough-looking sergeant poked his head into the room. He politely interrupted our conversation to ask if we could please encourage Roy to eat more, so he would stop losing weight.

In addition to making life easier for their wards, the kindness showed by the guards, nurses, and other prison staff also benefited themselves. The suicide rate for prison guards is nearly 40% higher than for the average of all other professions. Longtime prison guards have an average life expectancy about 20 years less than the general public. We've already seen how acting with kindness can build resilience in powerful ways. That's why cultivating kindness and compassion among prison workers is vital for the well-being not only of the incarcerated, but of the workers themselves.

Prioritize Kindfulness in Our Constantly Changing State of Mind

I'm going to use the metaphor of a glass-bottomed boat to illustrate how to prioritize kindfulness, even as our state of mind constantly changes. Through the floor of a glass-bottomed boat, passengers can see the ocean floor with its diverse landscape and beautiful variety of sea life. The glass is like the meditative-mind—it did not create the colorful scene in the sea below, it just gave us the access to see with clarity what was there all along. In the same way that the glass allows us to see the deeper ocean life, meditative-mind allows us to see deeper parts of ourselves, including our profound instinct to be kind and make our sense of "us" more inclusive.

But what happens when we walk over our glass? It might get a little dirty. If we walk over it a lot, or if we have muddy shoes, it might get very dirty. Of course, the dirtier the glass gets, the harder it is to see the beautiful ocean below. This is what happens when we experience mind-wandering throughout the day. Maybe with a little low-keyed mind-wandering the glass is just a bit smudged. With agitation, it's getting hard to see the ocean floor through the dirty footprints. Feeling disturbed and acting with unkindness, the glass is covered in mud, completely cutting off your beautiful view of the present moment. And being out of touch with the peacefulness of the present moment stands in the way of us expanding our kindness circle.

But the glass isn't ruined forever. You can see through it again just by cleaning it off. Mindfulness gives us brooms, mops, scrubbers, and cleaning sprays that can clear away even the biggest mess. Sometimes a gentle tool, like shifting attention to breathing, is all it takes to wipe away the dust. Other times things are really difficult, and we may be so deeply disturbed that it takes all our tools—plus support from a friend, partner, or therapist—to be able get that glass clear again and to act on our opportunities to be kind.

Nobody's glass stays clean all the time. For each of us, every day is a constant process of mind-wandering (smudging up the glass) and mindfulness (wiping it clean again). In a typical day, we might experience some relaxation after five minutes of morning meditation, then get slightly agitated by a traffic jam. We might indulge in some pleasant daydreaming during a meeting, then share a quiet and intimate conversation with a sick friend. Losing our work in a computer crash is disturbing, while listening to music at bedtime sets the stage for evening meditation.

For all of us, watching that glass get dirty and wiping it clean again is an unending process, which is another way of saying that our state of mind is always changing. The frequency and magnitude of the changes depend partly on what's happening in our physical world, but also on the effort we put into our own personal kindfulness practice toward others and ourselves. The more we practice shifting our attention to mindfulness and kindness during the day, the more our changing states of mind (conscious and unconscious) will revolve around kindness and our intention to expand our kindness circle. I cannot over-emphasize the importance of being able to quickly notice when you are mind-wandering and are able to then immediately shift to mindfulness. It can be as easy as taking one cleansing breath.

If we've been engaged in intense negative thoughts and acts over a relatively long period of time, shifting to sensing-mindfulness or even low-key mind-wandering can be very difficult. The crowd of negative thoughts walks all over that glass-bottomed boat, covering it with footprints. Think about how you felt at work or in school when you had to work late into the night to take on a second shift or prepare a report. Even after you finished your work and collapsed into bed, you might have found yourself unable to slow the flood of stressful thoughts. Again, practicing mindfulness may not provide immediate relief, but it can ease the transition and prepare your mind to relax when things are calmer. Once we calm down, we will be more willing and more able to expand our circle of kindness to co-workers, strangers, and others. Expanding our circle is deeply rewarding and makes us grateful.

try it now

What have you noticed about how your own state of mind keeps changing from positive to negative to neutral over the course of a day—or even a few hours? In your practice journal, write about this experience, and discuss how your changing state of mind has affected your feelings, as well as your intention to be kindful toward others. For example, consider writing about a time when your intention to be kindful was disrupted by the momentum of your thinking and emotions.

Expanding Our Circle of Kindfulness at Work

The effects of bringing compassion and kindness into the workplace can be dramatic. Dennis Tirch, a psychologist and the founding director of The Center for Compassion Focused Therapy, works with business leaders. In one case, he worked with a CEO who had begun mindfulness and compassion training to deal with personal problems. Even after her concerns about her personal life were resolved, she remained in compassion-focused coaching to help her resolve some thorny issues at work. Her firm was being restructured, and she had to make a decision that would affect the firm's shareholders and employees. After engaging her compassionate mind, she chose to take steps that would preserve thousands of jobs and ensure the long-term viability of the business, rather than make changes based on short-term profit. While this choice might have seemed less than aggressive in maximizing immediate gains, her decision led to much greater return on investment in the longer term for her shareholders, the preservation of the welfare of thousands of families, greater public goodwill, and a strengthened corporate culture.

Research on the importance of kindness across many workplaces was summarized by Emma Seppälä, the Science Director of the Stanford Center for Compassion and Altruism Research and Education, and Kim Cameron, University of Michigan management professor, in an article for the Harvard Business Review. They identified six characteristics of a positive—or kind—workplace:

- "Caring for, being interested in, and maintaining responsibility for colleagues as friends.

- Providing support for one another, including offering kindness and compassion when others are struggling.

- Avoiding blame and forgiving mistakes.

- Inspiring one another at work.

- Emphasizing the meaningfulness of the work.

- Treating one another with respect, gratitude, trust, and integrity."

How can a boss nurture these six characteristics? They can foster positive social connections, show empathy, go out of their way to help, and encourage people to speak up—especially about their problems.

Looking for some quick, simple tips for how both employees and bosses can act with kindness? There are many lists of tips on the Internet. Try some of these:

- As an icebreaker for any work event, ask individuals to share an act of kindness.

- Compliment people who you see act with kindness.

- When giving a talk on any topic, mention kindness.

- Introduce a colleague to a contact in your professional network.

- Be a cheerleader for someone else's idea or project.

- Be constructive in your criticism.

- When you ask someone about their work, really listen to the answer.

- Tell your boss what you appreciate about them.

- Share praise with a co-worker's boss, and their boss's boss.

- Give a glowing but honest recommendation.

- Give someone else a break over a disagreement; give them the benefit of the doubt.

- Share your expertise. Better yet, be a mentor.

- Admit when you're in the wrong (it helps other people feel better about their mistakes!).

- Don't complain and don't gossip.

- Congratulate others on their accomplishments.

- Share a positive thought about something going on at work, especially acts of kindness.

But what is meant by a more productive workplace? Seppala and Cameron define it as organizational effectiveness that includes financial performance, customer satisfaction, employee engagement and productivity. A kind (positive) workplace improves relationships and creativity, attracts and retains employees, and buffers against stress, which improves health and employee "bounce back" following adversity. Finally, kindness is contagious in the work place.[54]

Unfortunately, unkindness is also contagious. Lund University psychology professor Eva Torkelson found that rudeness in the workplace spreads if nothing is done about it.[55] But let's look more closely at what is meant by unkindness in the workplace. In her article *Workplace incivility: A review of the literature and agenda for future research*, Oregon State University management professor Pauline Schilpzand described two types of unkindness:

- Negative behaviors such as aggression, deviance, bullying and abusive supervision.

- Incivility such as talking down to others, not listening, and making demeaning remarks. Incivility is less intense and not as clearly aggressive as negative behaviors.

Furthermore, Schilpzand and her team reported that 50% of the workforce experiences incivility at least once a week. Incivility is estimated to cost companies $14,000 per year per employee.

Multiple research studies on incivility in seven countries and in 16 different types of workplaces point to incivility being pervasive worldwide. Incivility can cause worry, avoidance or retaliation, emotional distress, depression, disengagement from work with lowered motivation and lowered satisfaction, higher turn-over, absenteeism, quitting, and, unkind behavior toward customers.[56]

Adam Grant, the Saul P. Steinberg Professor of Management at the Wharton School of Business, spent years studying success and productivity in the workplace. In his book *Give and Take*, he identified four personality types in the workplace. There are doormats (who always say "yes" even at their own cost), takers (who take advantage of others), and matchers (who are always keeping score about who "owes" whom). The most kindful workplace personality type is the sustainable giver. This person reaches out to others with kindness, supporting peers while setting reasonable boundaries.[57] Of the four types, the sustainable givers—those who practice kindness—experience the greatest happiness and success at work. Which type are you? Think about how being more mindfully kind in the present moment could help you shift from being a "doormat" or a "matcher" to a "sustainable giver."

I discovered that the four types are not just found at work. At home I was a matcher, keeping track of whose turn it was to make the bed and do the dishes. Once I realized that I was a matcher, I began weakening that habit, and just made the bed when it needed to be made, or washed the dishes when I saw they were dirty. Stopping myself from keeping score all the time made me happier, and it made my wife happier as well. Remember, kindness can play a central role in each moment of personal relationships, just as it does in each moment at work.

The issue of how to help others without becoming a doormat is often relevant both inside and outside the workplace. With mindful kindness, at times we decide to acquiesce to do what someone else wants, and at other times we might decide to not do those things. If we have reasonable boundaries for taking care of ourselves and stick to them, we can protect ourselves from becoming a doormat.

try it now

Do you identify with one of the four personality types, or are you a mix? Think about these four types to describe your personality, at home or at work, and write about how it makes you feel in the **Kindness/Gratitude** or **Unkindness** section of your practice journal. Next, write about how you might become more of a sustainable giver in the **Kindness/Gratitude** section.

Expanding Our Circle of Kindfulness by Including the "Other"

As humans, we have an inherent inclination to be kind toward those close to us and, at times, even to act with kindness toward strangers. But when is the last time you acted with true kindness toward a homeless person, someone who was mentally ill, or someone whose political views you consider abhorrent? In fact, as members of a society that values material goods and success through wealth or professional accomplishments, we seldom are encouraged to expand our circle of kindness to those seen as "others."

I'll be the first to admit that when I was younger, kindness ended where unfamiliarity and fear of vulnerability began. Setting myself apart from "the other"—including people who differed from me because of race, religion, or sexual orientation—freed me from a sense of responsibility for their well-being.

Extend kindness to those who may seem like "the other."

A rationalization I learned growing up was that the "others" who were criminal, poor, or homeless brought their problems on themselves; they were violent, lazy, or dishonest. To be blunt, the "others" deserved to have a hard life and were not worthy of my kindness. This negative mind-wandering made me feel condescending and even resentful that they took such poor care of themselves, or were living off food stamps and housing subsidies. These feelings were unpleasant and suppressed any inclination I may have had to treat them with kindness—or to be open to receiving kindness from them.

There is a cost for harboring ill will toward an "other" group. Elizabeth Page-Gould, professor of psychology and the Canada Research Chair of Social Psychophysiology at the University of Toronto, included this statement in her article, *Warning: Racism Is Bad for Your Health*: "Harboring racist feelings in a multicultural society causes daily stress; this kind of stress can lead to chronic problems like cancer, hypertension, and Type II diabetes." [58]

Leaving my small and ultra-conservative hometown for the University of Illinois was an eye opener for me. While many from my hometown discouraged me from going to the University of Illinois because it was "full of communists," when I arrived, I found just the opposite—idealistic young people deeply disturbed by the needless death and destruction of the Vietnam War. This was the first of many times when I have realized that my rationalizations for blaming and ignoring "the other" were unjustified. In the late 1960s, I consulted on a large federal education project called Follow Through serving low-income schools serving white, African American, Latinx, and Native American elementary students. In these various settings, I had the honor of working with incredibly skilled and dedicated educators of color. And at the same time I saw the challenges of teaching children, many of whom were neglected or abused at home. Many had seen violence; some had witnessed the murder of a family member, friend, or stranger. Children who experience trauma experience mental damage that physically affects the brain, analogous to how physical disabilities affect the body. Many of these children attend school only sporadically and drop out before graduating. I began to understand why adults who grow up without gaining the knowledge, skills and work habits to thrive in society are viewed as "others."

I learned even more about my prejudiced rationalizations for blaming the "other" after I retired, when my mindfulness practice had matured, and I had more time to learn close-up about a different group of "others." My partnership with prisoners, which includes corresponding with men convicted of violent crimes, and mentoring their efforts to practice kindfulness behind bars, gave me a new perspective on a group considered outcasts by most of society. Of course, when individuals commit violent crimes, they must be held responsible, which can include serving time in prison. However, I found that many of the men I corresponded with had significantly changed since committing their crimes, and I believe they desire to live peaceful, honest lives. Throughout this book, you've been reading about the experiences of Roy, Tad, and Cody, in their own words. By now, you too may have come to see them not as "others" but rather as human beings who were abused over and over as children, and yet could transform themselves into kinder, more mindful and compassionate men while behind bars in maximum security prison.

Another of my learning experiences was volunteering as a food server at a homeless shelter. The shelter provided a safe place for people to sleep on nights when the temperature dropped below freezing. I was able to look each person in the eye and greet them as human beings while I served them as they moved along a counter in front of me. They were always polite and grateful for the food and a dry, warm place to sleep on a freezing night. Each man and woman was a person with hopes and suffering. One evening, a guest in a wheelchair needed three men to lower him to his sleeping mat. Only then did I think about how, on nights warmer than 30 degrees, he would sleep sitting up in his wheelchair with a tarp over his head to keep the rain off. In that moment, I was overwhelmed by gratitude for all my comforts!

I also learn about compassion from our two daughters, who as adults have been deeply involved in social justice organizing for Native Americans, African Americans, immigrants, and the LGBTQ+ community. Their work continues to open our eyes to the history of these groups and the discrimination they still experience.

A special "other" is the abused child, whom I often observed when working in low-income schools. Without at least one caring adult to teach personal responsibility and social skills, many abused children grow up and find themselves in jail, homeless, and abusing their partner and their own children. Parent training programs exist that transform dysfunctional families into nurturing families, a profound kindness. I have had the privilege to serve as president of the board of GenerationPMTO, an international non-profit that provides effective, evidence-based parenting training for clinicians to use with adults who have been neglectful or abusive toward their children. This training benefits both the adults and the children. One study found that parents who completed the GenerationPMTO training were able to take their children out of foster care and reunify the family an average of 350 days earlier than parents who received a traditional treatment.

Many adults who have received this training, including homeless mothers and fathers, have shown continued dedication to learning effective parenting skills.[59] But this training has been made available to only a small fraction of the parents who could benefit. Too many agencies do not adopt evidenced-based practices. Voicing your support for this type of effective, evidence-based parenting training is a way to act with kindness to both adults and children. It is one of the two most important ways to change the downward spiral of many troubled children and families. The other way is to support a caring, effective education for children, starting from pre-kindergarten.

Many people with privilege have empathy for those suffering from the effects of poverty, discrimination, or abuse. In contrast, these same privileged individuals often have little sympathy for those who hold different political or religious beliefs. We treat as "others" those who follow the "wrong" political party or have the "wrong" religious beliefs.

Disagreements over politics and religion can be very heated. Being kind does not mean you have to agree with the other person's position, but rather listening with mindfulness to see if there are areas of possible understanding. Listening with an open mind and looking for common ground are acts of kindness that can reduce acrimony and increase civility in our society.

Sometimes we treat those who are dying as "others." Sitting with my mother as she died was a memorable opportunity to open my heart to other people near death. I volunteered at a hospice center, where I had the opportunity to spend time with half a dozen dying men. I was even able to participate in the Buddhist ritual of washing and dressing the body of men immediately after they died. Getting to know several people just before they died means that those who are dying are no longer "others" to me.

try it now

In the **Kindness/Gratitude** section of your practice journal, write about how you plan to make your circle of kindness more inclusive of an "other" group.

Religions Call for Being Kind to "Others"

Major religions instruct us to treat others with kindness.

While our aversion to making connections with people we consider "other" may be deep seated, the call to do better and reach across the divide is nearly as old as civilization itself. Every major religion instructs us to treat others—especially the weakest members of our society—with kindness. All religions encourage us to treat the "other" with fairness and kindness. As the Old Testament says in Zechariah 7:9-10, "Judge fairly, and show mercy and kindness to one another. Do not oppress widows, orphans, foreigners, and the poor."

Kindness is taught in some form in all religions. Here are some examples:

Jesus: "Love your enemies." "Do to others as you would have them do to you."

Apostle Paul: "Love is patient and kind. Love is not jealous or boastful or proud or rude. It does not demand its own way. It is not irritable, and it keeps no record of being wronged. It does not rejoice about injustice but rejoices whenever the truth wins out. Love never gives up."

Saint Basil: "He who plants kindness gathers love."

Moses: "Love your neighbor as yourself."

Muhammad: "Kindness is a mark of faith, and whoever is not kind has no faith." "There is a reward for kindness to every living thing."

Gandhi: "The simplest acts of kindness are by far more powerful than a thousand heads bowing in prayer."

Buddha: "To be kind is more important than to be right. Many times people don't need a brilliant mind that speaks but a special heart that listens."

Dalai Lama: "Only the development of compassion and understanding of others can bring us the tranquility and happiness we all seek."

Confucius: "Act with kindness but do not expect gratitude." "Forget injuries; never forget kindness."

Because kindness is central to all religions, it forms a basis for interfaith dialogue and a way to bring differing religions together around a common purpose: a kindness purpose.

Christians have the Bible, Buddhists have the precepts, Jews have the Torah, and Muslims have the Koran, all of which urge practicing kindness to the poor. The Golden Rule teaches, "Do unto others as you would have them do unto you." In today's world, we might refine the Golden Rule to go one step further: treat others as *they* want to be treated—not the way we want them to treat us; in other words, see the world through their eyes, not our own.

Building habits that expand our circle of kindness can help us forge stronger connections with others. And acts of kindness that cross these barriers can be profound in a way that we might never experience when we limit our kind acts to those who are closest to us. Getting past my rationalizations about "others" is an ongoing process for me, and it probably will be for you as well. You may find it difficult to choose to connect with others; to experience them as fellow human beings. Think of expanding your circle of kindness as building a habit that will challenge you in many ways over a long period of time. When you catch yourself being judgmental toward an "other," take one cleansing breath.

FROM THE OTHER SIDE

Roy wrote about how many prisoners have had relatives treat them as "others" and abandon them:

More and more guys in here are finding themselves alone, as in their people are cutting them loose. Their families don't answer the phone; they have them blocked. They don't write any more. I know...two white guys whose people have said, "F-'em." They've all got life or life without parole...when I talk to them their hearts are crushed...They aren't asking for money, just an "I still love you" postcard. I've seen friends stick by friends in here better than so-called family. It's always been a place where the occasional "Dear John" letter shows up, but the last couple of years it's enough to be shocking. You can hear the hurt and loneliness in their voices.

try it now

In your practice journal, write about a positive experience in which you extended the reach of your kindness to an "other."

Our ability to extend the reach of our kindness sometimes depends on our stage in life, which was discussed in Step 10. New parents raising one or more young children might find it enough of a challenge just to be kind to their own family members, let alone think about the fate of prisoners or refugees. Yet even under these stressful circumstances, it's possible to take one cleansing breath and reach out with kindness to these outsiders, maybe just by offering the human dignity of eye contact and a nod to a homeless person as you walk by. After all, when we extend kindness and respect in this way, we are modeling for our children and loved ones that the very notion of "other" is wrong, and that our kindness belongs to all people and living things, for their sake and ours.

Or maybe you're a young person, and instead of kids, your stressor is the long hours you put in at your job as you launch your career. Of course, you can always start by practicing kindness with co-workers and friends. You can work up to connecting with "others" in small ways, like keeping a stash of protein bars in your bag to offer to homeless people you pass in the street, or by looking for ways to donate your professional skills pro bono to a local nonprofit group or a family in need.

Maybe you're retired and don't have the disposable income to give to charity, but you have free time to volunteer at a soup kitchen, animal shelter, or meals-on-wheels program.

While thinking about ways to expand your circle of kindness, remember to take care of yourself in terms of building kind habits (positive social relationships, financial stability, exercise, healthy nutrition, music, art, dance, sports, spending time in nature, crafts, and rest) and weakening unkind habits.

Sometimes we cannot be kind to the "other," or even to a family member, when being kind would bring us more suffering than we can bear. The challenge is to find a way to be kind, while also taking care of ourselves. A friend recently wrote to me about how she was struggling with a decision to limit ties with her father:

I am not planning to see my dad this Christmas. We have a long history of misunderstanding one another, and I know I am supposed to embrace those who are different from me, including those who have different political views. To me, though, what he believes in aren't merely different politics but different morals, and those morals are in conflict with my and my only child's— his only grandchild's—best interest. For instance, my child was born with insulin-dependent diabetes and needed the Affordable Care Act law to pass so she could get insurance. Her life, the life of his only grandchild, depended on it! But he opposed it, then wrote me a mean letter after the law passed, where he told me my child's ability to finally get health insurance was going to ruin our country. He also refused to go see her when she was in a hospital in a coma, even though he was healthy, wealthy, and was only an hour away. So I don't want to be near my dad. I don't have peace about it in either direction, whether I stay away or go see him. But I also don't want to open myself up to even more heartache than I already experience, by being around him. I wrote him a letter with as much kindness as I could muster but received a defensive nasty reply. He's my dad and I love him, so I still communicate with him; just sometimes, I need to protect myself.

---

try it now

In the **Kindness/Gratitude** section of your practice journal, write about how you have extended kindness to an "other" (someone who is very different from you in outlook, background, or socio-economic status). How did extending kindness to a person in that group make you feel?

Including the Earth in Our Circle of Kindness

The climate of the Earth, the quality of our air, the cleanliness of our water, the well-being of plants and animals, and the health of our forests and other landscapes are all deserving of our kindness. The obvious reason for being kind is that our very survival depends on the quality and quantity of water, air, climate, plants and animals. Of course, as we've already seen, being in forests, oceans, and the rest of the natural world also enhances our health and gives us joy, contentment, and gratitude.

Humankind has never-before-heard-of power over the future of our natural world. Mindful kindness is needed more than ever

While individuals cannot change the way governments and corporations treat our natural world, we can let them know our concerns by supporting organizations and candidates advocating for policies that support responsible use of natural resources. On a personal level, we can reduce our personal consumption of fossil fuels, meat, and other resources.[60]

One small step I take is to turn off unneeded lights in my home, which also gives me many opportunities each day to practice mindfulness. My wife, Linda, drives an electric car to reduce her carbon footprint. Maybe our greatest opportunity for earth-kindness has come through actions we have taken on forestland we own: planting about 80,000 trees and creating two conservation easements for oak habitat.[61]

Converting Compassion to Kindness

Maybe you truly feel compassion for our natural world and for the "others" in our society. However, compassion without action is not kindness. Of course, knowing of a hardship and feeling concerned is a first and essential step. But feeling compassion for others does not solve their problem.

When a group of San Francisco nuns who ran a soup kitchen for the homeless faced eviction because they couldn't keep up with the city's rising rents, protesters used them as an example of how gentrification was forcing out longtime residents and appealed to Silicon Valley executives to intervene in the gentrification that was forcing out these longtime residents. The business leaders were supportive, and talked about the importance of compassion, but they took no action whatsoever. Meanwhile, the self-help superstar Tony Robbins took action. Robbins, who was once homeless himself and is known for his philanthropy, bought the nuns their own space for a soup kitchen to continue their mission of feeding the hungry. While we cannot afford to buy a storefront to support our kind intentions, Robbins' gift shows how we can back up our compassion with acts of kindness that make a real difference.

Small acts of kindness can make a real difference too. In one of the booths at the Eugene Saturday market called an empathy tent, volunteers listen—just listen—to anyone who wants to talk. One woman was in despair and broke out in tears, several times, as she told her story. The listener, himself recently wounded by a break up, cried as well. As the woman left, she mentioned that she had been feeling so sad that she'd been contemplating suicide, but after the listening session, she no longer felt hopeless.

A small act of kindness can make a real difference.

FROM THE OTHER SIDE

One of the most powerful truths about kindness is that it can benefit the giver as much as the receiver. I was reminded of this when I received this letter from Tad a few days after his release from prison:

I knew what type of family I have! But, now that I am able to see them face-to-face, my heart only bleeds more sympathy for them. They are bitter, mean individuals. The element of kindness is nowhere to be found in most of them.

When I went to visit my mom & stepdad to pick up some of my artwork & property, as soon as I walked in their apartment, my heart hit the floor. The way they lived was devastating, such filth filled their place. My mother looked so pain-strickened, it was sad. She asked me if I still loved her. Yes, was my answer. But how she was living was sickening.

My stepdad looked like the walking dead! A man I once had so much hatred for, on the day I saw him and my mom for the first time in over 15 years, I told him to come give me a hug. And while hugging him, I told him, "I forgave him." No more hate inside for that man. I even told him, "I loved him." That was something I never thought I would do. BUT, I did it! All that practice in [prison] paid off. Years of hatred within myself turned to complete understanding of need, compassion & kindness.

try it now

Write about or reflect upon a time you felt compassion toward an "other," but ignored the opportunity to act with kindness. In the **Unkindness** section of your practice journal, write about how ignoring the opportunity made you feel, and about how you might act with kindness if the opportunity arises again.

A World of Kindfulness

Not only can we expand our circle of kindness as individuals, we can also join groups that are dedicated to expanding circles of kindness. In his books *Rebooting Capitalism: How We Can Forge a Society That Works for Everyone* and *The Nurture Effect: How the Science of Human Behavior Can Improve Our Lives and Our World*, Tony Biglan, senior scientist at Oregon Research Institute describes and documents a range of evidenced-based practices that can increase people's well-being in virtually every aspect of our society, from early childhood education to corporate practices.[62] Looking beyond our individual actions of kindfulness, the books give specific ways we can join with others to support the development of nurturing environments, including communities with a culture of kindness. However, in *The Goodness Paradox*, Richard Wrangham, Ruth B. Moore Professor of Biological Anthropology at Harvard University, reminds us that humans are unique as a species because they evolved to show unusual tolerance and kindness toward their in-group and an unusual level of violence toward their out-groups. As noted earlier, one of humankind's greatest challenges is developing tolerance, if not kindness, toward our "out-groups."[63]

Expanding mindful kindness can transform our world and "turn weapons and electric chairs into flower arrangements."

Wrapping Up

Our kindfulness practice shapes our constantly changing state of mind, which in turn determines our interest in and capacity to expand our circle of kindfulness. Learning to be mindfully kind to those close to us (and to ourselves) sometimes seems almost impossible—even more impossible when we need to call on the Kindful Options in difficult times. So is it reasonable to assume we have the energy to build kindful habits for embracing others? The surprising answer is that the payoff for going beyond empathy to action makes the effort worthwhile. Opening ourselves up to others enriches our lives, as I described in *Saint Badass: Personal Transcendence in Tucker Max Hell.*[64] The kindful tools I used to embrace these men "on the other side" are the same tools I use to better my life and the lives of those around me, and to take better care of our earth. Moreover, my prisoner friends are using these tools to help other prisoners become more mindfully kind. Once kindfulness reaches a tipping point in who we include as "us" in the world, we will all have more security and a sense of belonging, with less violence and heartbreak.

try it now

Having come this far, are you ready to invigorate your Kindful Vow for how love wins by giving new emphasis to extending the reach of your kindness beyond your comfort zone? If so, you can do this alone, with a loved one, or as part of a group. To invigorate your vow, read the vow again. When you get to the third part, "I intend to expand the reach of my kindfulness by..." finish the sentence by describing your specific intention for one of the groups you might consider "other"—like prisoners, the homeless, the poor, the dying, or those facing discrimination.

～

checking in

Look at the list below of some of the practices you've learned. Which of these kindful practices have you found the most useful in your life? In the **Kindness/Gratitude** section of your practice journal, write about your experience using one or two of these practices. Name the practice, then write about what prompted you to use it, and what happened afterward, including how it made you feel, and what the result was:

- Meditation

- The three breaths (including deeper and slower)

- The Experience-then-Return Loop

- Sensing-mindfulness

- Mindful micropractices

- Asking for help for those in need

- Calling up memories of joy and gratitude

- Taking on the role of a kindful practitioner, detective, or warrior

- Acting with kindness to someone or yourself

- Getting together with someone you care about

- Being engaged/having fun

time for reflection

Which kindful practice would you like to use more often? Why? How might you use it more often?

STEP 12
Practice Makes 'Permanent'

All of humanity's problems stem from man's inability to sit quietly in a room alone.

— BLAISE PASCAL, *PENSÉES*

People crave distraction. In fact, University of Virginia psychology professor Tim Wilson found that when left alone in an empty room for just 15 minutes with nothing to do, 12 out of 18 men and 6 out of 24 women would voluntarily give themselves a painful electric shock, rather than simply sit quietly with their thoughts.[65]

So if by now you've tried a little meditation or learned to enjoy moments of sensing-mindfulness and the experience of meditative-mind, take a moment to acknowledge the progress you've made. Think about what your life was like when you first made the decision to pick up this book. Maybe you were someone who spent long periods dwelling on your worries or resentments; or who focused on yourself so much that you were blind to the needs or feelings of others; or who expressed your negative thoughts by lashing out with unkindness toward the people closest to you. Maybe you were even someone who would shock yourself just for a distraction from your own thoughts.

You've come a long way. You've made progress in coping with upsetting and even miserable thoughts and emotions, lessening the need for external distractions. You've also added a number of tools to your toolbox—like sensing-mindfulness, the Three-Breath Method, and Experience-then-Return Loop. This book has presented these and other tools to help you live more mindfully, practice kindness toward yourself and others, stay resilient when things get difficult, and learn from your hard times. Your next step is a big one: the rest of your life. This is where the real work comes in. It's one thing to learn about these ideas and give new techniques a try. It's another to make them a part of your life, day after day, week after week, month after month, until they become the habits that define who you are. The practice of kindfulness is most helpful when it becomes an integral part of your identity. Still, even after years of practice we will make mistakes in practicing kindfulness. Mistakes are inevitable; we will never be perfect. Even as I was working on the final edits for this book, I realized that my practice of martial arts was more of a chore than a pleasant kind habit. I was always thinking about how I could improve my tai chi movements. What had once been a pleasant kind habit was a source for negative mind-wandering. Using soft-eyes, I shifted my gaze from side to side as I went through my tai chi moves. Within a few moments, I broke into a broad grin that returns whenever I practice tai chi with sensing-mindfulness. In fact, this broad grin arises many times during the day. Admitting to our mistakes is painful. Yet, learning from our mistakes is how love wins.

Recognize that your kindfulness practice is endless; fulfill your pledge in the Kindful Vow; be relentless in your intentions to be mindfully kind; and transform these ideas into ever more powerful habits by committing to practice them every day. At some point, you will realize that you are being mindfully kind many times during the day, without thinking about it. Mindful kindness has become a habit! This means you have weakened some of your unkind habits and are less focused on yourself. You'll notice a shift toward "how to be kind" and a shift away from "how to get what I want."

FROM THE OTHER SIDE

As Tad approached the end of his 15-year sentence, he prepared to leave his student, Chris, behind. Tad realized the importance of teaching Chris to extend his kindful practice to others in Tucker Max, where Chris will spend the rest of his life.

Chris & I were having a discussion on "friendship" and the respon-
sibilities it holds. I tried to get him to understand, if him & I are

friends then it's BOTH of our responsibilities to conduct ourselves in an honorable virtuous manner, to produce a real mindful friendship. We must also be mindful of others that claim or state, they're our friends.

Leadership is the most characteristic quality I tried to build in Chris, in the short time we spent together. His willingness to sacrifice and serve (humble) will make him into a great leader. But, with leadership comes great responsibility. "Be wise as a serpent, but kind as a dove."

Two Paths

Every person practices kindfulness differently. For some people, it's helpful to approach a new practice gradually. Others like to dive into the deep end. Either way, it's important to continue your practice of mindful kindness after you finish this book. With that in mind, I've prepared two guides, or Paths, to take you deeper into your practice. If you're someone who thrives on ritual or routine, Path 1 is designed to help you take the kindness practices you've learned here and make them part of your daily life. If you like variety and enjoy always trying something new, try the 31 Days of Kindfulness in Path 2. And if you really want to take your practice deeper, try both!

Regardless of the path you select, keep a practice journal. One of your most valuable tools in the physical world, your journal is the place where you can write down ideas, keep track of your practice, note the outcomes you experience, and explore the feelings that arise. Looking back, it can help you see how you have changed your kind and unkind habits.

Path 1: Daily Practice

1. Set a morning routine.

   a. Describe a kindness you will do today.

   b. Meditate for 10 minutes (20 when you can).

   c. Perform one of your morning activities as a mindful microspractice (for example, washing your face, making the bed, brushing your teeth, or dressing).

   d. Invigorate your Kindful Vow. Say aloud or to yourself:

> *I will be more kindful to myself by...*
> *I will be more kindful in all my relationships by...*
> *I will extend the reach of my kindfulness by...*

2. During the day, be kind to yourself and kind to others (the Renew-then-Serve Cycle) by working on strengthening a kind habit or weakening an unkind habit. In addition, implement one or two of the following:

- Calling upon the detective and warrior.

- Shifting into sensing-mindfulness, either one at a time or rotating through several, one after another.

- Practicing and deepening the Three-Breath Method. Or just taking one cleansing breath.

- Using the Experience-then-Return Loop in dealing with agitated thoughts and emotions.

- Calling up memories of joy and appreciation that trigger your gratitude.

- Asking for help for others.

- Spending time being engaged and enjoying fun activities.

3. Set an evening routine.

   a. Reflect on or write about how your practice went during the day:

- How were you kind to others (serve)? Think about your kind and unkind habits: What went well? Why? What did not go well? Why? What will you do differently in the future?

- How kind were you to yourself (renew)? For example, are you strengthening a pleasant kind habit or weakening an unkind habit? Perform one of your evening activities as a mindful micropractice (for example, washing your face, brushing your teeth, putting your clothes away, or dressing for bed).

b. Name two things you are grateful for and two things you did well.

c. Meditate for 10 minutes (20 when you can) before going to bed.

try it now: Path 1

Follow Path 1 for five days (or more). In the **Kindness/Gratitude** section of your practice journal, write about what you did for your morning routine, your kindful practitioner actions during the day, and what you did for your evening routine.

Path 2: 31 Days of Kindfulness

Do the following practices, one each day, for a month. If you find a particular practice helpful, feel free to keep it up—no need to stop after just one day. And if your kindful habits need more reinforcement after the 31 days are up, you can always do them again!

Day 1: Take time to renew: be kind to yourself. Before moving on to others, start nurturing kindness from within. In what ways are you unkind to yourself? Pick one thing and, for today, show yourself the kindness you deserve. Select a kindness that you feel confident you can carry out, like stopping to stretch after an hour of steady work. Or take a moment to reflect on something you have accomplished, even something small, such as being friendly to a new co-worker.

Day 2: Start tiny habits. Start moving toward your kindness goals with something so small it will be easy to do. Look service workers in the eye when you speak with them. Touch your partner on the arm when you greet them. Give your dog's head a stroke every time you feed him.

Day 3: Reflect on your kindness toward loved ones. Is there something unkind you do that affects someone close to you? What are you willing to do to be kinder to him or her today? Simply acknowledging to yourself something unkind you have done to the person is a first step. Then decide how you might act with kindness toward that person today.

Day 4: Practice gratitude. When you wake up, before you go to bed, and any other time, name three things for which you have feelings of gratitude. Keep those feelings active for half a minute or more. Starting and ending your day with this gratitude practice will set the tone for your day and for restorative sleep. When you start with gratitude, you create a perspective that allows kindness to flourish and attract even more gratitude. Also, you can name things you are grateful for when you notice negative mind-wandering.

Day 5: Ask for support. Ask family or friends to help you in your effort to be more kind. Be specific: Tell them you'd like them to give you a reminder or signal when they see you starting to carry out an unkind habit. Asking for support is not only something we do for ourselves, it also gives someone else the opportunity to practice kindness by helping you.

Day 6: Expand your circle. Today, focus your attention on the homeless, prisoners, vulnerable children, and the less fortunate—the "others" of our society. Think about how you can make a gesture of kindness to someone from one of these groups today. Say hello, smile, give food or clothing, volunteer, write a letter, or stand up for social justice.

Day 7: Renew by appreciating yourself. Take a moment during the day to reflect on three things you are grateful for about yourself, such as your health, the way you treat another person or pet, or how another person treats you. Build kindness toward yourself by savoring the joy and appreciation of the things you are grateful for.

Day 8: Be of service to someone close. Take your focus off yourself by looking for an opportunity to help someone close to you, such as by finishing a chore they usually do, bringing them a cup of coffee or tea, or cleaning up after them.

Day 9: Take one cleansing breath. Just stopping to take that cleansing breath can do wonders for our mood and mindfulness. Concentrate on the physical sensation of that breath instead of the thoughts and emotions that were on your mind a moment ago.

Day 10: Be mindful in your actions. Focus on micropractices. Infuse activities (like brushing teeth, sipping tea, eating, and driving) with mindfulness, giving all your attention to the physical sensations of what you are doing at that moment. Say your Kindful Vow before starting an activity.

Day 11: Serve by offering encouragement. Think about someone in your life whom you have not encouraged in their efforts or success (envy or resentment may be the underlying reason), or maybe just haven't extended yourself to express support. If you cannot speak directly to this person, send an email, or even just speak your words of encouragement out loud, wherever you are.

Day 12: Make a deeper connection. Life is busy. It can be easy to forget to connect to yourself and your spiritual center with your deeper values of truth, love, compassion, insight, and intuition. Take time today to practice meditation or just sit silently. You can start with five minutes, or make it longer if you like.

Day 13: Make amends. Think about a time you imposed your opinions, preferences, or ways of doing things (possibly disguised as needs) on another person in such a way that you caused the person unhappiness. Think about how to make things right. If constructive, tell that person you are sorry for what you did. If you cannot speak directly to that person, or if contacting them would cause them more pain, just say out loud what you would like to tell the person. If you don't remember imposing your opinion on others, be vigilant today and notice if you do it. When it happens, acknowledge it by saying you are sorry. Also, you can ask someone close to you if they have seen you impose your opinion on others.

Day 14: Renew by enjoying music mindfully. When you are alone, listen to a piece of music you care about while you are multitasking—such as reading or having a snack. Now stop everything else you are doing, close your eyes, and listen to the same music again. Notice how much more fully you experience and enjoy the music.

Day 15: Set your intention to stop an unkind habit. Think about what small habits you have that might be inconveniencing or bothering the people close to you—habits like being late, leaving clutter around, or making noise. Pick one, and tell the person who's affected by your habit about your plan to change it. Then, follow through over the next several days.

Day 16: Serve by hearing the other side. We all have moments where we want to be right and really don't listen to the other person's point of view. When you find yourself in a disagreement today, take a moment to stop thinking about the argument you want to make, and pay attention to what the other person is saying. You don't have to let someone take advantage of you, but you can always acknowledge that you are listening with words like, "I hear what you are saying," "That's an important point," or even, "I understand more why you feel that way." After carefully considering the other person's argument, respond in a considerate manner.

Day 17: Respond with kindness. When strangers or acquaintances reach out for help, give them a kind response. You may not always have the time or resources to give them everything they are asking for, but you can always give them kindness. This may mean handing a protein bar instead of money to someone who is begging, or offering encouragement when you're not able to meet a request to volunteer. You can respond to others with kindness even while honoring your own boundaries.

Day 18: Look for opportunities to serve. The key to kindness is to be aware. Many acts of kindness are straightforward, such as complimenting another person on their work, or putting money in a stranger's expired parking meter. But chances are, you will notice many other opportunities for kindness if you are paying attention. Keep this question in the front of your mind today: How can I be kind right now? By being on the lookout, you will notice new ways of being kind, moment by moment.

Day 19: Renew by being mindful with eating. When you are alone, eat a snack while you are reading, listening to music, or watching TV. Now stop what you are doing, close your eyes, and begin eating again. Notice how your experience changes when you give it your full attention. Whether you struggle with healthy eating or not, give yourself the kindness of allowing yourself to fully taste and enjoy your meals today.

Day 20: Be kind with feelings. We can become so wrapped up in our emotions that it clouds our perspective and judgment. Today, when a difficult feeling like anger or fear arises, take three deep breaths. After the third breath, return to the intention you had before the emotion arose. Emotions are like waves. They rise up, crash down, and wash away again. They are meant to move and not get stuck. Remind yourself to use the 90-second Experience-then-Return Loop when a raw, difficult emotion rises up in you. Don't let it get stuck inside you.

Day 21: Let the kindness flow. For today, identify a friend or family member who needs support and shower them with extra kindness. Be creative. Be generous and abundant with your kindness. Notice how it changes your outlook for the day and how you feel doing it. Also notice how the person received it and what you think it meant for them.

Day 22: Start to change old patterns over several days. It's hard to weaken habits when temptation is all around you. For the first day, set yourself up for success by avoiding the old patterns that contributed to your unhealthy or unkind habits. If you're trying to cut back on sweets, don't put them in your cart in the grocery store. If you don't want to gossip, remove yourself from conversations where it is happening.

Day 23: Start building your skills over several days. Start learning a new skill that will help you to be more kind. There are many resources that can help you develop skills around communication, child rearing, and relationships. If you need more ideas, visit www.feedkindness.com, which offers resources related to mindful self-care, mindful couples' relationships, mindful parenting, mindful co-worker relationships, and mindful community participation.

Day 24: Renew by celebrating your victories. Be kind to yourself today by celebrating a victory, large or small. Take a moment to reflect on how much progress you've made since you first picked up this book. Think of just one step you have taken to weaken an unkind habit or to overcome a challenge that had been holding you back. Congratulate and reward yourself.

Day 25: Look on the bright side. Stop five times during the day and notice something positive.

Day 26: Give yourself a prompt to follow through on a new habit, such as the habit you selected for Day 23. Choosing, learning, and establishing a new habit takes consistency. Help yourself remember to follow through on your intentions by setting up reminders or prompts. A sticky note on the fridge, an alert on your phone, or a card on your pillow can help keep you on track of a new habit, such as naming three things you are grateful for when you go to bed at night.

Day 27: Practice the three R's: rest, recharge, refuel. Be kind to yourself by setting aside the time you need to rest and sleep, recharge by doing whatever gives you energy, and refuel with healthy food and drink. These "Three Rs" will help you feel balanced and focused throughout the day, so make sure you're getting enough of each. Chances are, you'll be giving your body something it's been needing for a long time.

Day 28: Serve by listening. Give someone the gift of your full attention. When you really listen to someone, they feel heard, acknowledged, and understood. Listen without interrupting and don't start thinking about your response until the person is finished. Rephrase and repeat what they said, so they know you really heard them. Ask questions. Listening in this way is a kindness that not only builds your connection with others, it brings you fully into the present moment.

Day 29: Give genuine praise. Many people go through life without their talents, hard work, or special qualities ever being recognized. That's why hearing praise can feel so good—especially when the praise is genuine and specific. Today, pay attention to those around you, and give someone praise when you notice something worth recognizing. Don't fake it or comment on something superficial, like their looks, but find a specific action or character trait to acknowledge.

Day 30: Serve by being kind to the Earth. Our planet sustains us—from the food we eat, to the air we breathe. And yet, it can be all too easy to take our clean, healthy environment for granted. Today, be kind to the Earth by giving back or at least acknowledging the many beautiful and important parts of our planet. Go outside and look at a tree or flowers. Give thanks for food and the wonder of how things grow. Then take it a step further and do something to protect and support our environment, such as recycling, picking up litter, starting a compost pile, or writing to lawmakers in support of better environmental protection.

Day 31: Forgive. We've come full circle. This 31-day challenge began with kindness to yourself because all change starts with you. For the final day, think of something that you regret and forgive yourself. Make amends, if necessary, but then let yourself off the hook. Stop carrying around the heavy load that may be adding weight to your life. Only by letting these burdens go can you move forward to offer kindness to the people in your life.

try it now: 31 Days of Kindfulness

Follow the 31 Days of Kindfulness. In the **Kindness/Gratitude** section of your practice journal, describe what you did on each day, including how you felt.

use technology to boost your kindfulness

Your phone offers many apps and other handy tools to prompt you to be mindful and kind. You can use iPhone Reminders, Google Reminders, Facebook Reminders, or other apps you customize to prompt mindfulness practices and acts of kindness. You can set notifications or reminders for the activities from the 31 Days of Kindfulness or any of the activities from Path 1.

Try setting a reminder for a time to meditate in the morning or to make brushing your teeth a mindful micropractice. Or create an alert to prompt you to take a break and stretch three times during the day. The activity reminders can be set for the times that work best for you and can also be set to repeat at that time over several days.

Our Stage in Life Influences How We Put Our Purpose into Practice

Studies have shown that when people are contributing to a higher purpose, they are likely to have a healthier outlook on life and be more resilient to stress. Of course, putting into practice our purpose of being a kindful practitioner can look different in each stage of life—from youth, to working and raising a family, to the empty nest, aging, loss, and dying. If you want to focus on a certain aspect of your stage in life, you might want to follow Path 1: Daily Practice. You can customize Path 1 for your stage, including how you select your micropractices, what you include in your kindful vow, what you focus on during the day, how you serve and renew, and what you select for gratitude. And yet, for every stage, being a kindful practitioner helps you cope in the present moment.

This section offers only one idea for each stage. For each of the six stages that follow, there are numerous resources available; I refer to some of them. You might want to be the detective and look more deeply into additional resources for your stage in life.

Youth—Set Your Purpose

According to Washington University psychology professor Patrick Hill and West Virginia University developmental psychology professor Nicholas Turiano, having a purpose is associated with greater longevity at all ages, including youth.[66] A number of international studies, such as one by Montclair State University family science and human development professor Miriam Linver, report that youth who have a sense of purpose enjoy specific benefits.[67] Unfortunately, research also suggests that having a sense of purpose is rare. Clark University psychology professor Seana Moran found that only 26% of 270 youth aged 12 to 20 expressed a purpose.[68] According to William Damon, author of *The Path to Purpose: How Young People Find Their Calling in Life*, "The biggest problem growing up today is not actually stress; it's meaninglessness."[69] The implication is clear for youth: There is great value in having a clear (and positive) purpose, such as being a kindful practitioner.

Working and Raising a Family—Seek Balance

Often, people who are working and raising a family face conflict between their purposes. They struggle to give equally to their career, their relationship with a partner, and child rearing. These are three important purposes. The challenge is how to find balance among the three, which will be more manageable when both partners have the purpose of being a kindful practitioner. That purpose is also important for singles and single parents. Balance is particularly challenging for women who still bear a heavier load than men in balancing work, child rearing, and relationships.[70] Amy Morin, psychotherapist and author of *13 Things Mentally Strong Parents Don't Do*, has the following self-care recommendations for kindful practitioners who are busy parents:

a. Set aside your pride. Take on the warrior mind and ask for help.

b. Don't be a doormat, but also don't be a matcher who is constantly keeping score with your partner.

c. Don't neglect yourself. Mindful kindness helps you renew.

d. Use mindfulness to free yourself from guilt over not doing a good enough job as a parent, partner, or employee. For example, being kind does not mean your child will always be happy. Everyone is unhappy sometimes, including children.[71]

Empty Nest—Look to Other Relationships

When the last child leaves home, some parents suffer from "empty nest syndrome." Coping with the emotional fallout of all your children leaving home can, for a time, become a person's primary purpose. You can take on the role of the detective to find ways to change your situation. There are many ways to shift your attention away from the change in your family to serving and renewing, such as these ideas from Step 9:

1. Be with those you care about, including staying in touch with your child, and possibly spending time with other parents who are now empty-nesters.

2. Focus on your renewal; spend time in engaging and fun activities. Set an intention of seeing how the empty nest gives you freedom to engage in activities you did not have time for before your last child left home. Maybe you can take up pottery or piano.

Loss—Cope with Grieving

Loss may come through a break-up, divorce, or the death of a spouse or another loved one. Not surprisingly, practicing the role of a kindful practitioner earlier in your life prepares you for this kind of difficult transition, not only with coping strategies, but also by giving you the warrior mindset and the detective's skills to find specific actions to take.

Sheryl Sandbergs' book *Option B* offered helpful research findings and personal experiences for those in the immediate aftermath of the loss of a loved one. Sandberg's husband died unexpectedly, leaving her with two young children. Early in the book, she explains the damage done by the three Ps: personalization, pervasiveness, and permanence.

Personalization means you think the loss is your fault and you feel guilty. With pervasiveness, you believe that the loss will virtually destroy every aspect of your life. Permanence means that you are convinced that the initial horrible feelings will last forever.[72] Another helpful book for dealing with the immediate aftermath of the loss of a loved one is *The Year of Magical Thinking* by Joan Didion, which chronicles her changing feelings and experiences during the first year following the unexpected death of her husband.[73] Many of my friends have found it helpful in coping with their grief.

Aging—Be Proactive

First, an encouraging finding for aging individuals who have kind self-care habits and are consequently in better health. Heidelberg University psychology professor Oliver Schilling reported they maintain positive affect longer as they age, and their negative affect holds off until closer to the time of death.[74] These positive outcomes likely result from being a kindful practitioner: having close caring relationships with family and friends, helping others, and engaging in self-care kind habits such as exercise, healthy eating, and stress management.

However, even if we enjoy our retirement years, once aging leads to physical and mental declines, we often see a decrease in those positive feelings, and an increase in negative ones. According to the National Council for Aging Care, getting older is associated with declines in several areas: bones, heart, brain and nervous system, senses, skin, sex life. This is the time when the proactive value of being a kindful practitioner becomes evident. You can take steps to mitigate these declines with changes like a proper diet, physical activity, challenging brain activities, having a positive outlook, being proactive about health and safety, and by doing things like getting a flu shot and keeping floors clear to prevent falls.[75]

Dying—Deal With Your Anxiety

As we face death, many people understandably turn inward. Even so, as my friend Jeremy showed us, we can still be kindful practitioners toward others. One of the most important ways to be mindfully kind to ourselves when facing death is to make an effort to shift our attention away from our anxiety about dying. Reducing our anxiety about dying is about more than just eliminating an unpleasant feeling. Anxiety about death seems to be at the core of a number of mental disorders including hypochondriasis, panic disorder, and anxiety and depressive disorders.[76] University of Illinois psychology professor Ryan Ritter reported that, for many people, limiting this anxiety may not be as difficult as commonly perceived. It turns out that the dying are actually more positive toward death than those who are merely thinking about death. Most surprising was the finding that the feelings of terminally ill patients and men on death row approaching death were not as unpleasant as would be anticipated.[77]

Note about a broken heart: It's important to note that the loss of a loved one, the empty nest, aging, and dying all involve the break of an important connection. When the connection is lost, we are no longer giving and receiving kindness with that other person. The loss of the connection means the feel-good chemicals—three neurotransmitters in particular—are no longer present, and we are in fact going through withdrawal from those chemicals. You might think of this withdrawal as what many call a broken heart.

try it later

In thinking about your stage in life, what does it mean to you to be a kindful practitioner? What action might you take to become more mindfully kind? Describe this action in your practice journal.

Five Elements of Happiness

Positive psychology researcher Martin Seligman breaks down happiness into five elements:

1. **Positive emotions** come from the feel-good chemicals released in our body when we are kind, receive kindness, or observe kindness. Close caring relationships are a reliable source of constructive emotions.

2. **Engagement** comes when mindfulness allows us to feel absorbed in what we're doing. Close caring relationships offer repeated opportunities for engagement.

3. **Relationships** become close and caring from all the ways we are kind to others and thereby create an authentic connection with them.

4. **Meaning** comes from our purposeful existence as a kindful practitioner, often involving our close caring relationships.

5. **Achievement** occurs when our purpose is supported by skills of change, skills of action and skills of character, producing a sense of accomplishment and success. One of life's greatest achievements is having many close caring relationships.[78]

Of course, that means we can also define unhappiness according to the absence of these elements.

People of all ages, from toddlers to adults, experience happiness when being kind to another person. Simon Fraser University psychology professor Lara Akin found that children younger than two expressed more happiness when they gave a treat to someone else than when they received a treat themselves. Even more interesting, they were happier giving away their own treats—and thus reducing their stash—than giving away treats that didn't belong to them.[79] University of British Columbia psychology professor Elizabeth Dunn and Harvard Business School professor Michael Norton reported a similar phenomenon in adults around the world, with studies showing that spending money on others gives people a bigger boost to happiness than splurging on themselves.[80]

try it now

In your journal, write about how working on the exercises in this book has affected each of the five elements of happiness in your life: positive emotions, engagement, relationships, meaning, and achievement.

～

review: comparing your kind and unkind responses

Think about how you would kindly and unkindly respond (mentally or with an action) when a person's slow driving on a curving road is causing you to be late.

～

A Life of Kindfulness

You're almost at the end of this book. But really, that means you're at the beginning of a new life of kindfulness. Think about the changes you have made over the past days, weeks, or months, and how different your life is now. Perhaps you're less troubled by negative mind-wandering or have broken some old habits and built new ones. Your changes may have been small and simple, but sometimes those kinds of changes are the ones that can have the most profound and long-lasting impact. You may still slip up sometimes and miss opportunities for kindness, but now you are more aware of these moments. Hopefully you are also more aware of how the other people in your life are affected by your kindness, and perhaps how they are showing you kindness in return.

How can you expand your understanding of kindfulness? Keep practicing, keep meditating, and give it time. Reflect on how much you trust your kindful practice and how that trust encourages you to learn how to be even more kindful. This openness is vitally important as you move through the stages of your life, from youth to dying.

If you return to this book in a couple of years and browse through it again, you are likely to find that the explanations and practices outlined here have new meaning for you. And if you keep a practice journal, looking back on what you have written will give you another perspective on how much your understanding of kindfulness has deepened. I'm reminded of a talk by a Buddhist teacher from Shasta Abbey. Shortly after hearing the talk, I met the teacher and thanked him for his excellent lecture. Two years later, I listened to a recording of that same lecture. When I met with the teacher again, I told him, jokingly, how his teaching had grown so much deeper over the past two years! Of course, it was not the teaching but my understanding that had changed.

As you continue your practice of mindful kindness, you will develop a deeper understanding of how it strengthens your intimate relationships, infuses your life with a sense of purpose, and serves as a critical component of positive emotions, engagement, relationships, meaning, and achievement—the five elements of happiness. So, enjoy a life of mindful kindness and happiness.

CONCLUSION
Share the Gift of Kindfulness

You may have thought you were finished with *How Love Wins*. Not quite. Having learned ways to be mindfully kind to yourself, to those close to you, and to 'others' as well, a powerful cycle has begun—your kindfulness today triggers feelings of well being and gratitude that will make you even more motivated to continue your practice of kindfulness tomorrow.

But we have more to do than just be kindful toward ourselves and others. We need to share the gift. (I hope this book has given you the gift of understanding the immense value of kindfulness and of actually being more kind.) We share the gift of kindfulness with friends by encouraging them to be more kind to others. As you have learned in this book, when we are more kind, we benefit. In turn, when our friends are more kind, they benefit.

Serving as an example of kindfulness to others can set the stage for conversations with friends and community members about how they can make kindfulness more central to their own lives—and, eventually, to continue spreading it outward. Earlier chapters pointed out the importance of responding to a person's comment by asking to hear more, agreeing, making an encouraging comment, or offering interesting relevant information, by asking caring questions about what is important in the person's life, and by taking seriously the other person's opinions and preferences. All these skills contribute to what can be referred to as

nutritious conversations. They are a way to spread kindfulness in many different conversations, such as with family, friends, and colleagues at work, church, and service clubs. We read a lot about nutritious meals, but what is meant by a nutritious conversation? A nutritious conversation takes a kindness perspective, discussing the kind acts of ourselves, others, and organizations. A nutritious conversation covers a variety of topics, most importantly the well being of family, friends, colleagues and our community. In contrast news from the media and from conversations about politics, crime, and environmental damage leave many of us feeling discouraged (if not depressed) and sometimes helpless. A nutritious conversation does not eliminate 'bad news' but rather manages it to tilt toward kindness. We need to take in enough local and national/international news to inform us to be responsible citizens, taking action by voting, volunteering, donating to non-profits, and protesting injustice. Similarly, conversations about the hardships of our friends, colleagues, and even strangers give us information that allows us to know when and how to help. Malnourished conversations focus largely on 'discouraging' news with little time spent on kind news or on the kind actions we might take to help those in need. Malnourished conversations leave us with indigestion, feeling hungry for something positive.

For those of us leading a privileged life, sharing the gift of kindfulness in the ways described in this book, such as nutritious conversations, is our responsibility. To quote the Bible (Luke 12:43), "From everyone who has been given much, much will be demanded; and from the one who has been entrusted with much, much more will be asked." Indeed, because of our privilege and good fortune, we should expect much of ourselves.

try it later: nutritious conversations

For your next couple of conversations, write in the **Kindness/Gratitude** section of your journal your estimate what percent of your conversations were nutritious. Then describe how you intend to make your next conversation more nutritious—by decreasing the focus on bad news that does not inform kind action and increasing the focus on kind news and planning kind acts. Implement your plan and write about what happened in your journal.

Since focusing our own lives on mindful kindness, Linda and I have begun another way to share the gift besides nutritious conversations, to "pay it forward," by encouraging others to be more kind to those close to them and even to strangers. We host Spreading Kindness dinners at our house to share ideas and experiences with like-minded friends. We've noticed that many people have a "comfort zone" around encouraging other to be more kind. One longtime married couple we know agreed that kindness was a foundation of their marriage, and readily embraced the challenge of encouraging others to be more kind, starting with their circle of friends.

But their reaction was different when I steered the conversation to encourage sharing the gift with those outside our comfort zone such as the prisoners I mentor in Tucker Max. When I told our friends about how mindful kindness transformed the lives of these men, they responded, not surprisingly, with wariness about dealing with murderers. They could not envision themselves being kind to men in a maximum-security prison, let alone encouraging these prisoners to be more kind. Most of us have a familiar comfort zone based on income, caring relationships, and a clean, beautiful environment. However, many of us do not really understand the difficulties faced by people who have never had the privilege of this way of life, like the men in Tucker Max. Realizing that for many of us, making this leap to share the gift of kindness with the "others" will be challenging, we try to communicate the benefits we've received personally from our relationships with the prisoners and others who are outside our comfort zone.

Special Challenges To Sharing the Gift

In sharing the gift of kindfulness, we may find teenagers and young adults underestimate the importance of kindness. On the other hand, elderly adults may value kindness but because they have lost friends and love ones, there is a reduction in their opportunities to practice kindness. Moreover, many individuals of all ages may be reluctant to engage in community volunteer activities, to extend the reach of their personal kindness to 'the others' and to encourage even their friends to be more kind. Understand that you will need to employ patience as you work to encourage your friends to first incorporate mindful kindness as a main purpose in their lives and then to "pay it forward," encouraging others in their lives to be more kind. Be careful though. Sharing the gift does not mean giving unasked for advice for how to be more kind to others

Another challenge in sharing the gift is maintaining our humility. In Step 2 Harry Walters, Navajo historian, explained that the question, "How you are doing?" is not just about you, but also your family and community. I had the privilege of spending a week with a small group on Harry's traditional homestead. I asked him many questions and for the first day or two found his answers confusing. Then it dawned on me. His answers were stories and in fact the stories did answer my questions. I learned that 'my' way of answering questions is not the only or the best way. I learned to be humble. In working to build a culture of kindness, we must be careful to avoid arrogance about knowing how best to understand and spread kindness.

"Each One Teach One"

In the South before the Civil War, African American slaves shared knowledge with each other through a system called "Each One Teach One." When one person learned to read, he or she was expected to pass on that knowledge by teaching another slave. I think this is a powerful idea that can also be applied to teaching kindness.

The prisoners I work with are experts in the "Each One Teach One" approach to spreading kindness. As each prisoner has learned about mindful kindness and put it into practice, he has shared the gift by teaching others, sharing a copy of *How Love Wins*, or leading by example. Ten years after I began corresponding with Roy Tester, a dozen other prisoners I write to are now practicing kindfulness in some way. For example, Roy taught RJ about mindful kindness. RJ is in prison because of child molestation, one of the most horrible of crimes. RJ's practice of kindness lead him to confess to me that he was an uncontrolled child molester and, as a kindful practitioner, wanted me to help him never be released from prison. I interacted with the prosecutor's office in Pierce County; his new confessions will result in him spending the rest of his life in prison and thereby never again molesting a child. RJ's practice led him, so far, to guide seven other men through *How Love Wins* to learn how to be more mindfully kind: Timothy, ML, Charles, Jerry, Steffen, James, and Victor.

Hopefully some of these men will share the gift by helping others learn about and practice mindful kindness.

Sharing the Gift of Kindness With Your Community

Sharing the gift with one person at a time as in "Each One Teach One" is an excellent approach. But for those of us who can, it would also be valuable to motivate larger numbers of people to act with mindful kindness, to help create communities with a culture of kindness. A culture of kindness shifts more and more 'others' to the category of 'us.' To contribute to a culture of kindness in the Eugene-Springfield area, where I live, a small group of volunteers launched a Spreading Kindness Campaign. Besides sponsoring Spreading Kindness dinners and other activities, we also organized a citywide workshop on kindness. We invited members of diverse communities and had over 150 participants to kick off the Spreading Kindness campaign. It was held on the 20th anniversary of the 1998 mass shooting at our local Thurston High School, where the second school shooting in the US occurred. The gathering recited a peace pledge that was written by three local fifth graders the day after the shooting. The pledge was led by one of the authors of the pledge (now an adult), her teacher, two principals, and current students who continue reciting the pledge; the pledge has been recited continuously for the last 20 years:

"To honor those students who have lost their lives to school violence, the students of Centennial School pledge to be violence free. We will not be verbally or physically mean to others. We will not gossip or spread rumors. We will respect everybody and their abilities. We will show respect by using kindness."

After that event, I and a dozen others formed a steering committee to launch a campaign to make Eugene and Springfield cities of kindness. Cities of Kindness[81] is a national movement to build local cultures of kindness in which more individuals are kinder (to themselves and others) more of the time, and in which organizations (governmental, business, religious, non-profits, and schools) encourage and support kindness. Our steering committee reached out to Tom Tait, recent mayor of Anaheim, CA and a national leader in the cities of kindness movement, for advice. Mayor Tait described how the Anaheim campaign focused on changing the culture through encouraging acts of kindness. For example, Anaheim citizen volunteers create appreciation baskets for every city employee. Each of the 3000 employees received two appreciation baskets over the past three years. The poverty level as measured by free and reduced lunch is 88%. 60% of the students are English Language learners. Yet the safety rating for this medium sized urban school district is A-. The superintendent reported that suspensions dropped by half and gang activity has dropped as well. Because of the culture change in Anaheim's schools, President Obama invited Mayor Tait to the White House to talk about how a culture of kindness can reduce school violence. In the past several years, because of the school kindness climate, the Dalai Lama, the spiritual leader of Tibet, has visited Anaheim many times. Our primary advisor from Anaheim, other than Tom Tait, is Nathan Zug, pastor of Community Presence at Magnolia Baptist Church and an Anaheim Police Department chaplain.

Our local campaign to make Eugene and Springfield cities of kindness in Oregon is attempting to systematically spread the message about the importance of kindness in our personal lives, at work, at school, and through the community. You can read about the surprising success of this campaign at SpreadingKindnessCampaign.org. Who knows? Cities of Kindness might be the next significant evolutionary transition, as defined by evolutionary biologist David Sloane Wilson in his book, *This View of Life*.[82]

WHAT TO SAY WHEN PEOPLE ASK ABOUT KINDFULNESS

As you share the gift of kindfulness with others, you might find yourself answering questions about the meaning of kindfulness. Here are five commonly asked questions and suggestions for how to answer them:

Q: What are the benefits of kindness?

A: Having mostly kind habits contributes to close, caring relationships that in turn contribute to a longer, healthier, loving and happier life.

Q: What does mindfulness mean?

A: Mindfulness means paying attention to what we intend to do in the present moment, being nonjudgmental, and not adding distracting thoughts.

Q: Why is mindfulness important?

A: Mindfulness keeps or focus on our intention in the present moment (rather than rehashing the past or imagining the future), brings us contentment, makes us more aware of how our actions are affecting others, decreases our unhappiness, enables us to weaken unkind habits, and helps us be more genuinely kind to ourselves and others.

Q: Why might I want kindfulness to be a primary purpose in my life?

A: Having kindfulness as a primary purpose is a powerful way to foster your well-being and the well-being of everyone touched by your kindness—at home, at work and throughout your social world.

Q: What is the value of a city having a culture of kindness?

A: When kindness is prominent in our personal lives, at work, at school, throughout the community and in government, civility, safety, and a sense of common purpose grows as does the reach of our kindfulness, making 'us' more inclusive.

Putting It Altogether

Mindful kindfulness affects all the important parts of our life: relationships, health, personal development, career/our calling, and recreation.

Relationships. A primary focus of this book is on how mindful kindness is critical to establishing and maintaining close caring relationships with our spouse/partner, family members, friends, co-workers, and even 'others.' These relationships provide our foundation for building our career, taking care of our health, pursuing personal development, and benefiting from recreation. At one time or another, our relationships will be challenging. This book gives several examples of how you can apply the foundation skills of change, action and character in your relationships. And, of course mindful kindness can guide you in breaking unkind habits and building kind habits.

Your calling/career. For a good part of our lives, most of us will spend much of our time in a work environment. While there will be differences in the degree to which we can use mindful kindness at work, in all work situations—as an employer or as an employee—we want to be a sustainable giver, a person who reaches out to others with kindness, supporting peers while setting reasonable boundaries.

Health. Health involves nutrition, exercise, rest, stress management, and not harming yourself with unkind habits such as substance abuse and violence. Having mindful kindness as a primary purpose helps you more clearly see what your health goals and habits should be as well as what unkind habits you need to deal with. Changing your habits involves the same set of skills as you apply with respect to relationships and the work place.

Personal development. Personal development is a life long process, through which we regularly decide the degree to which our kind and unkind habits are in line with our life goals. The mindful kindness skills taught in *How Love Wins* can support both religious and humanitarian personal development goals.

Mindful kindness skills provide us with the critical ability to non-judgmentally observe our behavior and those of the people around us so we have the awareness to identify the effects of our habits and the effects of the habits of others. Clearly seeing how our habits are affecting others sets the stage for us to make the most important changes in our lives, strengthening kind habits and diminishing unkind habits.

Recreation. Recreation includes activities outside of work that bring emotional satisfaction of some sort, such as pleasure or a sense of accomplishment. Recreation includes demanding physical activity—such as running and skiing—and less strenuous activities—such as playing cards, walking, gardening, and arts and crafts. Except for passive activities such as watching TV, recreation can be seen as making an effort to be more skilled, for example in skiing or in playing cards. From the perspective of *How Love Wins*, recreation includes many of our pleasant kind habits, which are essential ingredients for our renewal. They not only make our life more pleasant, but also can be employed to decrease our stress in difficult times.

Community. Community includes government, businesses, non-profits, faith-based organizations, schools, and more. These entities vary in their commitment to kindness, the reach of their kindness, their competence and their fairness. It is often said that it takes a village to raise a child. The looming question is what motivates a village to want to raise a child?

Let Mindful Kindness Drive Your Life

A metaphor for understanding the central role mindful kindness can play in our life is to think of the important parts of our life and our community as the systems that make up a car and the roads it travels on.

Our purpose—mindful kindness—is the driver. Our personal development includes the steering wheel that allows us to move toward kind habits and the brakes that stop unkind habits. Health is our engine. It allows us to speed up in building kind habits and go slow in the vicinity of unkind habits. Relationships require many parts: lights to clearly see where we are going and to allow others to see us clearly; the exhaust system to let off necessary toxic emotions and thoughts; the lubrication system to smooth out differences that are causing friction; and the cooling system that brings the temperature down when we are overheated. Our career is the fuel system that gives us energy to keep moving. Recreation is the music system that can lighten our mood or energize us. The community is the system of streets and highways that allows our car to travel from place to place.

What happens when we lack purpose? Possibly the driver never starts the car or drives around aimlessly. What if our purpose is to gain status and money? Or we are driven by anger? The driver races the engine, often has to break, frequently honks the horn at other drivers, and may be under the influence of alcohol, uppers, or downers. The music is loud and the road is full of potholes. As we can see, there is a clear advantage to having mindful kindness in the driver's seat.

As Roy Tester said, "It's just an Awesome Groove, helping others."

Wrapping up

Sharing the gift means just that: sharing. With Spreading Kindness dinners and other activities, we are not pushing people to carry out certain acts of kindness. Rather we are encouraging other people to increase kindness in their lives, in whatever way they see fit, and in turn encourage their friends to increase their kindness.

Your friends may want to hear your story about what you have learned and how being more mindfully kind has affected your life. Your story may be about major changes or it may be about minor changes. All changes matter. Small kindnesses and large kindnesses can change the world. And with the ripple effect some of those you encourage to act with mindful kindness will then talk to their friends about the importance of them acting with mindful kindness.

try it now

Describe how you helped someone learn about mindful kindness and how you supported them in applying it in their life and in sharing the gift with others in their life. Or, think of someone you know who might be interested in your mindful kindness practice. What would you tell them about how mindful kindness has changed your life?

Glossary

Backsliding

The lapse in attention that occurs after a period of mindfulness when an old trigger once again provokes an unkind habit.

Detective

A person who takes on the detective role searches for effective ways to change the physical world to solve a problem in the physical world.

Empathic joy

The emotion that arises when one experiences delight or excitement for the happiness and success of others.

Experience-then-Return Loop

When misery arises, we experience the emotion for 90 seconds (without thinking about the misery), and then return to our intention with mindfulness, using the Three-Breath method if need be.

Foundational skills

Three sets of skills that you call upon when building kind habits and weakening unkind habits:

1. Change your physical world and/or mental world

2. Take on the role of detective, warrior, or kindful practitioner

3. Develop a growth mindset, conscientiousness, patience, and humility

Kindful

Combining a kind and mindful state of being.

Kindful Cycle

A series of skillful actions to practice when facing serious challenges characterized by **negative mind-wandering** (see Step 1):

1. Engage the **Three-Breath method** (see Step 5) and **sensing-mindfulness** (see Step 7).

2. Ask for help for others.

3. Reflect on the inspiring kindness of others.

4. Act constructively in the physical world: Act in a manner that is constructive and directs your attention away from your negative mind-wandering.

Kindful practitioner

A person who takes on the kindful practitioner role makes efforts many times every day to practice mindful kindness.

Kindful Vow

I intend to:

Be mindfully kind to myself

Be mindfully kind in all my relationships

Expand the reach of my kindfulness

Kindness practices

Kindness includes seven practices, each of which benefits both the giver and receiver: forgiveness, gratitude, empathy, compassion, altruism, generosity, and cooperation.

Kindness plan

To make a plan for how to be kind, choose a kind habit that you want to develop and answer the following questions:

- What is the kind habit you have chosen to develop? How will it manifest itself in both your physical world and mental world?

- Who are you hoping to help by strengthening this habit?

- Who will you ask for support, if anyone?

- What detective work will you need to do, if any?

- How, if at all, will you use the mind of the warrior?

- What skills of character (growth mindset, conscientiousness, patience, and humility) will you need most?

- What action will you take to build the kind habit in your mental world?

- What action will you take in your physical world?

Low-keyed mind-wandering
A state of mind in which thoughts range from slightly unpleasant to neutral to pleasant. However, low-keyed mind-wandering can be harmful if we are distracted when we are driving, working around rapidly moving machine parts, or in other potentially dangerous situations. On the other hand, low-keyed mind-wandering can contribute to creativity, consolidating memory, and even happiness. In contrast, people are usually unhappy in the more intense levels of mind-wandering, called negative mind-wandering.

Meditation
The practice of focusing your attention for a length of time to transform the mind. Meditation brings about improved concentration, clarity, and calmness.

Meditative mind
A state of deep calmness. Thoughts, emotions, and sensations may arise, but they instantly pass away without you needing to engage mindfulness.

Mind-wandering
The state of mind that drifts away from one's intention and instead attends to unrelated, distracting thoughts.

Mindful micropractice
A familiar, daily activity or chore that is performed from start to finish as an exercise in mindfulness.

Mindful with emotions

The state of mind in which one is able to experience the emotion of the present moment without reverting to unthinking, habitual responses and without getting caught up in distracting thoughts.

Mindful with thoughts

The practice of keeping one's attention on what one intended to think about, without engaging in distraction and mind-wandering.

Mindfulness

The practice of paying attention on purpose to cultivate a mental state that is present, non-judgmental, and free of thoughts that distract us from our intention.

Mindful-Kind cycle

The mindful-kind cycle begins with mindfulness, which reduces mind-wandering and increases our awareness of our inclination to be kind. This inclination leads to an increase in our kindness and reduces our unkindness. The benefits resulting from more kind acts and fewer unkind acts include an increased number of chemical messengers that create positive feelings within us, appreciation from others for our kindness, and less stress. These benefits in turn motivate us to be more mindful, and being more mindful allows us to increase our kindness and the cycle continues.

Negative mind-wandering

Unkind thoughts and emotions that distract us from our specific intention, cause unhappiness, and, at times, lead to unkindness. The two levels of negative mind-wandering are misery (more intense) and agitation (less intense).

Order of Buddhist Contemplatives (OBC)

The OBC is an international monastic order of men and women who, together with lay ministers of the Order and congregations and affiliated meditation groups, are dedicated to practicing the Serene Reflection Meditation tradition of Buddhism, also called Soto Zen.

Roles (See **Kindful practitioner**, **Detective**, and **Warrior**)

Sangha

Thich Nhat Hanh explains sangha as being a community of friends practicing the dharma (the teaching) together to bring about and maintain awareness, understanding, acceptance, and love.

Sensing-Mindfulness

The practice of shifting our attention away from thoughts to our senses of touch, sight, smell, and hearing. This method of awareness and focusing on the present moment includes: soft-eyes, sharp-eyes, soft-ears, and soft-contact.

Sharp-Eyes

Focusing all your visual attention on a specific object. Both an intense focus on an object (sharp-eyes) and a very broad field of vision (soft-eyes) take considerable concentration. Sharp-eyes is a form of sensing-mindfulness, which reduces mind-wandering.

Skills of action

This foundational skill group involves the ability to assume the role we need to play to make meaningful changes (kindful practitioner, detective, and warrior).

Skills of change

This foundational skill group involves the ability to make a shift in your mental or physical world.

Skills of character

This foundational skill group includes having a growth mindset, conscientiousness, patience, and humility in order to see meaningful change through to completion.

Soft-Contact

Relaxing tense muscles and directing all your attention to your sensation of touch. Directing all your attention to touch is a form of sensing-mindfulness, which reduces mind-wandering.

Soft-Ears

Directing all your attention to take in sounds from a number of sources, not focusing on any one source. With soft-ears, your range of listening is broad, including the periphery, yet you are not focusing on a particular source from within your audible field. Directing all your attention to your full array of sounds is a form of sensing-mindfulness, which reduces mind-wandering.

Soft-Eyes

The practice of relaxing one's focus to take in not only what is in one's direct line of sight, but also the peripheral vision. Soft-eyes is a form of sensing mindfulness, which reduces mind-wandering.

Three-Breath Method

The practice of redirecting attention away from mind-wandering by focusing on the physical expansion and contraction of the abdomen as you take each of three breaths.

Tonglen

A Buddhist meditation practice of sending and receiving in which you ask for help for others.

Trigger

An external occurrence that provokes a habitual behavior.

Unkind habit

A regular behavior or tendency that is inconsiderate or even cruel, causing harm to oneself or others, whether intentional or unintentional.

Unmindful

A mental state that dwells on the past or future, that wanders aimlessly, and/or that gives attention to distracting thoughts. See **Mindfulness**.

Unmindful-Unkind cycle

The unmindful-unkind cycle begins with negative mind-wandering. We are so self-absorbed with distracting thoughts and emotions that we are unaware of the negative consequences of our unkind habits and unaware of our inherent inclination to act with and receive kindness. Because of negative mind-wandering we act with less kindness and more unkindness. With less kindness and more unkindness we do not have these benefits: the boost from the chemical messengers, appreciation from the recipient of the kindness, and a drop in stress. Without these benefits we lack of motivation to be mindful, which means the negative mind-wandering continues or becomes even more negative and the cycle begins again.

Warrior

A person who takes on the warrior role maintains mindfulness and acts with kindness in the face of significant adversity.

Resources for Mindfulness and Kindness

Greater Good Science Center
https://greatergood.berkeley.edu/

This site provides links to organizations that "promote social and emotional well-being through research, practice, or both." Categories of organizations include:

Altruism & Heroism
Anti-Racism & Tolerance
Empathy
Family & Couples
Forgiveness
Gratitude
Happiness
Mind & Body
Mindfulness
Work & Career

Feed Kindness Starve Harm:
Practicing Mindful Kindness in Personal Situations
https://feedkindness.com/resources/

This Resources for Mindful Living link provides examples, activities, and research findings for using mindfulness to clearly see and change unkind habits while cultivating kind habits in a variety of personal situations: self care, couples, friends, parents, and co-workers.

Making Mindful Kindness Part of Community Participation
https://feedkindness.com/resources/mindful-community-participation/

This Feed Kindness Starve Harm link provides examples, activities, research, and resources for how to practice mindful kindness while serving your community.

Working toward Social Justice Using Mindful Kindness
https://feedkindness.com/resources/mindful-social-justice/

This Feed Kindness Starve Harm link provides examples, activities, research, and resources for how to practice mindful kindness while working toward social justice.

Kindness Ideas

KindSpring

http://www.kindspring.org/ideas/

KindSpring provides kindness ideas across different themes, including For Friends and Family, For Yourself, and For the Elderly.

Random Acts of Kindness Foundation

https://www.randomactsofkindness.org/kindness-ideas

Random Acts believes in spreading kindness throughout schools, communities, and homes. They provide ideas in many categories including ideas you can do for strangers, ideas just for you, ideas you can do at work, ideas to show kindness to your neighbors, and ideas for your community.

Buddhism and Prisons

Compassion Works for All

http://www.compassionworksforall.org

The mission of Compassion Works for All is "to offer healing and hope by living and teaching compassion, especially to the disenfranchised and people in prison."

Engaged Buddhism Resources from DharmaNet International

http://www.dharmanet.org/

This organization provides information about engaged Buddhism in many aspects of society, not just prisons.

National Buddhist Prison Sangha

https://zmm.mro.org/national-buddhist-prison-sangha/

The National Buddhist Prison Sangha is a nationwide network of Buddhist volunteers. Their mission is "to sustain a correspondence program in Zen Buddhist practice with inmates across the country in prison facility settings."

Prison Mindfulness Institute
http://prisonmindfulness.org

The mission of the institute is "to provide prisoners, prison staff, and prison volunteers with the most effective, evidence-based tools for rehabilitation, self-transformation, and personal & professional development. In particular, we provide and promote the use of proven effective mindfulness-based interventions (MBIs)."

Saint Badass: Transcendence in Tucker Max Hell.
See https://www.feedkindness.com/books-and-more/saint-badass/ for information about this book.

Prisons and Prison Reform

The Real Cost of Prisons Project
http://www.realcostofprisons.org

This project "brings together justice activists, artists, researchers and women and men directly experiencing the impact of mass criminalization who are working to end the carceral state." The site includes writing, comix, and music created by prisoners.

Yes! Magazine
https://www.yesmagazine.org/topic/social-justice/criminal-justice-reform/

The Criminal Justice Reform section of Yes! magazine provides articles about improving, reforming, and abolishing prisons.

Increasing Compassion

Jinpa, T. (2015). *A Fearless Heart: How the Courage to Be Compassionate Can Transform Our Lives.* New York, NY: Penguin. Part 2 is particularly helpful.

Salzberg, S. & Kabat-Zinn, J. (2002). *Lovingkindness: The Revolutionary Art of Happiness.* Boulder, CO: Shambhala.

Inspirational Movies

Inspirational movies based on true stories
http://www.imdb.com/list/ls0539264b82/

The author of this list recommends 90 inspirational movies including The Great Debaters, The Vernon Johns Story, McFarland USA, Invictus, A Civil Action, and Selma.

IMDb: Movies Tagged "Inspirational"
https://www.imdb.com/search/title/?keywords=inspirational

This link provides a list of recommended inspirational movies.

Notes

Preface

1. My lay ordination master was Rev. Master Jiyu-Kennett, who in 1963 received the Dharma Transmission from Koho Zenji, abbot of Sojiji, one of the two head training temples for Soto Zen in Japan.

Introduction

2. Mineo, L. (November 2018). Over nearly 80 years, Harvard study has been showing how to live a healthy and happy life. Retrieved from https://news.harvard.edu/gazette/story/2017/04/over-nearly-80-years-harvard-study-has-been-showing-how-to-live-a-healthy-and-happy-life/.

3. Thomas, A.G., Jonason, P.K., Blackburn, J., Kennair, L.E., Lowe, R., Malouff, J.M., Stewart-Williams, S., Sulikowski, D., & Li, N.P. (2019). Mate preference priorities in the East and West: A cross-cultural test of the mate preference priority model. *Journal of personality.*

4. Gottman, J. M., & Levenson, R. W. (1999). What predicts change in marital interaction over time? A study of alternative models. *Family Process, 38:* 143–158.

5. Gable, S. L., Gonzaga, G. C., & Strachman, A. (November 2006). Will you be there for me when things go right? Supportive responses to positive event disclosures. *Journal of Personality and Social Psychology, 91*(5): 904–917.

6. Welch, D. (2015). *Love factually: 10 proven steps from I wish to I do.* Austin, TX: Love Science Media. See pp, 62–63.

7. Nelson, S.K., Layous, K., Cole, S.W., & Lyubomirsky, S. (2016). Do unto others or treat yourself? The effects of prosocial and self-focused behavior on psychological flourishing. *Emotion, 16*(6), 850-61.

8. Fredrickson, B.L., Grewen, K.M., Coffey, K.A., Algoe, S.B., Firestine, A.M., Arevalo, J., Ma, J., & Cole, S.W. (2013). A functional genomic perspective on human well-being. *Proceedings of the National Academy of Sciences of the United States of America, 110*(33), 13684-9.

9. Gouin, J., Carter, C.S., Pournajafi-Nazarloo, H., Glaser, R., & Kiecolt-Glaser, J.K. (2010). Marital behavior, oxytocin, vasopressin, and wound healing. *Psychoneuroendocrinology, 35*, 1082-1090.

10. Li, Y., Pan, A., Wang, D., Liu, X.R., Dhana, K., Franco, Ò., Kaptoge, S.K., Angelantonio, E.D., Stampfer, M.J., Willett, W.C., & Hu, F.B. (2018). Impact of Healthy Lifestyle Factors on Life Expectancies in the US Population. *Circulation, 138*, 345–355.

11. Harding, K. (2019) *The Rabbit Effect: Live Longer, Happier, and Healthier with the Groundbreaking Science of Kindness.* New York, NY: Atria Books.

12. Bartlett, M.Y., & DeSteno, D. (2006). Gratitude and prosocial behavior: helping when it costs you. *Psychological science, 17*(4), 319-25.

13. Karns, C.M., Moore, W.E., & Mayr, U. (2017). The Cultivation of Pure Altruism via Gratitude: A Functional MRI Study of Change with Gratitude Practice. *Front. Hum. Neurosci.*.

14. Emmons, R.A., & Stern, R. (2013). Gratitude as a psychotherapeutic intervention. *Journal of clinical psychology, 69*(8), 846-55.

Step 1

15. Gottman, J.M. (1994). What Predicts Divorce?: The Relationship Between Marital Processes and Marital Outcomes.

16. Gottman, J.M., & Silver, N. (1999). The Seven Principles for Making Marriage Work.

17. Killingsworth, M. (July 2013). Does mind-wandering make you unhappy? Retrieved from http://greatergood.berkeley.edu/article/item/does_mind_wandering_make_you_unhappy.

Step 2

18. Origin unknown. According to Mother Teresa's website (http://www.motherteresa.org/08_info/Quotesf.html), she has been mistakenly identified as the origin of this quote.

19. https://www.fosterpurpose.org/about

20. Aknin, L.B., Hamlin, J.K., & Dunn, E.W. (2012). Giving Leads to Happiness in Young Children. *PloS one.*

21. https://www.mindsetworks.com/science/

22. Muraven, M. (2010). Building Self-Control Strength: Practicing Self-Control Leads to Improved Self-Control Performance. *Journal of experimental social psychology, 46*(2), 465-468.

Step 3

23. https://www.gottman.com/ blog/3-research-based-tips-for-a-happy-and-healthy-relationship/

24. Darwin, C. (1871). *The Descent of Man.* (p. 88) Retrieved from https:// charles-darwin.classic-literature.co.uk/the-descent-of-man/ebook-page-88. asp

25. Fredrickson, B.L., Grewen, K.M., Coffey, K.A., Algoe, S.B., Firestine, A.M., Arevalo, J., Ma, J., & Cole, S.W. (2013). A functional genomic perspective on human well-being. *Proceedings of the National Academy of Sciences of the United States of America, 110*(33), 13684-9.

26. Tang, Y., Tang, R., & Posner, M.I. (2013). Brief meditation training induces smoking reduction. *Proceedings of the National Academy of Sciences of the United States of America, 110*(34), 13971-5.

27. Lim, D., Condon, P., & DeSteno, D. (2015). Mindfulness and Compassion: An Examination of Mechanism and Scalability. *PloS one.*

28. Sandstrom, G.M., & Dunn, E.W. (2014). Social Interactions and Well-Being: The Surprising Power of Weak Ties. *Personality & social psychology bulletin, 40*(7), 910-922.

29. http://www.brucekalexander.com/articles-speeches/ rat-park/148-addiction-the-view-from-rat-park

30. http://www.shinrin-yoku.org/shinrin-yoku.html

31. Li, Q. (2018). *Forest Bathing: How Trees Can Help You Find Health and Happiness.* NY, NY: Viking.

32. Yeager, R., Riggs, D.W., DeJarnett, N., Tollerud, D.J., Wilson, J., Conklin, D.J., O'Toole, T.E., McCracken, J., Lorkiewicz, P.K., Xie, Z., Zafar, N., Krishnasamy, S.S., Srivastava, S.K., Finch, J., Keith, R.J., DeFilippis, A.P., Rai, S.N., Liu, G., & Bhatnagar, A. (2018). Association Between Residential Greenness and Cardiovascular Disease Risk. *Journal of the American Heart Association.*

33. Park, S., & Mattson, R.H. (2009). Therapeutic Influences of Plants in Hospital Rooms on Surgical Recovery.

34. Goldstein, P., Weissman-Fogel, I., & Shamay-Tsoory, S.G. (2017). The role of touch in regulating inter-partner physiological coupling during empathy for pain. *Scientific Reports.*

Step 4

35. https://obcon.org/

36. https://shastaabbey.org/

37. http://throssel.org.uk/

38. https://liveanddare.com/types-of-meditation

39. Jabr, F. (2013). Why Your Brain Needs More Downtime. Retrieved from https://www.scientificamerican.com/article/mental-downtime/

40. Konrath, S., Fuhrel-Forbis, A.R., Lou, A., & Brown, S.N. (2012). Motives for volunteering are associated with mortality risk in older adults. *Health psychology : official journal of the Division of Health Psychology, American Psychological Association, 31*(1), 87-96.

Step 5

41. A music video can be found at https://youtu.be/awzNHuGqoMc

42. McGonigal, K. (2011). *The Willpower Instinct: How Self-Control Works, Why It Matters, and What You Can Do To Get More of It.* New York, NY: Avery.

43. Bolte Taylor, J. (2008). *My Stroke of Insight: A Brain Scientist's Personal Journey.* New York, NY: Viking.

44. Linden, D. (2015). *Touch: The Science of Hand, Heart, and Mind.* New York, NY: Viking.

45. Kleiber, B.A., Jain, S., & Trivedi, M.H. (2005). Depression and pain: implications for symptomatic presentation and pharmacological treatments. *Psychiatry (Edgmont (Pa. : Township)), 2*(5), 12-8.

46. Brown, C.A., & Jones, A.K. (2010). Meditation experience predicts less negative appraisal of pain: Electrophysiological evidence for the involvement of anticipatory neural responses. *PAIN, 150,* 428-438.

47. Andrews, P.W., & Thomson, J.A. (2010). Depression's Evolutionary Roots. Retrieved from https://www.scientificamerican.com/article/depressions-evolutionary-roots/

Step 6

48. Talhelm, T., Zhang, X., Oishi, S., Shi-min, C., Duan, D., Lan, X., & Kitayama, S. (2014). Large-Scale Psychological Differences Within China Explained by Rice Versus Wheat Agriculture. *Science, 344*, 603-608.

49. Martin, R. (2015.) 5 Ways to Deal with Angry People. Retrieved from https://www.psychologytoday.com/us/blog/all-the-rage/201506/5-ways-deal-angry-people

50. For more details on these ways, see https://www.wikihow.com/Deal-With-a-Rude-Family-Member

Step 7

51. Tsafou, K., Ridder, D.T., Ee, R.V., & Lacroix, J.P. (2016). Mindfulness and satisfaction in physical activity: A cross-sectional study in the Dutch population. *Journal of health psychology, 21*(9), 1817-27.

52. Deepak Chopra's audio body-scan can be found at https://youtu.be/1zHaZJpLdBk.

Step 10

53. Brooks, D. (2011). *The Social Animal: The Hidden Sources of Love, Character, and Achievement.* New York, NY: Random House.

Step 11

54. Seppälä, E., Cameron. K. (2015). Proof That Positive Work Cultures Are More Productive. Retrieved from: https://hbr.org/2015/12/proof-that-positive-work-cultures-are-more-productive.

55. Holm, K.L., Torkelson, E., & Bäckström, M. (2015). Models of Workplace Incivility: The Relationships to Instigated Incivility and Negative Outcomes. *BioMed research international.*

56. Schilpzand, P., Pater, I.E., & Erez, A. (2016). Workplace incivility: A review of the literature and agenda for future research.

57. Grant, A. M. (2013). *Give and Take: Why Helping Others Drives Our Success*. New York, NY: Viking. TED talk available at https://www.ted.com/speakers/adam_grant. Grant, A. & Rebele, R. (2017) More On Being Generous Without Being a Doormat. Retrieved from https://hbr.org/2017/02/more-on-being-generous-without-being-a-doormat

58. Page-Gould, E. (2010). Warning: Racism is Bad for Your Health. Retrieved from: https://greatergood.berkeley.edu/article/item/why_racism_is_bad_for_your_health

59. Dishion, T.J., Forgatch, M.S., Chamberlain, P.A., & Pelham, W.E. (2016). The Oregon Model of Behavior Family Therapy: From Intervention Design to Promoting Large-Scale System Change. *Behavior therapy, 47*(6), 812-837.

60. To take on the role of the detective and learn more about kindness to the earth, go to: http://www.joinskc.org/spread-kindness/kindness-to-the-earth/

61. Read more at https://www.mckenzieriver.org/2015/12/its-the-trees/ and https://www.mckenzieriver.org/protected-lands/conservation-easements/native-oaks-ridge/

62. Read more at https://tonybiglan.com/thenurtureeffect/

63. Wrangham, R. (2019). *The Goodness Paradox: The Strange Relationship Between Virtue and Violence in Human Evolution*. New York, NY: Pantheon Books.

64. Read more at https://www.feedkindness.com/books-and-more/saint-badass/

Step 12

65. Wilson, T.D., Reinhard, D.A., Westgate, E.C., Gilbert, D.T., Ellerbeck, N.E., Hahn, C., Brown, C.L., & Shaked, A. (2014). Just think: The challenges of the disengaged mind. *Science, 345*, 75-77.

66. Hill, P.L., & Turiano, N.A. (2014). Purpose in life as a predictor of mortality across adulthood. *Psychological science, 25*(7), 1482-6.

67. Linver, M.R., Roth, J.L., & Brooks-Gunn, J. (2009). Patterns of adolescents' participation in organized activities: are sports best when combined with other activities? *Developmental psychology, 45*(2), 354-67.

68. Moran, S. (2009). Purpose: giftedness in intrapersonal intelligence.

69. Lobdell, T. (2011). Getting off the treadmill. Retrieved from https://www.paloaltoonline.com/weekly/morguepdf/2011/2011_11_18.paw.section2.pdf

70. Parker, K. (2015). Despite progress, women still bear heavier load than men in balancing work and family. Retrieved from https://www.pewresearch.org/fact-tank/2015/03/10/women-still-bear-heavier-load-than-men-balancing-work-family/

71. Morin, A. (2014). The Five Things Successful Working Parents Give Up To Reach A Work-Life Balance. Retrieved from https://www.forbes.com/sites/amymorin/2014/01/20/the-five-things-successful-working-parents-give-up-to-reach-a-work-life-balance/#463cf2b157ea

72. Sandberg, S. (2017). *Option B: Facing Adversity, Building Resilience, and Finding Joy.* New York, NY: Knopf.

73. Didion, J. (2005). *The Year of Magical Thinking.* New York, NY: Knopf.

74. Schilling, O.K., Deeg, D.J., & Huisman, M. (2018). Affective Well-Being in the Last Years of Life: The Role of Health Decline. *Psychology and Aging, 33,* 739–753.

75. How to cope with the aging process. Retrieved from https://www.aging.com/how-to-cope-with-the-aging-process/

76. Iverach, L., Menzies, R.G., & Menzies, R.E. (2014). Death anxiety and its role in psychopathology: reviewing the status of a transdiagnostic construct. *Clinical psychology review, 34*(7), 580-93.

77. Goranson, A., Ritter, R.S., Waytz, A., Norton, M.I., & Gray, K. (2017). Dying Is Unexpectedly Positive. *Psychological science, 28*(7), 988-99.

78. Seligman, M. (2011). The Original Theory: Authentic Happiness. Retrieved from https://www.authentichappiness.sas.upenn.edu/learn/wellbeing

79. Aknin, L.B., Hamlin, J.K., & Dunn, E.W. (2012). Giving Leads to Happiness in Young Children. *PloS one.*

80. Dunn, E. & Norton, M. (2013). *Happy Money: The Science of Smarter Spending.* New York, NY: Simon & Schuster.

Conclusion

81. https://cityofkindness.org/

82. Wilson, D.S. (2019). *This View of Life: Completing the Darwinian Revolution.* New York, NY: Pantheon.

About the Author

Doug Carnine is a lay minister in the Order of Buddhist Contemplatives at the Eugene Buddhist Priory, as well as a founding member of the Priory. A practicing Buddhist for more than 40 years, Carnine was ordained as a lay Buddhist in 1975. He is also a longtime practitioner of tai chi.

An award-winning professor of Education at the University of Oregon for almost 40 years, Carnine helped lead a social movement to increase the use of evidence in education. That work lead to him receiving a presidential appointment to serve on the board of the National Institute for Literacy. He is also the author of more than 100 scholarly publications, six books, and numerous teaching programs on subjects ranging from math and science to world history and English composition.

Since his retirement from the University in 2010, Carnine has focused on the study and practice of mindful kindness. His work inspired him to write *How Love Wins,* and, with four incarcerated co-authors, *Saint Badass: Transcendence in Tucker Max Hell.* He is currently serving as coordinator of the Campaign to Make Eugene and Springfield Cities of Kindness (SpreadingKindnessCampaign.org).

Carnine and his wife, Linda, also a lay Buddhist minister, have two daughters.